P9-CCC-172

PLACE IN RETURN BOX to remove this checkout from your record.
TO AVOID FINES return on or before date due.

DATE DUE	DATE DUE	DATE DUE
JAN 0 9 2006		
071306	MAR 1 7 2004	
APR 0 3 2012	1 5	

MSU Is An Affirmative Action/Equal Opportunity Institution
c:\circ\datedue.pm3-p.1

Sino-American Relations, 1949–71

Sino-American Relations, 1949-71

Documented and introduced by Roderick MacFarquhar

**Published for
the Royal Institute of International Affairs
by David & Charles Ltd**

DAVID & CHARLES
NEWTON ABBOT

E
183.8
.C5
m28
1972
c.2

0 7153 5793 X

First published in Great Britain in 1972
for David & Charles Ltd

Printed in Great Britain by
Redwood Press Limited Trowbridge Wilts
for David & Charles (Publishers) Ltd
South Devon House Newton Abbot Devon

Contents

B420310

v

Chronology

1949	June 30	Mao Tse-tung's "On the People's Democratic Dictatorship" published
	August 5	State Department issues White Paper on China
	October 1	People's Republic of China (PRC) inaugurated
1950	January 5	Truman statement on status of Formosa
	January 12	US votes against replacement of Chinese Nationalists (ROC) by PRC in UN
	January 14	All US official personnel ordered to leave China after seizure of American property in Peking
	June 25	Outbreak of Korean War
	June 27	Truman orders Seventh Fleet to protect Formosa
	October 14	Chinese troops begin moving into Korea
	November 2	Chinese and US troops clash for the first time
	November 28	Head of special PRC delegation addresses UN Security Council
1951	February 1	UN declares PRC an aggressor in Korea
	July 10	Truce talks begin in Korea
	November 27	Agreement reached on provisional cease-fire in Korea
1952	December 2	President-elect Eisenhower goes to Korea
1953	February 2	Chiang Kai-shek "unleashed"
	July 26	Korean armistice signed
1954	April 26	Geneva Conference opens to discuss Korea
	May 8	Geneva Conference turns to Indochina
	July 21	Geneva Conference reaches agreement on Indochina

1954	September 8	SEATO treaty signed
	December 2	US-ROC treaty signed
1955	January 10	Chinese air raids on Tachens
	January 29	Congressional "Formosa resolution" becomes law
	February 5	US announces ROC decision to evacuate Tachens
	April 23	Chou En-lai offers to talk with the US
	August 1	US-PRC ambassadorial talks begin
	September 10	US-PRC agreement on return of civilians
1956	August 6	PRC offers visas to US correspondents
	September 25	Ch'en Yi addresses Eighth Party Congress on foreign policy
1957	June 28	Major Dulles address on China policy
	August 22	US grants visas for correspondents to go to China
	November 17	Mao, in Moscow, proclaims east wind prevails over west wind
1958	August 23	Offshore islands shelled; Dulles warns PRC
	August 27	Chinese coastal radio threatens Quemoy with invasion
	September 4	Strong Dulles warning; PRC claims its territorial waters extend 12 miles
	September 6	Chou suggests resumption of Warsaw talks
	September 30	Dulles criticizes garrisoning of offshore islands
	October 6	PRC declares one-week cease-fire
	October 23	Chiang renounces force as principal means of liberating mainland
	October 25	PRC starts alternate-day bombardment of offshore islands.
1959	April 15	Dulles resigns; succeeded by Herter
	September 15	Khrushchev arrives in US for two-week tour
	September 29	Khrushchev flies to Peking for PRC tenth anniversary
1960	April 22	China's first ideological attacks on Soviet foreign policy
	September 6	Warsaw talks stalemated hereafter on issue of Taiwan
1961	December 15	China representation issue at UN voted an important question requiring two-thirds majority

1962	May 23	Kennedy indicates willingness to consider sending food to China as refugees flood into Hong Kong
	June 26	PRC informed at Warsaw US will not back ROC attack
	October 20	Major PRC offensive on disputed frontier with India
1963	July 25	Partial test-ban treaty signed
	November 22	Kennedy assassinated
	December 13	Hilsman makes major China policy speech
1964	August 2	Tonkin Gulf incident
	October 16	First Chinese nuclear test
1965	February 7	US starts to bomb North Vietnam
	September 2	Lin Piao's "Long Live the Victory of People's War" issued
1966	March	Senate Foreign Relations Committee hearings on China
	April 17	Rusk statement on China policy released
	May 10	Chinese third nuclear test contains thermonuclear material
	August	CCP Eleventh Plenum of the Eighth Central Committee sets Cultural Revolution guidelines
	October 27	PRC guided missile–nuclear weapon test
1968	May 2	Chinese correspondents invited to cover US Presidential campaign
	May 13	Paris peace talks on Vietnam open
	May 28	PRC calls for postponement of Warsaw talks until after US election
	November 26	PRC proposes February 20 for resumption of Warsaw talks
1969	February 18	PRC cancels Warsaw meeting
	March	Serious Sino-Soviet border clashes
	April 1	Lin Piao speech to CCP's Ninth Congress
	July 21	First Nixon relaxation of trade and travel restrictions concerning PRC
	July 25	Nixon outlines new Asian policy at Guam (Nixon Doctrine)
1970	January 20	Warsaw talks resume after two years
	March 18	Sihanouk overthrown in Cambodian coup
	May 20	Mao denounces US on Cambodia
1971	February	South Vietnamese troops move into Laos

Preface

THE NIXON VISIT to China may one day be seen as the most important international event of the 1970s. The first meeting of the heads of government of two of the great countries of the world, hitherto bitter enemies for more than two decades, must surely be a turning point in global politics. What is incontestable is the importance of the event in Sino-American relations. President Nixon and Premier Chou En-lai may conclude no agreements; the visit could be canceled as the result of a last-minute crisis. But even in the latter eventuality, one important achievement of the past year would remain: The leaders of the two countries have for the first time simultaneously demonstrated a willingness to meet and to talk in an effort to improve relations between their countries. That joint willingness will remain as a benchmark whatever happens in the next few months, and the belief that the invitation to President Nixon signalled the end of an era underlies the preparation of this volume. It seems an appropriate moment to describe and document the main developments and the critical issues of those twenty-two years of unremitting mutual hostility.

I have also thought it important to examine the immediate causes and implications of the breakthrough in 1971. A. M. Halpern traces the changes in Chinese foreign policy that permitted Chou En-lai to issue his invitation to Nixon. Donald Klein focuses on the men who have helped bring about those changes. Morton Halperin concentrates more on the future, examining the implications of Nixon's China policy for the US posture in Asia.

When preparing a volume in so cooperative an organization as

Chatham House, it is difficult to remember who has *not* helped in its production. But I would like to thank particularly James Fawcett who mobilized; Margaret Cornell who expedited; Eileen Menzies who organized; Hermia Oliver who edited tirelessly; Hilary Black of the Press Library and Carole Mann and Helen Roy of the Library who supplied cuttings, magazines, and reference works fast and frequently; Pat Trim who xeroxed endlessly; and Fiona Ilic, Louise Orr, and Dorothy Woollams who typed furiously. I am very grateful, too, to Mervyn W. Adams and other staff members of Praeger Publishers who worked hard to get the manuscript published quickly.

I would also like to thank Morton Abramowitz, A. M. Halpern, and Richard Wich for their advice on documentation; Edgar Snow, Stewart Alsop, and Anthony Lewis for kindly allowing me to reproduce excerpts from articles which have become documents; and Daniel Ellegiers for permitting me to use A. M. Halpern's article. The mistakes of omission and commission remain mine.

RODERICK MACFARQUHAR

London, January, 1972

PART ONE

Breakthrough in 1971

America and Asia: The Impact of Nixon's China Policy

Morton H. Halperin

THE SPECTACULAR and unexpected trip by the President of the United States to the People's Republic of China quite naturally has raised questions in American and Asian minds about US motives for the move, its impact on Asian politics, and its significance for the future of Sino-American relations and US relations with other Asian nations. This essay considers each of these questions in turn.

WHY THE NIXON TRIP?

To understand why the United States did not seek to establish relations with Peking at an earlier date and why President Nixon was able to move with relative freedom at home at the time he did, one must look largely to American domestic politics. To understand why the President decided to seek improvement in Sino-American relations, one must look largely to his conception of US national security interests and his view of how the world operates. To understand why the move was made as it was, one must look both to American domestic politics and to the President's style.

No foreign policy issue has been more entangled in domestic politics than American relations with China in the postwar period.

3

Prior to the establishment of the People's Republic in 1949, President Harry S Truman and his Secretary of State, Dean Acheson, were under intensive pressure from the right wing of the Republican Party and from conservative Democrats to provide further military and economic aid to the Chiang Kai-shek regime. Truman, recognizing that such aid would be ineffective and run the risk of gradually drawing the United States into military involvement in the conflict, refused to accept this advice since he was determined that under no circumstances would American forces be used in China. He paid the price of increasing Republican dissatisfaction, which ultimately ran the risk of threatening bipartisan support for the Marshall Plan and Truman's overall European policy.

As the Nationalists fled from the mainland, Truman was faced with growing pressures, both from the Joint Chiefs of Staff and from the Republican Party, to intervene to defend Taiwan. These pressures, too, Truman resisted. He and his Secretary of State carefully explained that Taiwan had been returned to China, and hence American involvement in the defense of Taiwan would be involvement in the Chinese civil war.*When war broke out in Korea, Truman, needing bipartisan support for his East Asian policy as well as the acquiescence of the Joint Chiefs of Staff in the American military intervention in Korea, felt it necessary to send the Seventh Fleet into the Taiwan Strait. It was this action, taken in the opening days of the Korean War, that is likely to have the most lasting effect on the evolution of Sino-American relations.

Any doubts in the United States about the sending of the Seventh Fleet into the Taiwan Strait were removed with the Chinese intervention in the Korean War. From that time forward, all Americans viewed China with a sense of betrayal. Americans had felt a special responsibility for China; Americans had wooed China and supported it but had seen it reject these overtures and send Chinese soldiers to kill American boys on the Korean peninsula.

Thus, from 1950 onward, there was widespread domestic support for the effort to isolate and contain Peking and ultimately to see the regime overthrown and replaced by an anti-Communist government. During the period of McCarthyism that followed, there was a search for the "traitors in the State Department" who had permitted China to "fall" to Communism.

The issue was clearly too hot to touch politically during the 1950s, even had Eisenhower or his Secretary of State, John Foster Dulles, had any desire to do so. In fact, both had strong personal feelings of animosity toward Communist China and eagerly reinforced the policy of containment and isolation.

President John F. Kennedy and most of his principal foreign policy advisors did not share these views about Peking. They recognized that the People's Republic of China was here to stay and that the United States should move toward some sort of diplomatic contact with the Peking regime and stop seeking its isolation from the international community. However, Kennedy quickly recognized the strong domestic pressures against any such move. The China Lobby had maintained its popularity, and Kennedy felt vulnerable to right-wing pressures. These concerns were brought home forcefully during his conversations in the transition period with the outgoing President and Vice-President. Both Eisenhower and Richard Nixon informed Kennedy that they would generally support him on foreign policy matters but would be obliged to speak out and attack him, should he make any move toward diplomatic relations or UN membership for Peking. Indeed, reporting this episode in his book, *Six Crises,* Nixon takes pride in his success in preventing Kennedy's left-wing advisors from moving him toward contact with the People's Republic:

> I then brought up the issue which I told him I had particular strong views—the recognition of Red China and its admission to the U.N. . . .
> In expressing my strong opposition to this policy, I pointed out that . . . what was really at stake was that admitting Red China to the United Nations would be a mockery of the provision of the Charter which limits its membership to "peace-loving" nations and what was disturbing was that it would give respectability to the Communist regime which would immensely increase its power and

prestige in Asia, and probably irreparably weaken the non-Communist governments in that area.[1]

In the Johnson administration, these domestic political concerns were reinforced both by bureaucratic pressures and by the war in Vietnam. The administration was painting the struggle in Indochina as necessary for the containment of China, and it was difficult to move toward accommodation with Peking. Only if China could be shown to be an expansionist and aggressor nation could the war in Indochina be justified to the American people. Moreover, Johnson tended to defer to Dean Rusk on most foreign policy matters. Rusk, a veteran of the India-Burma theater in World War II and a target for critics of the Korean War during his tenure as Assistant Secretary of State, was unwilling to recommend to Johnson any change in China policy.

Thus, the 1960s came to a close with the United States continuing to maintain its quite extraordinary policy of attempting totally to isolate China and prevent any contact between the two countries. It is true that most travel restrictions had been lifted, but this was largely at the insistence of the Supreme Court, which gradually ruled unconstitutional many US Government restrictions on the travel rights of American citizens. Trade remained prohibited until the end of the decade. Moreover, the United States was committed to efforts to prevent Peking's entry into the United Nations or its establishment of diplomatic relations with other nations.

At the same time, fundamental changes were under way in the general public attitude in the United States toward the People's Republic. As a result of the Sino-Soviet split, the disillusionment in the United States with the Vietnam war, and the acceptance of the analysis of China being done by American China specialists, the American people were ready for a new China policy. By the time President Nixon came into office, most Americans were prepared to accept the permanence of the People's Republic as an independent nationalist regime which was not a puppet of the Soviet Union and was indeed hostile to Russian influence. China

[1] Richard M. Nixon, *Six Crises* (New York: Doubleday, 1962), pp. 408–9.

was viewed not as an aggressive expansionist power but rather as a defensive and weak nation that aspired to be treated as a major world power. The memories of the Korean War had faded in the United States by 1969, and most Americans were prepared to accept the argument that the United States needed to find some way to help bring China into the world community.

Thus, President Nixon came into office at a time when change in American China policy was long overdue and when the domestic political situation made it particularly easy for him to act. There has been some adverse reaction from the right wing of the Republican Party to what he has done, but because it is difficult for anyone to charge that President Nixon is soft on Communism, he was much freer to act than a Democratic President would have been, even in the current changed political climate. Domestic politics, then, provided the setting in which the President could move on China policy if he wanted to do so.

The explanation for his decision to modify US policy toward China, however, lies in his conception of America's role in the world and the nature of diplomacy in the 1970s. Both President Nixon and his Assistant for National Security Affairs, Henry A. Kissinger, believe that future peace and stability depend primarily on the relationship between the United States and the Soviet Union. These are the only two countries with substantial nuclear capabilities and with conventional military power that can be projected throughout the world. They are also the only two countries with the military and economic resources to sustain large-scale conflicts that could threaten world peace. Thus, from the early stages of the administration, the focus has been on a strategy that came to be known as "linkage," namely an effort to negotiate with the Soviet Union on a broad range of international issues—from the Middle East to strategic arms limitation negotiations to Indochina to the security of Central Europe. It is this process of negotiation with the Soviet Union that is to yield the generation of peace that Mr. Nixon has promised the American people and the era of world stability about which Kissinger has written so much. Thus, relations with other nations are to be seen largely as they affect the overall relationship with the Soviet Union and contribute to world stability.

⟩⟨ It is in this context of Soviet-American relations that the decision to move toward establishing contact with Peking must be seen. The President seems to feel that agreements with the Soviet Union will be more likely if the Russians fear the consequences of the absence of such agreements. In this connection, while American relations with Peking are not, as the President said, specifically directed at any other nation, they are nevertheless seen by the administration as useful in prodding the Soviet Union into agreements on a broad range of questions. Moreover, only if the United States is prepared to have contact with all the major powers of the world can it be in a position to deal with the Soviet Union across the board and to establish procedures seen as consistent with the American interests and world stability.

⊦ Thus, the President's China policy is rooted in his concept of global diplomacy rather than in the so-called Nixon Doctrine. If the trip to China was aimed primarily at the Soviet Union, the Nixon Doctrine was aimed primarily at the American people. The Nixon Doctrine was designed, on the one hand, to convince the American people that the US role in the world would be reduced and, on the other, to encourage American allies—particularly in East Asia—to take greater responsibility for their own security. While seeking to convince Americans that the US role in the world should be reduced, the Nixon Doctrine also aimed at justifying continued American involvement. Thus, the Doctrine asserts that the United States will continue to meet all of its commitments and to help countries resist Communist aggression. The effort seeks to convince the American public that while the American role is diminishing the United States still needs to maintain a substantial military capability and to concern itself with events in East Asia because of the threat from China and the Soviet Union. America's allies, it is hoped, will be persuaded that the United States is more likely to remain involved if they make a greater contribution to their own security. From the perspective of these latter two objectives, President Nixon's trip to Peking and the changed policy toward China are not at all helpful. As will be discussed below, and as must have been clear to the President and his advisors, the dramatic change in China policy serves to disquiet America's allies and to add to the concerns stemming from the Nixon Doctrine. The President's trip makes it harder to sustain domestic support for the degree of involvement in Asia that the President apparently wants to have.

If we now ask why the new policy toward China has unfolded as it has, we need to look toward the President's style in relation to bureaucracy as well as to American domestic politics. Both Nixon and Kissinger have a great distrust of entrenched governmental bureaucracies, particularly the State Department. They believe that career bureaucrats have a limited vision and that they cannot be relied upon faithfully to execute the policies laid out by the President. Moreover, they have learned that bureaucracies tend to leak information to the press. Individuals who are opposed to a policy initiative under consideration are likely to inform the press about it before it has reached the official declaration stage, in the hope that publicity will modify or block the proposal.

In order to avoid these dangers, when the President is fully committed on an issue, he and Kissinger will work alone to devise a strategy, drawing for expertise and staff work on a few members of Kissinger's entourage. Kissinger will then seek to execute it without informing the State Department. This was the pattern followed when the Soviet Union showed signs of seeking to establish a base in Cuba that could be used to refuel Soviet nuclear submarines. While the rest of the American Government tended to view this move with relative equanimity, Kissinger and the President decided that it was a serious threat to American security. Kissinger was dispatched to talk with Soviet Foreign Minister Gromyko, then visiting the United States, and negotiated an arrangement under which the American Government claims that the Russians agreed not to establish such a submarine base. The pattern reappeared in the Strategic Arms Limitation Talks (SALT). When the talks appeared to be bogged down, Kissinger apparently carried out private negotiations and the result was the President's dramatic announcement on television that an agreement had been reached with the top Soviet leaders that both governments would concentrate on negotiating an ABM limitation while at the same time limiting certain strategic offensive forces.

It is not surprising that, in the delicate negotiations for the Presidential trip to Peking, Nixon and Kissinger moved with their usual secrecy and without consultation with the bureaucracy. They must have feared that a leak to the American press might have led to a denunciation by right-wing groups before the administration was ready to announce its dramatic move. They also must have been concerned that the State Department would insist upon consultation with American allies, thereby delaying and perhaps forcing the cancellation of the proposed trip. Until it was certain that the President's trip could be arranged, there must have seemed little purpose in risking adverse publicity, particularly given the President's disdain for the advice and effectiveness of his foreign policy advisors in the bureaucracy.

Moreover, secrecy allowed the President to make another of what is now becoming a tradition of surprise Presidential television announcements. In domestic political terms, the process is very effective. The mystery surrounding the announcement of his appearance increases public interest, and the President has a large and curious audience. The statement that he was going to China and that Henry Kissinger had just returned was an event of major domestic political importance, and the trip may have valuable political benefits unless it becomes clear that it has failed to produce long-run benefits. If domestic politics and the President's style provide an explanation for the secret manner in which the arrangements for the trip were made, it is nevertheless true that they added to the cost of the proposed move in terms of America's relations with its Asian allies.

EFFECT ON ASIAN POLITICS

The immediate effects of the announcement of the President's trip to Peking cannot be divorced from the fact that it occurred without prior consultation. Since the President was not prepared to tell his own Vice-President or Secretary of Defense what he planned to do, he could not very well consult with leaders of foreign governments. This secrecy was bought at a high price.

The greatest problems created by the President's trip were in Japan. In order to understand the problem, it is necessary to consider briefly the state of American-Japanese relations and the role of the China issue in Japanese domestic politics.

Relations with China had been a critical aspect of US relations with Japan since the early 1950s when Secretary of State Dulles told Prime Minister Yoshida that the US Senate would not ratify the treaty ending the American Occupation of Japan unless the Japanese Government agreed in advance that Japan would deal with Nationalist China rather than with Communist China. Yielding to this pressure, Yoshida sent a letter to Dulles indicating that if the U.S. Senate ratified the treaty, Japan would open negotiations with Chiang Kai-shek leading toward a peace treaty. The Japanese kept their word and signed a treaty of peace with the Nationalists rather than with the Peking government. Thus forced to bind themselves to the Nationalists, the Japanese feared that they would wake up one morning to find that the United States had changed its policy toward Peking, leaving the Japanese out on a limb.

The concern of successive Japanese governments about this issue was compounded by the fact that China has been and remains an important issue in Japanese domestic politics. All the opposition political parties and major newspapers, as well as important elements within the ruling Liberal Democratic Party, have been pressing for some time for a normalization of relations with Peking. They have charged that the Japanese Government has not moved on this question out of undue deference to the United States. In fact, the Sato government's reluctance to establish formal diplomatic relations with the People's Republic is based as much on Japan's relations with Taiwan as on an unwillingness to break ranks with the United States. Nevertheless, the Japanese have always recognized that they would have to move if the United States did, and they have always desired to move first.

Recognizing the importance of the China issue to the Sato government, the United States had begun consultations with Japan on the specific issue of the China seat in the United Nations. These negotiations had been going on for some time when the Kissinger trip and the planned Presidential visit to the Chinese mainland were suddenly announced. The negotiations involved what had been described in the Japanese press as "intimate and frank" discussions. Japanese leaders were confident that they knew the precise thinking of the Nixon administration on China and that the two governments were determined to work out a common policy. This sense of cooperation is the key to Prime Minister Sato's consternation upon learning only minutes before the President's announcement that, unknown to him and to the American officials with whom the Japanese Government was consulting, the United States had been working out plans for Henry Kissinger to go to China and to arrange for a Presidential visit. The "frank" consultations Sato thought he was having with the United States were exposed as a sham.

Beyond this, however, many Japanese feel that the President's move confirmed their worst nightmare—that of an accommodation between Washington and Peking at the expense of Tokyo. Although it is unlikely that any such deal would be made, the concern persists.

Concern in Tokyo was reinforced a month later when the United States administered what became known as the "second shock," namely the unilateral American decision to impose a 10 per cent excise tax on imports and to suspend trading in gold. This step was soon followed by a US ultimatum on the question of an import quota on Japanese textiles and by the American insistence that Japan cosponsor the "important question" resolution designed to preserve Taiwan's seat in the UN General Assembly.

Although the Japanese Government has accommodated itself to these American initiatives, they have raised doubts in Japan as to whether the United States is in fact prepared to treat Japan as a major ally and a full partner in East Asia.

In other countries as well, the impact of the announcement of the Nixon trip, followed by American economic moves, has increased concern about the future of American policy. In Australia, concerns were highlighted by the fact that China had become a domestic political issue. The opposition parties had been pressing the Australian Government to move toward recognition of Peking and seized upon the American move as evidence that the United States was moving in that direction and leaving Australia behind.

In countries such as Korea, the Philippines, and Thailand, the way the visit to Peking was handled underscored the fears of leaders who had been concerned about the meaning of the Nixon Doctrine. Particularly because they were not informed in advance nor told afterward what had been discussed between Kissinger and Chinese Premier Chou En-lai, leaders of these governments could not but fear that some secret understanding had been reached with China at their expense or would be reached during the President's visit. In Thailand and Korea, the concern was particularly great. The Thai, who had been reassessing their policy because of the Nixon Doctrine and the American disengagement from Indochina, became increasingly worried that the United States might be preparing for a total withdrawal from the Asian mainland. The Koreans feared that Sino-American negotiations would focus on the Korean problem as one concrete issue that had traditionally involved the two powers and that they might feel was ripe for settlement.

THE FUTURE OF ASIAN POLITICS

It is easier to specify what the reopening of American contact with Peking cannot do and the dangers it holds for Asian politics than it is to specify the likely benefits.

Despite some wishful thinking in the United States, the President's trip to Peking is unlikely to have any appreciable effect on the Indochina war. Peking is very unlikely to be willing to persuade Hanoi to compromise on its terms for a settlement. Chinese public statements have made it clear that they will not put pressure on Hanoi, and Chinese leaders have almost certainly told American officials the same thing in private. Even if the Chinese were tempted to bring pressure on the Democratic Republic of Vietnam, the risks in such a move are considerable. It is one thing for the Chinese to be seen dealing with American imperialists and quite another for them to compromise their ideological position by seeming to throw away the interests of a key ally. Abandoning Hanoi would be tantamount to handing over Communist leadership in Southeast Asia to the Soviet Union. This Peking is not likely to be prepared to do. Moreover, even if the Chinese were to reduce or cut off aid to Hanoi in an effort to force it into a political settlement, the Soviet Union would be likely to fill the breach and enable Hanoi to carry on.

The publicity attending the President's trip has reduced some of the domestic pressure in the United States for a total American withdrawal from Vietnam. However, if it becomes clear that the President's trip has not advanced an Indochina settlement, this pressure will again increase.

The renewed contacts between Washington and Peking are no more likely to bring a settlement in Korea than in Indochina. Despite the concern of Seoul (and one may suppose Pyongyang) about these contacts, neither Peking nor Washington has the leverage on its ally to bring about a settlement between the two Koreas. Moscow remains the principal supplier of the North Korean regime. Moreover, it is unlikely that either Pyongyang or Seoul can be coerced into accepting the 38th parallel as a permanent political boundary and renouncing the use of force against its rival. A settlement of the Korean problem will have to await changes in Korean politics, whereby each government gradually accepts the other's legitimacy. Until that occurs, no deal by the superpowers can have an appreciable effect on the Korean situation.

Despite the hopes of the administration, the move toward China is not likely to have any major impact on Soviet-American relations. As the Russians have shown in dealing with the Indo-Pakistani war, they will continue to pursue what they view as their own interests in various parts of the world, even if this raises doubts in Washington about whether or not the Soviet Union is genuinely interested in a big-power détente. The two superpowers reached an agreement on Berlin in 1971 because both had a sufficient stake in reducing tensions there and not because the Soviet Union was concerned about the American *rapprochement* with China or because it wished to demonstrate its interests in peaceful relations with the United States. Agreements on SALT or in the Middle East will likewise be determined by the specific issues and pressures involved and not by Soviet fear of a Sino-American *rapprochement*.

When the President announced that Henry Kissinger had been to Peking and that he would follow, many observers assumed that some understanding on the Taiwan question must have been reached. In particular they assumed that Kissinger and the Chinese leaders had reached an understanding about Chinese admission to the United Nations. It soon became apparent that this was not the case when the United States went down to defeat in its efforts to maintain a seat for Taiwan in the General Assembly. There appears to be no more truth in the supposition that some understanding had been reached on the issue of Taiwan. American officials have made it clear that the United States intends to maintain its treaty commitments to the defense of Taiwan, and China has stated unequivocally that the issue is an internal affair of the Chinese people. It is doubtful that Peking and Washington will reach any agreement on this issue in the near future. Unless they do so, it will not be possible for them to establish formal diplomatic relations, although some lesser form of regular diplomatic contact is likely, including possibly a permanent American diplomatic presence of some kind in Peking.

Despite the seeming rigidity of both sides on the question of Taiwan, it appears that a solution might be reached if the United

States took a more flexible position on the issue along the lines laid out in a recent book by Richard Moorsteen and Morton Abramowitz.[2] They propose that the United States adopt a "one China but not now" policy, under which the United States would declare that, in its view, Taiwan is a part of China and should come under the control of the mainland. The United States would assert, however, that such a change in the *de facto* status of Taiwan should not occur by force but rather should be negotiated peacefully by the officials on Taiwan and the Chinese Government. The United States would continue to maintain its treaty commitment to Taiwan until this settlement came about but would not attempt to interfere with Peking's efforts to regain control by peaceful means.

In order to reach an understanding with Peking along these lines, the United States would almost certainly have to agree to withdraw all of its military units from Taiwan. This the United States should be prepared to do. Until the Vietnam war intensified, the United States maintained only a very small military presence on Taiwan. As that war winds down, the United States should be able to remove the forces that were introduced on the island to support Indochina operations. The remaining units, which are largely concerned with the supply and training of Taiwanese forces, could also be removed without any serious detrimental effects on Taiwan's military capability. In fact, the Nationalist forces are now strong enough to defend Taiwan against a Chinese Communist attack. Peking has made no effort to develop the amphibious and airborne capability it would need to invade a heavily defended island 90 miles off its coast. Politically, it seems unlikely that the Chinese would risk launching a military attack on Taiwan that might cause the Americans to intervene, no matter what American declaratory policy was. The American military capability to intervene in Taiwan would also not be affected by a US military withdrawal. The American power that would be

[2] Richard Moorsteen and Morton Abramowitz, *Remaking China Policy: U.S.–China Relations and Governmental Decision-Making* (Cambridge, Mass.: Harvard University Press, 1971).

used in defending Taiwan would come from the Seventh Fleet, which is not based in Taiwanese ports, and from airbases in Japan and Okinawa.

If the United States were prepared, as it should be, to assert unequivocally that Taiwan is a part of the People's Republic of China and to remove all of its military forces from Taiwan, the way might be open for a settlement of this issue. Such steps would not substantially increase the probability of a Chinese Communist military attack against Taiwan but would probably speed the day when a government on Taiwan would come to terms with the mainland government.

Beyond these more immediate questions, a dialogue between Washington and Peking is long overdue on more fundamental questions affecting the security and well-being of the peoples of China, the United States, and, indeed, of the rest of the world.

One set of issues concerns problems raised by the fact that both China and the United States are nuclear powers. The United States should begin to talk to Peking about reducing the risk of nuclear war and the effects of testing nuclear warheads. It is likely that, for a considerable period, Peking will not be seriously interested in these negotiations and rather will seek to develop nuclear parity with the United States and the Soviet Union. Nevertheless, the process of mutual education should not wait until treaties on fundamental arms control questions can be negotiated. In the shorter run, it may be possible to interest the Chinese in such measures as the treaty banning biological weapons.

The United States should also give serious consideration to the Chinese proposal to ban the first use of nuclear weapons. China is now the only nuclear power that has proclaimed unilaterally that it would never be the first to use nuclear weapons. In the case of Europe, the United States has been reluctant to issue a no-first-use declaration because of the German fear that Soviet conventional power can be deterred only by the NATO threat of the first use of nuclear weapons. In Asia, there is no such fear. There is no place along China's borders where China has an overwhelming preponderance of conventional military power. Moreover, it is unlikely that any Asian nation expects the United States to use nuclear weapons in its defense, and this question has not been an issue in US bilateral relations with any of its Asian allies. Thus, the United States should give serious consideration to the exchange of no-first-use declarations with China, even if it is not prepared to negotiate a world-wide no-first-use agreement.

The entry of China into the United Nations should also make it easier to bring Peking into negotiations on a whole range of nonpolitical matters involving space, weather, control of the sea beds, disease control, and matters of international pollution. Multinational agreements in these areas would mean very little without the participation of the government of one-quarter of the world's population, and the United States should, in its bilateral dealings with Peking, seek to interest it in joining the efforts that are under way in the United Nations and other forums.

The fascination Americans have always had with China, and the concern caused by the Chinese development of nuclear weapons, run the risk of creating a situation in which the United States appears to give priority to relations with Peking over relations with other Asian powers and in particular with Japan. In fact, in moving toward Peking, the United States appears to have lost track of the fact that relations with Japan will be much more important to American security and indeed to the security of East Asia as a whole than the bilateral relations between China and the United States. A militarized Japan would create far greater problems for Asia than China is likely to do in the next few decades. Economically, Japan can make a much more significant contribution to the development of East Asia than China possibly can. Japan is now the United States's largest overseas trading partner, and this trade will, for the indefinite future, be infinitely more important to the United States than any possible trade with the Chinese mainland. Thus, in seeking to improve relations with Peking, the United States should, more than it has in the recent past, weigh the consequences for relations with Japan. This does not mean that the United States cannot seek to improve relations with China; only that it must do so after the closest consultations with Tokyo and bearing in mind the much greater importance of relations with Japan.

For example, before moving toward the "one China but not now" policy advocated above, the United States should discuss the matter in detail with Tokyo. Fortunately, Japanese political leaders seem to be moving in the same direction. Japan has assured Peking in recent months that it accepts that Taiwan is a part of China, and the Japanese will probably be willing to go along with a "one China but not now" policy.

In dealing with other countries in East Asia, the United States should be sensitive to their concern that it is prepared to sell out their interests in an effort to come to an understanding with Peking. This problem will be particularly acute in relations with Korea. Korean leaders understandably fear that the United States may reach some understanding with Peking at their expense. In particular, the Chinese have been pressing for some time for a complete American military withdrawal from Korea. The United States has already withdrawn more than 20,000 men from Korea and is reported to be planning a total withdrawal over the next several years after the Korean military forces are built up. The arguments for such a withdrawal may be questioned on their own terms. A total American military withdrawal from Korea would increase the risk that either the South or the North would be tempted to launch military action. Moreover, such a withdrawal would raise the gravest questions in Tokyo as to whether or not the United States was reneging on a commitment to a country whose security is important to the defense of Japan. The American move toward China reinforces all of these concerns. It would thus make sense for the United States to postpone any plans for a total withdrawal from Korea and in fact to commit itself to maintaining American forces on the Korea peninsula until there is a fundamental change in the Korean political situation. At the same time, the United States should press the South Korean Government to move ahead with efforts to begin a political dialogue with North Korea.

In assessing the future, it is all too easy to assume that Asian

politics will largely be determined by the political relations between the superpowers. In fact, as in the past twenty-five years,
Asian politics is likely to be shaped largely by internal developments in the countries of the area. Superpower relations can
lead to wars causing great destruction, or they can contribute
to an environment that reduces the likelihood of interstate warfare
and increases the prospects for economic and political development. Since the superpowers do not have any incompatible vital
interests in Asia, it is to be hoped that the new Sino-American
contacts will reduce tension in East Asia and provide a climate
in which other nations can concentrate on economic and social
development. But that will occur only if there is not an American
withdrawal that ruptures American-Japanese relations and increases the sense of insecurity of small Asian nations. And it will
occur only if the United States comes increasingly to view China
as China sees itself, namely as a weak, poor, and developing
nation.

China's Foreign Policy Since the Cultural Revolution*

A. M. Halpern

TIME AND POLITICAL EVENTS have had their due impact on China's foreign policy. The transition from the combat phase to the reconstruction phase of the Cultural Revolution took place in the fall of 1968. Making all necessary allowances for the complexity of the situation, one can take the country-wide establishment of provincial revolutionary committees (September 5, 1968) and the meeting of the Twelfth Plenum of the Eighth Central Committee of the Chinese Communist Party (CCP) (October 13–31, 1968) as not only convenient but significant indices of change. The key objective of domestic political action had definitely passed from expelling a set of entrenched power-holders to establishing substantially new institutions.

As far as Chinese foreign policy has moved since the middle of 1968, it nevertheless moved comparatively slowly and deliberately. The pace of development has been more nearly comparable to that of the years 1952–56 than to other periods in the past.

* The ideas expressed in this article are those of the author and do not necessarily represent the views of either the Center for Naval Analyses or any other sponsoring agency. This article was presented at the tenth working session of the Centre d'Etude du Sud-Est Asiatique et de l'Extrême-Orient, Brussels, which was held in Bruges on November 8–9, 1971, on the theme "China After the Cultural Revolution." Bold-face numbers in parentheses are those of documents in Part Two below.

The atmosphere surrounding decisions and actions has been relatively unexcited, at least as compared with earlier critical transition periods—such as 1952–56, 1957–59, 1962–63, or 1965–66.[1] It is still by no means clear that the evolution has come to a climax, let alone to a point of completion.

Still, an overall pattern has begun to emerge. The catchwords by which one characterizes the pattern are not a matter of indifference. Some sources, especially journalistic, speak of a "return to normal." The prior history of PRC foreign policy, however, shows no single consistent pattern, but rather a series of adaptations to changing situations. The term "normal" succeeds only in diverting attention from the more serious business of analyzing the emerging pattern as an adaptation to yet another distinctive phase of world politics. Others describe recent PRC policy as "flexible." This term, too, referring to manner or style, risks begging the more important question of what objectives the policy may be aiming at. One can surely say, as a matter of observation, that Peking has developed a selective and highly differentiated approach in foreign relations, in sharp contrast to the rigidity and truncated scope of 1966–67. The questions that should be asked (and hopefully answered) are: What has been the PRC's recent analysis of the world distribution of power? How has it seen its role in this kind of world? What interests has Peking tried to *realize*, and what resources has it had available? If there is an underlying rationale or strategy to Chinese foreign policy in the current period, it is answers to these questions that would bring it to light.

It is worth looking back at both the stated rationale and the pattern of behavior of the PRC's foreign relations during the combat phase of the Cultural Revolution. The basic rationale, as originally stated in the November, 1965, article "Refutation of the New Leaders of the CPSU on 'United Action,' " was that:

[1] Briefly, 1952–56 was the period of transition to a policy based on the "Bandung spirit"; 1957–59, the period of incubation of the Sino-Soviet split; 1962–63, the transition to Sino-Soviet confrontation; 1965–66, the transition from claiming leadership of the Third World to claiming leadership of all revolutionary forces.

> The characteristic of the present world situation is that, with the daily deepening of the international class struggle, a process of great upheaval, great division and great reorganization is taking place. . . . Drastic divisions and realignments of political forces are taking place on a world scale.[2]

Put in other terms, the Chinese view was that a process of polarization was going on in all major subsystems of the world political structure: in the Communist subsystem, between "true Marxism-Leninism" (Chinese) and (Soviet) "revisionism"; in the Third World, between revolutionary countries or movements and those that were either nonrevolutionary or subservient to "imperialism" or "social-imperialism"; in the developed capitalist countries, between the revolutionary masses and the ruling classes. These several polarizing processes produced a division of the world into two types of forces, the popular (revolutionary) and the anti-popular (counterrevolutionary).

Peking defined its role as unity with and leadership of the revolutionary forces of the world under the aegis of Mao Tsetung thought. The opposing forces—the common enemies—were categorized as imperialism, revisionism (= social-imperialism), and all reactionaries (alternatively, the reactionaries of various countries). Accordingly, those with whom China kept close ties were mainly the so-called Marxist-Leninist parties throughout the world, especially those, like the Burmese, Thai, and Malayan Communist parties, who were engaged in armed struggle against incumbent governments. The various Palestinian resistance groups also qualified for Chinese approval and support. Despite their ties to the Soviet Union and their willingness to enter into negotiations with the United States, North Vietnam and the South Vietnamese National Liberation Front (later the Provisional Revolutionary Government) remained in Chinese eyes the primary focus of anti-imperialist struggle and continued to receive substantial Chinese help. Along with Albania, these came to be the only governments who could be described as highly esteemed allies of the People's Republic of China.

[2] *Peking Review*, No. 46 (November 12, 1965), p. 20.

PRC acceptance of diplomatic isolation was understandable not only in terms of the domestic situation of 1966–67, the turbulent early period of the Cultural Revolution, but also in terms of its bipolar view of the world. Even where state relations continued to be maintained, in almost all cases (Tanzania and Zambia excepted), the volume of contacts was reduced. Further, Peking cut itself off from practically all Communist-supported international front organizations and Third World institutions in which it had been active. Isolation could hardly go further. Yet, no substantial damage, either long-term or even short-term, to PRC interests can be shown to have resulted. On the contrary, there was a widespread malaise elsewhere in the world, as if China's self-isolation was an indication of some obscure pathology permeating the world political structure, and a consequent receptiveness to any Chinese initiatives that might signal a change in the situation. Further, when Peking reached the point of redefining its views and adopting different behavior, it was unusually free from prior commitments. It could reappraise its strategy from a virtual *tabula rasa* position and move in the directions and at the pace it would determine for itself—subject, of course, to environmental developments.

The first signs of reappraisal could be detected in the fall of 1968. In various declarations of that time, of which the communiqué of the Twelfth Plenum of the CCP (October 31, 1968) [3] can be taken as representative, two themes were conspicuously absent. There were no references to "great upheaval, great division, great reorganization." There were also no direct references either to China as the center of the world revolution or to Mao's thought as the sole reliable guide. This decrease in dogmatism signalled potential Chinese interest in seeking out points of common interest with a wider range of partners than its then existing set of clients. A substitute slogan was announced: "The world revolution has entered a great new era." While the same three enemies were listed (and, in fact, have continued to be listed in most official statements up to the present), the

[3] Supplement to *Peking Review*, No. 44 (November 1, 1968).

language of the declarations cast the two superpowers in the role of major enemies and gave less attention to the "reactionaries of various countries." There was a call for a broad united front of all oppressed peoples, which again showed potential interest in a wider range of contacts.

A more refined and complex statement on foreign policy was included in Lin Piao's report to the Ninth Congress of the CCP (April, 1969).[4] While the document is now dated, it retains some interest as identifying the problem areas that the Chinese felt they would have to deal with.

Apart from his detailed attention to the Sino-Soviet border crisis, Lin Piao essentially made the following points: First, China would support to the end revolutionary struggles against the three enemies. Second, the world situation was dominated by the superpowers, whether by their cooperation with each other or by their competition with each other. Third, the superpowers were vulnerable—"paper tigers"—especially to united action by the "oppressed nations." In connection with this point, the Lin Piao report reverted to the 1963 CCP polemical document, "Proposal Concerning the General Line of the International Communist Movement,"[5] to find a rationale. Lin revived the concept of the four types of contradictions in the world situation but now lumped the Soviet Union with the United States as having interests antagonistic to those of the oppressed nations, its own proletariat, other "imperialist" (i.e., developed) countries, and the socialist countries. These contradictions were "bound to give rise to revolution" (but surely not revolution in the same meaning as Mao-inspired armed struggle), which in turn would make it possible to prevent a third world war. Fourth (again borrowing the language of the 1963 proposal), Lin restated China's foreign policy as resting consistently on cooperation with socialist countries, support for the revolutionary struggles of all oppressed peoples and nations, and peaceful coexistence with countries having different social systems.

[4] *Peking Review,* No. 18 (April 30, 1969), pp. 30–34.
[5] *Ibid.,* No. 25 (June 21, 1963), pp. 6–22.

Although it was not hastily thrown together, the section of Lin Piao's report dealing with China's foreign relations was a patchwork, in which anyone could find almost anything he wished. In retrospect, its significance seems to lie in several points. While reaffirming a revolutionary perspective and mission for China, it confirmed the departure from the dogmatic Maoist bipolar view already evident in late 1968. It showed that the Chinese continued to regard themselves as a global power and to require a policy of global scope, at least in conception. It designated a variety of arenas in which China could act, and it took cognizance of opportunities for movement in state-to-state relations. It reasserted Chinese interest in all of the Third World. Most important, it designated the superpower duopoly as the central fact in the world situation and coping with the two superpowers as the PRC's problem of highest priority.

ENVIRONMENTAL FACTORS

A country facing massive problems of internal reconstruction, which China did in early 1969, should logically seek above all to reduce any threats to its security and to avoid involvement in war. If it had actually been able to make a completely fresh appraisal of its foreign policy, there were several logically possible choices that could have been considered. One would have been to seek protection by alliance with a great power. There is no evidence that the Chinese ever considered this option. They would have had little to offer or to gain in such alliance, but in any case their manifest attachment to independence would have been enough to rule it out. At the other extreme, they could choose the course of maximum expediency, playing as little a world role as possible and pursuing a narrow, short-range national interest policy. This course also does not seem to have been considered. The remaining major option was to play as big a part on the world stage as circumstances allowed.

The Lin Piao report of April, 1969 (71), indicated possible

courses of action but set out no definite tactical blueprints. At that point, the Chinese apparently estimated the world situation to be fluid. They evidently felt under no compulsion to move rapidly, even in the face of crises. The further development of their strategy and tactics depended in part on external events. Events that seem to have had a significant precipitating effect were the Sino-Soviet border crisis (1969), the Nixon-Sato joint communiqué (November, 1969), the Cambodian crisis (March, 1970), and the American–South Vietnamese incursion into lower Laos (February, 1971). While much remains obscure about the Chinese response to each of these events, some observations are possible.

The Sino-Soviet Border Crisis

Of the various speculations about the immediate origin of the border clash between the Russians and the Chinese on the Ussuri River on March 2, 1969, the least improbable is that Peking provoked it.[6] The Chinese handling of the incident clearly showed that they neither intended nor expected to provoke a war with the Soviet Union. Neither, in spite of their various psychological warfare ploys, did the Russians seek war wtih China. Both sides soon gave signs of wanting to reduce the tension, to the extent possible, by negotiations. Although it took six months to arrange the beginning of negotiations,[7] and although two years of negotiations had produced no tangible settlement of the immediate issue, the resulting change in the atmosphere of Sino-Soviet relations satisfied Chinese needs. There has been no important change in force deployments on either side of the border, but no important incidents either. The Chinese position,

[6] The incident involved a fire fight between Chinese and Russian military units at Chenpao (Damanskiy) Island, which both countries claim as their territory. A second engagement on March 15 was more likely a Soviet retaliatory gesture.

[7] On September 11, 1969, Premier Kosygin made an unscheduled trip to Peking where he conferred with Chou En-lai and others in the airport lounge. Formal talks between delegations headed by V. V. Kuznetsov and Ch'iao Kuan-hua opened in Peking on October 20, 1969.

as defined in October, 1969,[8] was to seek better state relations without compromising "ideological" positions, i.e., retaining freedom to make anti-Soviet political moves outside the context of bilateral relations. State relations have improved to the extent that ships of each country have resumed calls at the other's ports, a trade agreement has been signed, and there is minimal observance of normal civility on formal occasions. Critical tensions have been defused, the Chinese are able to keep the Soviet Union at arm's length diplomatically, they have more scope for relations with the East European countries, and for the present that seems to satisfy Chinese requirements.

An important side-effect of the Sino-Soviet quasi-détente was that it opened the way for resumption of Chinese relations with North Korea, which had been rendered practically nonexistent by the Cultural Revolution. The two countries have discovered a number of interests in common, especially vis-à-vis Japan. Contacts between them have been increasingly frequent, leading up to the recent agreement on Chinese military aid to North Korea. But coordination of foreign policies has in no sense resulted in North Korea's becoming dependent on China. North Korea's relations with the Soviet Union have not deteriorated, and the pattern of its relations with other socialist countries and Communist parties by no means duplicates China's.

Chinese tolerance of these differences represents a striking departure from the dogmatism of 1966–67, when the Chinese preferred to alienate all old friends who would not join in denouncing the Soviet Union and rendering obeisance to Mao's thought. The present relationship is also not as exclusive as in 1963–64, when the North Koreans (and even the North Vietnamese) almost matched China in their criticisms of the Soviet Union and its Communist Party (CPSU). The North Koreans continue to represent themselves as members of the socialist community, while the Chinese still officially regard that community as an instrument of Soviet social-imperialism. The customary Chinese formula de-

[8] See the Chinese Government statement in *Peking Review,* No. 41 (October 10, 1969), pp. 3–4.

scribes North Korea as the eastern outpost of anti-imperialist struggle, emphasizing its location in Asia, while the North Koreans also accept designation by others as the eastern outpost of the socialist camp. Similarly, the North Vietnamese refer to the socialist camp as one of the three revolutionary forces in the world, while the Chinese do not.

In 1963–64, it was reasonable to speak of an Asian Communist coalition, or even of an Asian wing of the Communist movement, though even at that time the coalition was not a complete Chinese imperium. Relations among the same elements today are a good deal looser, though still effective. Chinese relations of "mutual assistance and cooperation with socialist countries" do not in practice extend very far or deep. The point on which there is widest agreement is that the world Communist movement at present does not need a single center—not the Soviet Union, but also not China. In the context of structural change in the world movement as a whole, there is no basis for a united Asian wing, nor is there a compelling reason for China to put a high value on the socialist camp as such.

The Nixon-Sato Communiqué

The Nixon-Sato communiqué of November, 1969,[9] was a clear sign that the Sato government felt ready to claim for Japan a bigger, more active, more autonomous role in world affairs. Here, the Prime Minister was in accord with Japanese public opinion. Secondly, Sato designated South Korea and Taiwan as areas of special interest in terms of Japan's national security. In this the Prime Minister was moving much in advance of public opinion, which he presumably hoped to win over to support him.

Peking evidently felt that Japan had now attained new weight as a factor in the environment and that a response was required to deal in both the short and the long run with the implications of this development. A common evaluation of the Japanese challenge expedited the Sino–North Korean *rapprochement*. The two countries have conducted a sustained propaganda campaign

[9] See Secretary of State, *United States Foreign Policy, 1969–70* (Washington, D.C.: U.S. Government Printing Office, March, 1970), pp. 503 ff.

centered on the theme that Japanese militarism has been revived and that Japan will again inevitably pursue an imperialistic policy in Asia. In terms of countermeasures, China has taken on the main burden of trying to influence Japanese developments, with North Korea playing a minor role and with some of the PRC's client parties in Southeast Asia lending support on the level of propaganda.

It was not until September, 1970, that the Chinese tactical line vis-à-vis Japan assumed definite shape. Under the dogmatic Cultural Revolution approach, the Chinese had alienated the Japanese Communist Party (JCP) and precipitated splits in that party and in other Japanese organizations devoted to improvement of Sino-Japanese relations. Thereafter, only the most determinedly loyal Japanese supporters of Maoism (whom the JCP terms "blind followers") were hospitably received in Peking. The new approach rests basically on a broad united front tactic—an earlier Maoist tactic once known as "isolating the diehards and winning over the middle forces"—with the JCP still excluded from the front. The approach further involves the cultivation of dialogue, apparently fruitful, with a broad range of Japanese figures; pressures on Japanese business by denying trade to those who do not conform to Chinese conditions and by favoring some sectors of the business community to the disadvantage of others; exploiting the apprehensions of those opposed to Premier Sato's policies and thus stimulating controversy even within the government party; and finally offering in concrete terms proposals that, if acceptable to Japan, could turn tension into cooperation.[10]

[10] For Chou En-lai's interviews with representatives of visiting Japanese trade missions, in which he declared that China would not trade with Japanese firms that conducted trade with South Korea or Taiwan, see particularly Kyodo news dispatches from Peking, April 16 and 20, 1970. See also the March 1, 1971, joint communiqué of the Chinese and Japanese Memorandum Trade Offices, *Peking Review,* No. 11, March 12, 1971, pp. 24–25.

The PRC's conditions for normalizing relations with Japan have been stated on a number of occasions, with some variations in content. Of particular interest is the July 2, 1971, joint statement by the China-Japan Friendship Association and the Komeito (Clean Government Party), *Peking Review,* No. 28, July 9, 1971, pp. 20–21.

Peking's objectives can only be inferred. It seems clear that, first of all, the Chinese place some value on forcing Sato to relinquish his position as Premier sooner than he would do so voluntarily. Second, the Chinese evidently hope to change Japan's policies toward themselves, especially as regards Taiwan and Korea. Third, by stimulating controversy, the Chinese can hope to delay significantly, if not to forestall entirely, the implementation of some Japanese policies, especially in the national security area. Fourth, and most speculatively, the Chinese may have made an analysis of major social trends in Japan, according to which impending changes in Japanese public opinion and attitudes will support the prolongation of short-run changes in China policy at least into the middle run.

The new PRC approach to Japan has already shown some results and is likely to show more. Over the coming decade, however, it seems probable that the Sino-Japanese relationship will continue to be essentially competitive and to be perceived as such on both sides. As Japan functions more independently, China will continue to need a distinctive policy toward Japan, with side-effects on other Chinese policies. Thus, Japan should continue to be a factor in keeping the overall pattern of Chinese policy selective and differentiated.

The Cambodian Crisis

The Cambodian crisis of March, 1970, was a windfall for China. Whatever possibility there might have been for a negotiated settlement over Vietnam without China's participation or out of accord with Chinese wishes was ruled out. Peking was able to redefine the Vietnam problem as the Indochina problem, to acquire a more important role in the situation, and to reduce the role the Soviet Union could play. It was noteworthy that the Chinese handled the situation in such a way as to emphasize that it was an Asian problem to be handled by Asians. The situation played some part in promoting Sino–North Korean *rapprochement* and also in promoting some additional Southeast Asian support for the PRC's anti-Japanese posture. It also fitted well with Chinese slogans calling for the future of Asia to be determined not by outside powers but by the peoples of Asia.

In direct connection with the new situation in Indochina, Peking issued Mao's statement of May 20, 1970 (72). Since the statement contained very little that had not already been said by Chinese sources, it appeared at the time that it served mainly to confirm the PRC's commitment to the Indochinese coalition. In retrospect, two items stand out as more important. One was the emphasis on the ability of small countries to defeat big powers. If taken as an estimate of the facts, this is the equivalent of estimates made by others that the superpowers are not equipped to control the internal affairs of the developing countries. The second was the slogan which declared that while "the danger of a new world war still exists, . . . revolution is the main trend in the world today." This slogan remains the most often quoted portion of the May 20th statement. It represented a new development in comparison with Lin Piao's report to the Ninth Congress, which envisaged the two possibilities that either a world war would give rise to revolution or that revolution would prevent the war. It superseded the slogan issued for National Day (October 1), 1969, which called on the people of the world to "use revolutionary war to eliminate any war of aggression" launched by "any imperialism or social-imperialism." [11]

Taken in the May, 1970, context, the statement that revolution is the main trend might have signified either that China no longer felt immediately subject to Soviet military threat or that Peking was confident of a favorable outcome in Indochina, or both. In a broader perspective, especially taking into account the frequent repetition of the slogan, it may have reflected a more general estimate that it was now possible to place greater weight on the political aspect of political-military opposition to the two superpowers.

[11] *Peking Review,* No. 38 (September 19, 1969), pp. 3–4.

Laos

The outcome of the February, 1971, incursion into Laos was described by both China and North Vietnam as a victory of great strategic significance for their side. Such statements were issued often enough and in sufficient detail to indicate that their authors were committed to this estimate, whether the raw military facts supported it or not. It can be taken for granted that the phrasing of President Nixon's April 7, 1971, television speech ("a reasonable chance to survive" for South Vietnam),[12] though ignored in public, was carefully noted in private by the Chinese and the North Vietnamese. Shortly afterward came the presentation by the Neo Lao Hac Sat of a new formula for a settlement in Laos,[13] followed by the seven-point proposal of the South Vietnam Provisional Revolutionary Government in July.[14] Peking immediately made public its endorsement of the latter proposal. The contrast with the PRC's previous handling of similar proposals —which was typically to ignore their existence—was marked.

While we cannot know for certain what calculations North Vietnam or China made concerning the Laotian incursion, it seems beyond doubt that these calculations were directly connected with ping-pong diplomacy and the opening of Sino-American dialogue.

GENERAL PERSPECTIVES

Besides the precipitating effect of crises like those described above, there is evidence—some from Chinese rhetoric, some from behavior—of ongoing changes in the PRC's general perspectives on world affairs. The impact of crises, by and large, is to force decisions, to precipitate reappraisal of particular situations and to redefine opportunities for subsequent action. In addition, the

---

[12] *New York Times,* April 8, 1971.
[13] New China News Agency, May 16, 1971.
[14] *Ibid.,* July 4, 1971.

Chinese have been engaged in constructing an estimate of the whole world situation and of their role in it.

Peking has by no means abandoned its interest in or support of its clientele of the Cultural Revolution period, whether these are Marxist-Leninist parties or revolutionary movements. But as it enlarged the scope of its external relations, which necessarily involved dealing with others as between states, it could no longer sustain a concept of international relations as exclusively synonymous with international class struggle. Fervent adoration of Mao and devotion to Mao Tsetung Thought as the acme of Marxism-Leninism could no longer be the essential and sufficient qualification for acceptance as partners. In public dialogue with states that valued their relations with the Soviet Union, China did not require them to denounce modern revisionism and limited itself to attacking the Soviet Union not by name but in the transparent guise of "some persons."

In practice, some movements supported by Peking have improved their organization during the past three years (e.g., the Thai, Philippine, and Malayan movements), while others have lost ground (e.g., the Burma Communist Party and the Palestinian movement). Up to the middle of 1970, Chinese media regularly reported on the activities of these movements and frequently quoted their statements. From that point on until recently, they have largely discontinued the practice. In an interview in May, 1971, with Arab journalists, Chou En-lai hinted that the extent of future Chinese support might be contingent on performance.[15]

Lin Piao's report to the Ninth Congress dealt with the Third World as consisting essentially of the "oppressed peoples and nations." The emphasis at that time and for some time afterward seemed to be on the revolutionary, anti-superpower potential of these peoples and nations. Revival of the concept of "four contradictions" [16] could not fail to recall that in earlier polemics the Chinese had advanced the thesis that the underdeveloped countries were the "hinge of revolution." In actual dealings with such

[15] Published in *An-Nahar*, Beirut, May 29, 1971 (and translated in Foreign Broadcast Information Service, hereafter FBIS).

[16] (1) Between oppressed nations, on the one hand, and imperialism and

countries, the Chinese have adapted themselves to the fact that the Third World countries are not all identically situated and that complete Third World unity cannot be realized. An external measure of the change in approach might be the comparative frequency of the slogan that describes China as the "best and most reliable friend of all the oppressed peoples." Chinese statements have several times contained approval of nonalignment,[17] and during the visit to China of His Imperial Majesty Haile Selassie of Ethiopia in October, references to Bandung and the Ten Principles formulated there, as well as the Five Principles of Peaceful Coexistence (first enunciated in the Indo-Chinese agreement on Tibet of April 29, 1954) were conspicuous.[18] These rhetorical changes can be taken as signs of Chinese interest in state-to-state relations and Chinese adaptation to the needs and interests of other nations.

In geographical terms, the revival or expansion of Chinese relations with countries of the "intermediate zone" has occurred in Africa, Latin America, and the Middle East, as well as with countries of what was once described as the "second intermediate zone," namely, Western Europe.[19] The end of 1970 was something of a turning point. In relation to the Middle East, the Chinese

---

social imperialism on the other (i.e., USSR); (2) between proletariat and bourgeoisie in capitalist and revisionist countries; (3) between imperialist and social imperialist countries and among the imperialist countries; (4) between socialist countries on the one hand, and imperialism and social imperialism on the other.

[17] For an early example, see the joint communiqué on the establishment of diplomatic relations with Cameroun in *Peking Review*, No. 15 (April 9, 1971), p. 9. Other relevant examples are Li Hsien-nien's speech at a June 9 banquet in honor of Yugoslav Secretary of State for Foreign Affairs Mirko Tepavac, *Peking Review*, No. 25 (June 18, 1971), pp. 4–5, and the July 30 communiqué on the visit of the Government Delegation of Sierra Leone in *Peking Review*, No. 32 (August 6, 1971), pp. 23–24.

[18] See *Peking Review*, No. 42 (October 15, 1971), pp. 5–7, and for additional detail NCNA news releases, October 5–13, 1971.

[19] Since the establishment of the People's Republic in 1949, the Chinese have regularly referred to the underdeveloped (Third World) countries, viewed as an area that imperialism seeks to dominate, as the "intermediate zone." In 1964, shortly after France recognized Peking, Foreign Minister Ch'en Yi introduced the term "second intermediate zone" to refer to Western Europe.

endorsed the claims of the petroleum-exporting countries as against Western consumers. In relation to Latin America, the Chinese supported demands for a 200-mile limit on fishing rights. Statements such as these might deserve little attention except for being made by Peking. In these cases, China was identifying its interests with the state interests of others, interests of a specific character, which could hardly be called revolutionary interests except by an extraordinary extension of the meaning of the term. Further, the statements coincided in time with others related to China's conception of its status as a power, to be examined below.

By contrast, Peking has done very little about state relations with the Asian countries. This is not for lack of receptivity by those countries. Since early 1969, almost all the Asian countries have openly and repeatedly stated that they hoped for normal relations with China, subject usually to the condition that Peking would guarantee not to intervene in their domestic affairs. There are several possible explanations for Chinese tardiness in making an overt response to these advances. There was no urgency of time in responding to standing invitations. It is precisely in Asia that Peking is most committed to anti-government movements.[20] The sudden drop in attention to Asian revolutionary movements after mid-1970 could be taken as a signal of a negative order that the Chinese were disposed to consider state relations, but there was no immediate follow-up in action. Perhaps most important, the approach the Chinese would take to the Asian countries would depend on the state of the Vietnam situation, which in turn would depend on the state of Sino-American dialogue. When these two elements in the situation became somewhat clarified, China made some moves in political relations with Burma and in economic relations (with political overtones) with Malaysia.

The evolution of the Chinese approach to revolutionary movements and the Third World was necessarily related to a similarly evolving approach to the two superpowers. China's role in the

---

[20] Peking's handling of the Ceylon and Bangla Desh crises in 1971 reflected special circumstances surrounding each case.

world would be defined basically by its choice in this area. If the Chinese modified or largely discarded the dogmatic Cultural Revolution view of the world as polarized between "popular" and "anti-popular" forces, there were a number of alternatives theoretically open to them. They could have adopted an isolationist position, pursuing narrow national interests based on pure expediency. But the Chinese Communists have consistently thought in grand terms and valued a role in the world exceeding their capability rather than falling short of it. It was predictable that they would see their role as opposition to, perhaps rivalry with, the two superpowers.

Another theoretical alternative was alliance with either of the superpowers against the other. This choice could have been ruled out on various grounds, of which Peking's attachment to independence of action is in itself enough. A third alternative was to enter the power political game as the aspiring third great power. This might entail either maneuvering between the United States and the Soviet Union, uniting in an opportunistic way with one or the other according to the issue involved, or trying to establish a monopolistic sphere of influence equal to those of the superpowers. But China does not have the resources to sustain either of these roles. Further, with the emergence of Western Europe and Japan as autonomous power centers, the concept of tripolarity could have only a tenuous basis in fact. The real world in which China must function was clearly going to be a multipolar one.

While maintaining a posture of opposition to the superpowers, the Chinese had to defuse critical tensions and reduce, if they could not eliminate, potential threats to their security. It is a fair surmise that Peking's interest in direct relations with the superpowers does not go much beyond this. China achieved this much in relation to the Soviet Union toward the end of 1969. It was no accident that the first visible signs of *rapprochement* with Yugoslavia became apparent at that time. Defusing tensions with the United States has taken longer, largely because of the Indochina problem. It was again no accident that *rapprochement* with Burma and Malaya coincided in time with ping-pong diplomacy.

Rhetorical clarification of China's concept of its world role came at the end of 1970. Coincident with its verbal support for the oil-producing countries and for the Latin American position on territorial seas, Peking declared that it abjured the standing of a superpower and opposed the power politics practiced by the two superpowers. The declaration was rather disingenuous. China has not sworn off power politics of all kinds but has chosen a pattern of power politics consonant with its real capabilities. The Chinese now represent themselves as a medium-size power, declare that all countries, big and small, are equal, and are engaged in identifying, wherever they can find them, particular interests they have in common with medium and small countries. They further justify this approach as the practical way for all such countries to resist the hegemonistic policies of the superpowers and resurgent Japan.

Whatever reservations one may have about the genuineness over a longer period of a modest Chinese view of their world role, they have in the past months followed the tactics of accord with small and medium countries. In the process, the Chinese have accommodated themselves to the needs of their partners as often as they have demanded accommodation of their own needs. They have not tried to conceal all divergences of view with their partners—for example, in their joint communiqué with Romania. But there is a great and obvious difference in style and method from the not-so-distant past when the Chinese insisted on absolute doctrinal purity as a condition of partnership. The present pattern of Chinese behavior verges on being all things to all men.

The pattern of Chinese foreign policy is not yet complete or stable. For China genuinely to accept the fact of multipolarity is a major and unprecedented step. No one can be sure that the Chinese Communists can adjust, ideologically as well as tactically, to the standing of a medium power or to the idea that relations between nations are more valuable than international relations between classes. Nor can anyone be confident that the Chinese perceive the status quo in the world, especially in Asia, as sufficiently acceptable so that they will have more incentive to work within it than try to upset it. Finally, it remains to be seen whether China's dialogue with the superpowers and Japan will be conducted as an effort to secure a long-term peaceful and stable international environment or only as a tit-for-tat struggle under special conditions.

SUMMARY

By way of recapitulation, the problem-by-problem analysis of trends can be summarized in a chronological framework.

In late 1968 and early 1969, concurrently with the change from the combat phase to the reconstruction phase of the Cultural Revolution, programmatic statements indicated that Chinese foreign policy was being reappraised. There was, first, a de-emphasis of dogmatic Maoism and, second, a revival of theses and postures that had been stated in authoritative form in 1963. In the designation of enemies, attention was concentrated on the two superpowers, who were described as duopolistic, to the relative neglect of "all reactionaries."

The Sino-Soviet border crisis overshadowed other matters during most of 1969. Tentative resolution of the crisis was followed by the Sino–North Korean *rapprochement*. At the same time, Japan came into focus as a major adversary of China. The common problem of Japan contributed to Sino–North Korean solidarity, but coordination of foreign policy positions, by mutual assent, did not cover all areas. The Chinese stressed Asian Communist solidarity but rejected reintegration with the socialist camp. They did, however, pursue relations with Romania and Yugoslavia as well as Albania—i.e., with Eastern European countries who had points of difference with the Soviet Union.

In the wake of the Cambodian crisis, the Chinese made further efforts toward an alignment of Asian forces, with mixed success. At the same time, they indicated through the Mao statement of May 20, 1970 (72), that they no longer felt their own security to be imminently threatened. Chinese interest in the Third World as a whole, not only in the revolutionary Third World, thereafter grew, implying greater expectations placed on political opposition to the superpowers, as compared with armed struggle.

In mid-1970, Chinese public attention to Asian revolutionary movements decreased. Concurrently, Peking brought to a conclusion the negotiations for recognition by Canada by assenting to a formula regarding Taiwan that the Canadians could accept, since it required only that Ottawa "take note" of the Chinese position without necessarily endorsing it. Thereafter, using formulas that were increasingly easy for others to accept, China has revived or established diplomatic relations with a number of African, Middle Eastern, and European countries. Representation in the United Nations was obviously one of the interests at stake, but the purpose of locating common interests with other countries as against the superpowers and Japan was also served. In September, 1970, Peking launched a well-designed campaign to procure changes in Japan's China policy and national security policy.

At the end of 1970 and the beginning of 1971, the Chinese simultaneously declared that the People's Republic was not a superpower and that it identified itself with certain particularistic national demands of some Middle Eastern and Latin American countries. Following the South Vietnamese incursion into Laos of February, 1971, the Chinese displayed some expectation that the Indochina situation could be resolved to their satisfaction. The opening of a dialogue with Washington quickly followed. Thereafter, the Chinese declared more and more often that they regarded themselves in the role of a medium power with interests in common with all medium and small countries, expressed approval of nonalignment, and conducted an active friendly dialogue with many such countries. In the Asian area, however, the Chinese continue to support insurgent movements and have moved slowly in resuming or establishing state-to-state relations.

The pattern implied by these courses of action bears an uncomfortable, if incomplete, likeness to what used to be denounced as Liu Shao-ch'i's policy of *san-ho i-hsiao*—easing of the tactics of struggle in relations with imperialism, revisionism, and all reactionaries, and reduction of assistance to the underdeveloped countries. There is some evidence of discontent on the part of China's revolutionary clients and within the Chinese Communist leadership as well.

In regard to the revolutionary clients, the discontent is shown by the wording of their messages honoring the twenty-second anniversary (October 1, 1971) of the founding of the People's Republic. Whereas the Romanian, North Vietnamese, and some other messages spoke of the significance of the Chinese revolution in terms of its having tipped the balance of world power in favor of the socialist camp, the Malayan, Thai, and some other Asian Party messages made no such reference but stressed the importance of the Cultural Revolution and described the impact of the founding of the People's Republic only in terms of its making China the main bulwark of world revolution.[21]

Since April, 1969, some articles of a programmatic nature have seemed to revive the dogmatic revolutionary view of the world. The chief ones were the April, 1970, article on the 100th anniversary of Lenin's birth[22] and the March, 1971, article on the centennial of the Paris Commune.[23] I have not referred to either of these in discussing general trends because they appear to have been deviations from the main line and to have had no discernible impact on foreign policy.

In July and August, 1971, the formula "great upheaval, great division, great reorganization," which had been absent from Chinese statements since October, 1968, suddenly reappeared. A nonauthoritative press article at the beginning of 1970 had stated that this turmoil had been the characteristic of world developments in the 1960s, implying that the policy of that decade was no longer valid.[24] In his July 11 speech at a Peking mass rally in honor of the tenth anniversary of the Sino-Korean

[21] See NCNA and other press releases September 30, 1971, *et seq.*, as carried in FBIS.
[22] *Peking Review*, No. 17 (April 24, 1970), pp. 5–15.
[23] *Ibid.*, No. 12 (March 19, 1971), pp. 3–13.
[24] See "Victorious Years and Bright Prospects," *Ibid.*, No. 2 (January 9, 1970), pp. 18–22.

Treaty of Friendship, Cooperation, and Mutual Assistance, Politburo member Yao Wen-yuan stated, in direct contradiction to
this view, that the world situation was currently still in the period
where the formula fully applied. Huang Yung-sheng (at that
time a Politburo member and Chief of the General Staff of the
PLA), in a speech on August 18 at a banquet honoring a North
Korean military delegation, also used the phrase. On August 27,
Chou En-lai stated at a meeting in honor of the Cambodian revolutionary figure Ieng Sary that the current world situation was
characterized by "great upheaval" but conspicuously omitted
the last two-thirds of the formula.[25]

Similar discrepancies in the use of such phrases have in the
past proved to be indicators of controversy, and hence there is
reason to suspect that some members of China's leadership still
cling to the dogmatic revolutionary view of a bipolar world.

There is thus evidence, by no means conclusive, that the general trend of Chinese foreign policy is subject to some amount
of pulling and hauling by both external and internal forces. Chou
En-lai, however, appears committed to the multipolar analysis
and the strategy based on it. He is at an age where it is appropriate
for him to consider by what legacy he wants to be remembered
in Chinese history. A foreign policy that is adjusted to multipolarity but does not demean China's revolutionary mission may
be that legacy, or a large part of it.

[25] For Yao Wen-yuan's speech, see *ibid.,* No. 29 (July 16, 1971), pp.
12–14. For a summary of Huang Yung-sheng's speech see *ibid.,* No. 35
(August 27, 1971), p. 29. Huang did not repeat the formula in his remarks
at a September 9 banquet celebrating the twenty-third anniversary of the
founding of North Korea. For Chou's remarks, see *ibid.,* No. 36 (September 3, 1971), p. 12.

The Men and Institutions Behind China's Foreign Policy

Donald W. Klein

WHEN THE MEN in Washington and the men in Peking began
their esoteric communications or "signals"—each side seeking
some sort of accommodation—it is not difficult to imagine that
the Americans saw themselves in contact with Chou En-lai. Mao
Tse-tung, of course, must have sanctioned so significant a change
in policy. But once a decision was taken, few would doubt that
Chou would be in the pilot's seat. To a large degree, this was
all *déjà vu* for Chou. He had been the central figure who, in
1955 at Bandung, had called for the Sino-American ambassadorial
talks. Begrudgingly, the stern Mr. Dulles accepted the invitation,
but within two years the talks had come to little and hopes for
a *rapprochement* lay dormant for well over a decade.

It seems extraordinary that Chou and his familiar team still call
the shots a decade and a half after the 1955 initiative. But more
extraordinary is the fact that this same team first dealt with
Americans three decades ago—in the Nationalist capital at Chungking and in the Communist capital of Yenan. Before elaborating
in detail, we might define in rough outline Chou's "team." Never
large in numbers, it consisted of a small group led by Chou to
Chungking to coordinate Nationalist-Communist cooperation in the
war against Japan. It included Chou's wife, Teng Ying-ch'ao, as

43

well as such familiar present-day figures as Ch'iao Kuan-hua, Peking's chief envoy to the twenty-sixth UN General Assembly, and Huang Hua, China's permanent representative to the Security Council. It also included Ch'iao Kuan-hua's wife, Kung P'eng, who was as familiar to Western newsmen and diplomats as her husband, and who was an Assistant Minister of Foreign Affairs in Peking until her death in 1970. Still others were Wang Ping-nan, Chang Han-fu, and Ch'en Chia-k'ang, but these three were purged during the Cultural Revolution.

During the early 1940s, and especially after Pearl Harbor, Chou En-lai's coterie in Chungking devoted much time to cultivating Americans—apparently upon the correct assumption that the United States would emerge as the Western nation most deeply involved in Asia following Japan's defeat. These same considerations apparently governed the red-carpet treatment accorded the US military-diplomatic team sent to Yenan in 1944. American interests were more short-range; the United States wanted a first-hand assessment of the help the Yenan Communists might render in closing the circle on Japan. It is noteworthy that Yeh Chien-ying, one of Yenan's top generals, was among those who spent a good deal of time conferring with Americans in 1944. Mao Tse-tung himself, it should be noted, also gave freely of his time in 1944 in talks with American military and diplomatic figures.

The complex triangular Nationalist-Communist-American relations in 1944–46 were viewed with considerable misgivings by Yenan, but ties between the United States and Yenan were sufficient to gain Communist participation in a truce arrangement in early 1946. This was worked out by General George C. Marshall, and it provided for an "executive headquarters" in Peiping (as it was then called) with representatives from the American, Nationalist, and Communist sides. Chou En-lai, as always, was the major figure. Throughout the first half of 1946, in Chungking, Nanking, and Shanghai, he was in almost constant negotiations with General Marshall. In the meantime, the executive headquarters in Peiping worked on the day-to-day details. There, the Communist side was led by General Yeh Chien-ying, and high on Yeh's staff was Huang Hua, who doubled as Yeh's private secretary and head of the Communist press section. The Marshall Mission, of course, aborted by mid-1946. But even three years later, with the Communists secure in their victory over the Nationalists we find Huang Hua sounding out the last American ambassador to China on the possibility of US recognition of the yet-to-be-born People's Republic of China. Four years later, however, soon after the Korean War Armistice, Huang Hua was at Panmunjom engaging in bitter verbal duels with his American counterpart.

The next chapter in US-China relations began in mid-1955 with the inauguration of the ambassadorial talks in Geneva, which were transferred to Warsaw in 1958. For nine years, Wang Ping-nan, a veteran member of Chou En-lai's circle, conducted these talks—first with U. Alexis Johnson, and then with Jacob Beam, and lastly with John Cabot. In all, Wang took part in 120 meetings before his replacement in 1964 by Wang Kuoch'üan. The ambassadorial talks began on a hopeful note when both sides agreed to release the nationals of the other side held in its country. The talks were conducted with little rancor, but for the most part no progress was made on the crucial issues (e.g., the status of Taiwan). However, these periodic negotiations occasionally served both sides as a useful "safety valve," which helped keep the lid on situations that could have led to serious Sino-American confrontations. But, with the launching of the Cultural Revolution in 1966 the Warsaw talks lost much of their significance. There were post–Cultural Revolution indications that they would be revitalized; however, they were in effect pre-empted in 1971 by the Kissinger visits to China. As of 1972, the Warsaw talks still exist on paper, but it appears that they will be effectively replaced by higher-level negotiations which, on the Chinese side, may be handled by Peking's delegation to the United Nations.

This truncated version of American–Chinese Communist relations is scarcely sufficient to prove that Peking has some "American experts." Yet, it does demonstrate that, at senior levels, there are men with considerable—if somewhat dated—experience in negotiating with the United States. But much of this, from the Chinese viewpoint, is a negative lesson. To be sure, some Americans had cordial ties with these Chinese, such as the amicable relations between General Marshall and Chou En-lai. But in the final analysis, the Chinese apparently concluded that at best men such as Marshall were ineffective pawns in a basically anti-Communist policy worked out in Washington, or at worst double-dealers who wore a mask of personal cordiality but who were in fact willing agents of a hostile government. In any case, these same Chinese have come to the forefront in recent months as the United States and China have inched toward the settlement of many differences. It is, of course, not surprising to see Chou En-lai and Huang Hua, both seasoned diplomats, at the forefront in *any* important Chinese diplomatic maneuver. More striking, perhaps, is the "return" of Yeh Chien-ying to a foreign-affairs involvement. Following the Marshall Mission period, Yeh was concerned chiefly with domestic matters for two decades, but, given his past contacts with Americans, it does not seem a matter of chance that his "re-emergence" coincided with the Kissinger visits to China.[1]

A handful of men familiar with Americans does not, of course, prove that Peking was diplomatically prepared to move to center stage upon its entry into the United Nations in 1971. We must probe a little more deeply to see what stands behind Chou, Ch'iao, and Huang. Such a probe might well begin with the oft-repeated line from Washington, initiated two decades ago, that Peking was "isolated" from the realities of the world. This theme resulted from the Korean War embargo clamped upon China, which was indeed highly successful for a *few* years. But within a short time the ability to isolate China—diplomatically, militarily, or economically—became a piece of frozen rhetoric in Washington that the rest of the world increasingly ignored. The Bandung

[1] It is also possible that Yeh's re-emergence might have been more closely linked to the political fall of Lin Piao in the summer and autumn of 1971.

period, the new-found independence of a score of African nations, and the restiveness of de Gaulle were but a few of the factors that eroded Washington's enforced isolation upon China.

By the mid-1960s, Peking had formal diplomatic ties with fifty nations. This figure can be roughly doubled if one notes trade relations and the innumerable "unofficial" delegations—sports, cultural, peace, friendship—that roved around the world during these years. Lest this be regarded as something of an exaggeration to make a point, we can note that in 1970—just prior to Canadian recognition of Peking—more than three-fourths of Chinese trade was conducted with nations *not* having formal diplomatic relations with Peking. On the face of it, scores of Chinese must have gained diplomatic experience and first-hand knowledge of dozens of nations (North and South America largely excepted) during Peking's "pre–United Nations" period. But even such a common-sense hypothesis would have little meaning today if Peking had failed systematically to develop a corps of foreign service personnel, or if such a corps had been destroyed during the Cultural Revolution.

The Chinese did, in fact, create a tightly-knit foreign service corps. This achievement was already apparent by the end of the first decade of Communist rule.[2] By that time the majority of Peking's ambassadors had substantial experience abroad, there was a clear-cut pattern of in-service promotions generally unmarred by "political" appointees, and these efforts were buttressed by the growth of institutions offering specialized training for diplomats. These patterns continued through the mid-1960s, but they were cast in doubt early in the Cultural Revolution when virtually all senior diplomats were recalled. For the next two to three years, most of these men simply disappeared. Then, beginning in 1969, Peking returned to the world scene by send-

[2] For further elaboration of these points, see the writer's "Peking's Evolving Ministry of Foreign Affairs," *The China Quarterly*, No. 4 (October–December, 1960), pp. 28–39, and "The Management of Foreign Affairs in Communist China," in John M. H. Lindbeck (ed.), *China: Management of a Revolutionary Society* (Seattle: University of Washington Press, 1971), pp. 305–42.

ing senior diplomats abroad once more. Consequently, we are now in a position to make judgments about the quality of the foreign service in relation to the damage reportedly inflicted on it during the Cultural Revolution. Such judgments are difficult at best, but we might gain some broad insights by posing two questions: What has happened to the forty-two ambassadors who were abroad when the Cultural Revolution began, and what sort of diplomatic experience do the "new" (post–Cultural Revolution) ambassadors have?

Of the forty-two ambassadors in 1966, exactly half have been sent abroad again as ambassadors since 1969, and another eight are working in some phase of foreign affairs in Peking. About a quarter of these forty-two men are still not mentioned in the Chinese media, but it seems likely that some of them will return to active diplomatic work. Turning to post–Cultural Revolution ambassadorial assignments, we find that high standards of experience are again the norm. Of the 50 posts now filled, 1 is held by a former vice-minister of foreign affairs, 23 by men who were previously ambassadors, another 14 by former counselors (i.e., the second-ranking post in embassies), and eight more held other high-level posts (e.g., consul general; director or deputy director of a Foreign Ministry department). In sum, these 50 men have an average of about ten years in the diplomatic corps; on the negative side, only 4 of the 50 lack previous diplomatic experience.[3]

Backing up Peking's ambassadors is a Foreign Ministry whose structure is similar to most foreign offices around the world (see Appendix I). As elsewhere, most of the work is done by functional departments (e.g., the Protocol Department) or area "desks" (e.g., the Soviet Union and East European Affairs Department).

[3] As of December, 1971, China also has diplomatic relations with India, Laos, Uganda, Kenya, Burundi, Tunisia, San Marino, Iran, Belgium, Peru, Lebanon, Rwanda, Sierra Leone, Turkey, Senegal and Iceland. Envoys will presumably be sent to these nations in the near future. Peking also maintains diplomatic relations with the Sihanouk-led Cambodian government; however, because this is presently a government-in-exile in Peking, it has not been calculated in these figures.

On top of this structure is Foreign Minister Chi P'eng-fei and four vice-ministers. The late Ch'en Yi encountered considerable trouble during the Cultural Revolution from "ultra-leftist" factions, and was also in bad health until his death in 1972. As a consequence, he did not serve as Foreign Minister after the autumn of 1968 and afterward appeared very infrequently (but not as Foreign Minister). Chi P'eng-fei has served as the Acting Foreign Minister since April, 1971. He is a stranger to the outside world in contrast to the colorful Ch'en Yi. But Chi is no newcomer to China's diplomatic community. He was one of the first men Peking sent abroad in the early 1950s, serving as ambassador to East Germany. Moreover, Chi served for sixteen years as a vice-minister, and at the time of his elevation to Acting Foreign Minister he was the ranking vice-minister. Subordinate to Chi are three highly experienced vice-ministers: the previously mentioned Ch'iao Kuan-hua, and Han Nien-lung and Hsu I-hsin. Han had tours as ambassador in Pakistan and Sweden; he was an assistant-minister from 1958 to 1964, and has been a vice-minister since 1964. Hsu has had ambassadorial tours in Albania, Norway, and Syria, and has been a vice-minister since 1966. The only senior Foreign Ministry figure without extensive experience is Li Yao-wen, a former military man who became the fourth vice-minister in mid-1971.

Sino-American relations reached a new and dramatic stage with China's entry into the UN in 1971. Twenty-one years earlier, in 1950, a Chinese Communist delegation to the United Nations led by Wu Hsiu-ch'üan presented China's case regarding the Korean War and Chinese entry into that conflict. Between 1950 and 1971, Wu's group was the *only* Chinese Communist mission to set foot on American soil. A victim of the Cultural Revolution, Wu was not a candidate to lead the delegation in 1971. That role fell to Ch'iao Kuan-hua, who, incidentally, was one of Wu's aides in 1950 in New York.

Ch'iao's delegation demonstrated Peking's ability to field a first-rate diplomatic team. As already noted, the diplomatic experience of Ch'iao and his deputy Huang Hua predates, in effect, the establishment of the People's Republic in 1949. The multi-lingual Ch'iao has held several top diplomatic posts in Peking, and is currently a vice-minister of Foreign Affairs. Prior to Peking's entry into the United Nations, China participated in three conferences of global significance: the Geneva Conference of 1954, which ended French involvement in Indochina; the famous Bandung Conference in 1955; and the 1961–62 Geneva Conference on Laos. Ch'iao is the only senior Chinese diplomat who attended all three conferences. He was also at Chou En-lai's side in 1954 when Chou and Nehru articulated the "Five Principles of Peaceful Coexistence," and, a decade later, he accompanied Chou on his celebrated ten-nation tour of Africa. Diplomats and newsmen familiar with Ch'iao have a uniformly high estimate of his abilities.

Huang Hua, Peking's permanent representative to the Security Council, brings credentials to New York only slightly less impressive than his superior. He has a decade of experience in Africa as ambassador to Ghana and then to Egypt, which should stand him well in terms of the problems of African nationalism and the delicate Middle East situation. (Huang was in Cairo during the brief 1967 war with Israel.) Below Ch'iao and Huang are three representatives to the United Nations, Fu Hao, Ch'en Ch'u, and Hsiung Hsiang-hui.[4] (Ch'en is concurrently deputy representative under Huang to the Security Council.) This trio offers the Chinese mission specialized knowledge of several important areas of the world. Ch'en has headed both the Soviet Union and East European desk and the West Asian and North African (i.e., Arab countries) desk in the Foreign Ministry. Fu Hao has eight years experience as a senior diplomat in India, and Hsiung is one of the few Chinese diplomats educated in the United States (at Western Reserve in Cleveland in the late 1940s). For five years in the 1960s, Hsiung headed the Chinese mission in London.

Below this top echelon are other experienced men. An Chih-

[4] Several members of Peking's UN delegation, including Ch'iao, Fu, and Hsiang, returned to China after the General Assembly session.

yuan had a long tour in Moscow, and, because strained Sino-Soviet relations caused Peking to withdraw its ambassador, he served as chargé d'affaires *ad interim* for several years. Another man, T'ang Ming-chao, lived for many years in New York where in the late 1940s he edited a Chinese-language newspaper. In the post-1949 years, he was frequently cast as an "unofficial ambassador" on his numerous tours abroad with friendship delegations. T'ang's daughter, T'ang Wen-sheng (also known as Nancy T'ang), is also with the UN delegation; utilizing her American education, she serves as interpreter for Ch'iao Kuan-hua.

The ranking secretary, well-educated Chou Nan, served in Pakistan and Tanzania and has a good command of English. Another secretary, Kao Liang, doubles as press officer; he was a newsman in India and Tanzania (and several other east African countries) in the 1950s and 1960s. Subordinate secretaries include Hsu Hsin-hsi, an attaché in Stockholm in the 1960s, and Chao Wei, who during the same years held a similar post in Tanzania. More recently, Chao has worked on Middle East and African affairs in Peking. The senior correspondent with the mission, Yeh Chih-hsiung, headed the London office of the New China News Agency during the 1960s.

The data above strongly suggest several points. First, Peking has placed high priority on its mission to the United Nations. It is staffed with top diplomats who have varied experience in a number of key points throughout the world, or who have counterpart experience on the critical "desks" in the Foreign Ministry in Peking. Secondly, the Chinese were fully aware that Washington would take careful note of the composition of the delegation. The Americans, presumably, would conclude that Peking was leading with its best foot forward and would have men of sufficient stature to deal—directly or indirectly—with Washington on Sino-American relations. This second point can also be put in a negative perspective. Low-level staffing by Peking, or the inclusion, for example, of ill-experienced army officers (who hold so many other posts in the Chinese hierarchy) might well have been a "signal" to Washington that China intended to play a "wrecking" role at the United Nations. It might also have suggested that elements in Peking opposed to a Sino-American *rapprochement* had sufficient strength to thwart such a *rapprochement.*

We have already demonstrated that Peking has a foreign service "establishment" roughly similar to most major nations. Less explicit, but perhaps more pertinent for Sino-American relations in the immediate years ahead, is the fact that the Chinese have an extremely well developed "unofficial" foreign service corps. (See Appendix II.) It must be remembered that, for the past two decades, Peking has been dueling with Taipei to establish itself as the "legitimate" government of China. And, because Peking has usually been quite flexible in foreign affairs, it has frequently used a number of unofficial organs to deal with nations with whom it did not have formal diplomatic relations. Nowhere is this more apparent than in foreign trade. As already noted, in recent years, China has conducted three-fourths of its trade with countries that did not have formal ties with Peking. The organizational solution for China was simple: the establishment of the "unofficial" China Council for the Promotion of International Trade. In virtually all walks of life, there are similar "unofficial" bodies. The use of such organizations will be steadily obviated as many nations break formal ties with Taipei and establish them with Peking, but it is easy enough for the Chinese to maintain this unofficial framework for the years immediately ahead.

It seems most unlikely that Peking and Washington will establish formal diplomatic relations in the near future. American domestic politics militate against such a short-range possibility. At the highest levels—as already demonstrated by Chou En-lai's reception of Kissinger and Nixon—it is clear that China will not feel constrained by the lack of diplomatic relations with the United States. But in day-to-day relations, the Chinese may very well be fastidious about the lack of such relations. That is, they may insist that Americans deal with Chinese through ostensibly unofficial bodies. To do otherwise, from the Chinese viewpoint, would be to reinforce the "two-China" formula that so deeply distresses them. Moreover, another great nation, Japan, figures in Chinese calculations. Clearly, and by a wide margin, the United States and Japan have more complex relations with Taiwan than any other nation or combination of nations. Thus, for Peking to sanction "normal" relations when they are not in fact normal with either Washington or Tokyo would perpetuate the "two-Chinas" situation.

There is no intent here to delve into all the facets of Sino-American relations. However, it might be noted in brief that the complex Taiwan problem is only one of Peking's concerns. To the degree that China wishes to trade, for example, with nations having highly developed economies, it might be argued that Western Europe would suffice—and thus the United States and Japan could be ignored. But there is much evidence that Peking wants to avoid overreliance on one nation or area. In short, there are compelling reasons why Peking desires to deal with America and Japan—and such reasons will probably suffice to override the "two-China" problem. If this assumption is correct, then it is likely that Peking will, in its dealings with Washington, operate along lines employed for so many years in its "unofficial" ties to Japan: that is, a fairly high level of relations conducted by unofficial bodies.

In more concrete terms, what is the "Japanese formula"? It is the willingness of senior figures in the Japanese "establishment" (many of them holding government posts) to deal with China "unofficially." For example, a ranking member of the Sato's Liberal Democratic Party will deal with China in some other capacity—such as the head of a "friendship" delegation to China. If this same man works out a lucrative business contract, it is not officially endorsed by the Japanese Government—even though in Tokyo it will be common knowledge that the government stands behind the agreement. All of this, of course, is equally well known to the Chinese, who have been willing to play the game. Both the Chinese and the Japanese have nearly twenty years' experience in these semi-official contacts. The Americans can play the game, too. They have less experience, and doubtless certain Congressmen will raise objections.

We should not forget that much of the world's "relations" are conducted between individuals, organizations, or institutions in different countries. For example, student-exchange programs exist with only the minimum of governmental involvement (e.g., as regarding visas). To that degree, Americans can play the "unofficial game" as well as Chinese. But let us turn to a hypothetical situation (which is drawn from an *actual* situation involving China and Japan). Assume that China and the United States wish to formalize fishing rights close to each other's coasts. On the Chinese side, this could be handed by the China Fishery Association (ostensibly unofficial). No objections will be voiced in Peking; no official from a coastal province will argue that Peking is ignoring his province; no trade union official will insist that foreign fishermen are impairing the livelihood of his union members. On the American side, assume that the (hypothetical) Western States Fishery Association speaks for the United States. But no sooner is the agreement signed than the California governor denounces it; a Seattle labor leader threatens a strike; and seventeen US Senators insist that such arrangements require Senate ratification in the form of a treaty.

This example may be overdrawn. But it does suggest that the American penchant for legalisms may impede the development of Sino-American relations. In this sense, the United States is probably less well prepared than Peking to conduct semi-official relations. Rigidity on the American side will probably be most pronounced if the US Government tries to monopolize relations. On the other hand, there is ample room for flexibility if the United States utilizes the numerous educational institutions and private organizations that have a large fund of knowledge about China, as well as highly trained personnel.

Appendix I. Ministry of Foreign Affairs

Foreign Minister

Vice Foreign Ministers

Functional Departments *

Staff (or General) Office
Information Department
Protocol Department

Geographic Departments

Asian Affairs Department
Soviet Union and East European Affairs
Department
West Asian and African Affairs Department
West European, American, and Australasian Affairs Department

* It appears that one of the by-products of the Cultural Revolution has been a simplification of the structure of the functional departments. In addition to the above, there existed a few years ago the following departments: Personnel, International Affairs, Treaty and Law, General Services, Training, Consular Affairs, and Translation. Presumably, their functions have been absorbed by one of the above departments.

Appendix II. China's Unofficial Foreign Affairs Organizations

China has a number of ostensibly unofficial "mass" or "people's" organizations. Those devoted solely to foreign affairs are in List A. Others, in List B, are primarily for domestic affairs but are often active in international relations. Both lists are selective rather than comprehensive.

List A	*List B*
Afro-Asian Solidarity Committee	All-China Federation of Literary and Art Circles
All-China Returned Overseas Chinese Association	All-China Federation of Trade Unions
China Asia-Africa Society	All-China Journalists Association
China Council for the Promotion of International Trade	All-China Sports Federation
China Peace Committee	All-China Students Federation
Chinese People's Association for Friendship with Foreign Countries	All-China Youth Federation
Chinese People's Institute of Foreign Affairs	China Scientific and Technical Association
Friendship Associations (These include associations vis-à-vis all Communist nations except Yugoslavia, vis-à-vis Africa and Latin America, plus the following nations: Afghanistan, Burma, Cambodia, Ceylon, India, Indonesia, Iraq, Japan, Laos, Nepal, Pakistan, and the United Arab Republic.)	National Red Cross Society of China
	Political Science and Law Association of China
	Women's Federation of China

PART TWO

Sino-American Relations, 1949–71

Roderick MacFarquhar

I. Points of Departure

FRIENDSHIP between the Americans and the Chinese Communists was hardly to be expected when the People's Republic of China (PRC) was set up on October 1, 1949. Memories of the past were too freshly bitter; visions of the future were too radically divergent. Yet the two governments might have established a *modus vivendi;* mutual recognition was not unthinkable. But as it turned out, the Truman administration had only nine months in which to shed its major misconception regarding the Chinese Communist government and to educate its Republican critics. It had not accomplished these tasks by the time the Korean War broke out, and then it was too late.

As early as April, 1949, a Communist official called Huang Hua—destined to become the PRC's first permanent head of mission at the UN in 1971—raised the question of recognition with the American ambassador in the recently captured Nationalist capital, Nanking. The ambassador was Dr. Leighton Stuart, a man with long experience of China, principally in the field of education; he had been president of Peiping's Yenching University when Huang Hua had studied there. Stuart temporized. The question of recognition would have to await the establishment of a new government acceptable to the Chinese people and the international community.[1]

Dr. Stuart's cool response to his ex-pupil's inquiries may have added acerbity to Mao's pen when he derided fellow countrymen

[1] Tang Tsou, *America's Failure in China: 1941–50* (Chicago: University of Chicago Press, 1963), pp. 513–14.

who believed China could hope for anything from the West in an
article commemorating the twenty-eighth anniversary of the
Chinese Communist Party (CCP) published on June 30, 1949.
Entitled "On the People's Democratic Dictatorship" (1),[2] the
article expressed the hatred of imperialism that was to infuse
the foreign policy posture of the new regime, a hatred that accurately reflected nationwide resentment after a century of hu-
miliation at the hands of foreign powers.

For much of that century it had been Britain that had been
most detested by the Chinese as the chief Western imperialist
power exploiting their land. But with the entry of the United
States into the Pacific War after the Japanese attack on Pearl
Harbor, American influence became paramount in China. The
United States allotted large quantities of military and economic
aid to the Chinese Nationalist government, and Roosevelt made
great efforts to increase its international prestige. Chiang Kai-shek
was invited to the Cairo Conference in 1943 as the equal of the
American President and the British Prime Minister, Churchill.

Many American officials working in China, notably General
Stilwell, commander of US forces in the China-Burma-India
theatre, were dissatisfied with the use made of American weapons
and were critical of the passive strategy of Chiang Kai-shek. Some
felt that the Communists, bound in uneasy alliance to the Nationalists, were more vigorous and less corrupt. American liaison
officials were posted in the Communist capital, Yenan, and there
was a period of friendly collaboration there and in Chungking,
the Nationalist wartime capital, where Chou En-lai headed a
CCP mission. Chiang Kai-shek greatly resented these contacts
and, since Roosevelt had no intention of deserting his principal
Chinese ally, relations between the Americans and the Chinese
Communists inevitably suffered.

After the defeat of the Japanese, the Truman administration sent
General Marshall to mediate between the Nationalists and the
Communists in order to prevent civil war and promote coalition

---

[2] Boldface numerals in parentheses in this and following chapters refer to
the documents, which are numbered consecutively through Part Two.

government. But again, in the last analysis, the American administration was never likely to throw over its Nationalist allies in favor of Communists, especially at a time when the wartime friendship with the Soviet Union was being rapidly eroded by the cold war. When all-out civil war finally broke out in China in 1947, the Americans tried to help Chiang Kai-shek win.

American aid was in vain. By the time Mao wrote "On the People's Democratic Dictatorship," the Communists' victory was virtually complete, and it was time for him to start thinking about the international posture of the future Communist government. China's experience of imperialism and the Chinese Communists' experience of American intervention in the civil war had proved to Mao that the new regime had to "lean to one side" and place itself four-square in the Soviet camp—quite apart from ideological predilections that would have encouraged such a course anyway.

Yet, at this very moment, the Truman administration was preparing to dissociate itself from the clearly defeated Nationalists. On August 5, 1949, the State Department published an immensely long White Paper on *United States Relations with China, with Special Reference to the Period 1944 – 49*.[3] In his letter of transmittal to President Truman (2), Secretary of State Dean Acheson blamed the Nationalists' defeat on the military ineptitude of their leaders and the absence of a will to fight among their armies. More than $3 billion of American economic and military aid had been ineffective in bolstering the Nationalist regime. Nothing else the Americans reasonably could have done would have materially affected the result.

Acheson's considered judgment did not avert Republican charges that the Truman administration had "lost China." Senator McCarthy alleged treachery and conducted his notorious witch-hunt for Communists in government. The careers of a number of State Department China specialists were ruined.

[3] Republished in two volumes as *The China White Paper, August 1949* (Stanford, Calif.: Stanford University Press, 1967), with an introduction by Lyman P. Van Slyke.

Nor did Acheson's letter of transmittal have any better reception among the Chinese Communists. Naturally, Mao welcomed what he saw as an American confession of defeat and even an indication of the "decline of the entire system of imperialism." [4] But, he argued, the letter of transmittal did not indicate any sweeping change of attitude on the part of Washington toward the Chinese Communists; Acheson was not going to "act like 'the butcher who lays down his knife and at once becomes a Buddha' or 'the robber who has a change of heart and becomes a virtuous man.' " [5] Acheson had asserted that the Chinese Communists were subservient to the Soviet Union and that "a major portion" of the Chinese people might be exploited in the interests of Soviet imperialism. He had expressed the hope that China would eventually throw off this foreign yoke and that America "should encourage all developments in China which now and in the future work toward this end" (2). It was, understandably, an analysis that angered Mao.[6]

Acheson's position was flawed by a fatal contradiction. The White Paper had spelled out the indigenous nature of the Chinese revolution; yet, Acheson apparently took Mao's decision to lean to one side as proof that the Chinese leaders "had publicly announced their subservience to a foreign power, Russia . . ." (2). This implied that the actions of the Chinese Government were interpreted as part of the machinations of a Soviet-dominated international Communism whose activities in Europe had already caused the American and other Western governments much alarm; and this in turn meant that American attitudes toward the Chinese Communist regime would inevitably be influenced by the actions of Communists elsewhere. This was to be of decisive importance on the outbreak of the Korean War.

On January 5, 1950, three months after the proclamation of the PRC, President Truman announced that the US would not defend

[4] See "Cast Away Illusions, Prepare for Struggle" (August 14, 1949), reprinted in *Selected Works of Mao Tse-tung*, IV (Peking: Foreign Languages Press, 1961), p. 425.

[5] *Ibid.*, p. 428.

[6] *Ibid.*

the island of Formosa (Taiwan) where the remnant Nationalist forces had taken refuge (3). In his elucidation of the President's statement (4), Secretary of State Acheson rejected the idea of legal quibbling over the status of the island, and a week later, on January 12, he underlined the administration's attitude by describing an American defense perimeter that excluded Formosa (and South Korea) (5). The following month, the State Department pointed out to Congress (6) the unreality of alternative suggestions for the future of the island. Since the administration had earlier concluded that the Communists would be able to capture the island in the absence of American intervention,[7] the US was clearly prepared by early 1950 for the emergence of one, united, Communist China.

But the administration's policy continued to be contradictory. On the same day that Acheson excluded Formosa from America's defense perimeter, the US delegate to the UN stated that he could not vote for the replacement of Nationalist China by the PRC in the Security Council because his government still recognized the Nationalist government. The Americans did not wish to classify their negative vote as a veto and proclaimed themselves ready to accept the majority opinion, but, perhaps not surprisingly, the majority voted with the United States.[8]

The reluctance of the Truman administration to pursue its emerging China policy to a logical conclusion and recognize the new Chinese Government was partly the result of Republican attacks and an assumption of popular hostility to such a step.[9] Other factors were the maltreatment of American diplomats during the second half of 1949 and the seizure of US government property in Peking on January 14, 1950, which led to

[7] Tang Tsou, *op. cit.*, pp. 527–28.
[8] The speech of the US delegate can be found in UN, *Security Council Official Records,* Fifth Year, 460th Meeting: January 12, 1950, No. 2, p. 6. The rejection of the Soviet resolution led to the withdrawal of the Soviet representative from the Security Council. It was his continued absence at the time of the outbreak of the Korean War that permitted the Security Council to vote to resist the North Korean attack with UN forces.
[9] Tang Tsou, *op. cit.*, pp. 515–16.

a withdrawal of all American official personnel from China.[10] Underlying these proximate reasons was the schizophrenic analysis of the status of the new Chinese Government. Was it an independent authority to be appraised for recognition on the basis of its actions; or was it, as Acheson continued to assert (5), a Soviet puppet? Clearly the answer to this question must affect recognition policy. If Acheson anticipated that the Chinese people might one day rise in their wrath against the Communist government because of its subservience to Soviet imperialism, then there was a case to be made for not bolstering up a puppet regime by according it recognition.

In fact, though Stalin certainly exacted privileges for the Soviet Union in the borderlands, Acheson's depiction of the dismemberment of North China was hopelessly exaggerated. More importantly, Acheson completely misjudged the likely role of the Chinese leadership. Stalin's policy aroused resentment; it was not willingly agreed to by pliant tools. Acheson's misjudgement helped warp American China policy for years to come.

[10] *Ibid.*, pp. 516–18.

MAO SETS THE COURSE

1. Mao Tse-tung, "On the People's Democratic Dictatorship," June 30, 1949 (Extracts)

Imperialist aggression shattered the fond dreams of the Chinese about learning from the West. It was very odd—why were the teachers always committing aggression against their pupil? The Chinese learned a good deal from the West, but they could not make it work and were never able to realize their ideals. Their repeated struggles, including such a country-wide movement as the Revolution of 1911 [which overthrew the last imperial dynasty], all ended in failure. Day by day, conditions in the country got worse, and life was made impossible. Doubts arose, increased and deepened. World War I shook the whole globe. The Russians made the October Revolution and created the world's first socialist state. Under the leadership of Lenin and Stalin, the revolutionary energy of the great proletariat and labouring people of Russia, hitherto latent and unseen by foreigners, suddenly erupted like a volcano, and the Chinese and all mankind began to see the Russians in a new light. Then, and only then, did the Chinese enter an entirely new era in their thinking and their life. They found Marxism-Leninism, the universally applicable truth, and the face of China began to change . . .

Over a long period of twenty-two years, Chiang Kai-shek dragged China into ever more hopeless straits. In this period, during the anti-fascist Second World War in which the Soviet Union was the main force, three big imperialist powers were knocked out, while two others were weakened. In the whole world only one big imperialist power, the United States of America, remained uninjured. But the United States faced a grave domestic crisis. It wanted to ensalve the whole world; it supplied arms to help Chiang Kai-shek slaughter several million Chinese. Under the leadership of the Communist Party of China, the Chinese people, after driving out Japanese imperialism, waged the People's War of Liberation for three years and have basically won victory.

Thus Western bourgeois civilization, bourgeois democracy and the plan for a bourgeois republic have all gone bankrupt in the

65

eyes of the Chinese people. Bourgeois democracy has given way to people's democracy under the leadership of the working class and the bourgeois republic to the people's republic. This has made it possible to achieve socialism and communism through the people's republic, to abolish classes and enter a world of Great Harmony. . . .

All other ways have been tried and failed. Of the people who hankered after those ways, some have fallen, some have awakened and some are changing their ideas. Events are developing so swiftly that many feel the abruptness of the change and the need to learn anew. . . .

Up to now the principal and fundamental experience the Chinese people have gained is twofold:

(1) Internally arouse the masses of the people. . . . (2) Externally, unite in a common struggle with those nations of the world which treat us as equals and unite with the peoples of all countries. That is, ally ourselves with the Soviet Union, with the People's Democracies and with the proletariat and the broad masses of the people in all other countries, and form an international united front.

"You are leaning to one side." Exactly. The forty years' experience of Sun Yat-sen and the twenty-eight years' experience of the Communist Party have taught us to lean to one side, and we are firmly convinced that in order to win victory and consolidate it we must lean to one side. In the light of the experiences accumulated in these forty years and these twenty-eight years, all Chinese without exception must lean either to the side of imperialism or to the side of socialism. Sitting on the fence will not do, nor is there a third road. We oppose the Chiang Kai-shek reactionaries who lean to the side of imperialism, and we also oppose the illusions about a third road.

"You are too irritating." We are talking about how to deal with domestic and foreign reactionaries, the imperialists and their running dogs, not about how to deal with anyone else. With regard to such reactionaries, the question of irritating them or not does not arise. . . .

"We need help from the British and the U.S. governments." This, too, is a naive idea in these times. Would the present rulers of Britain and the United States, who are imperialists, help a people's state? Why do these countries do business with us and, supposing they might be willing to lend us money on terms of mutual benefit in the future, why would they do so? Because their capitalists want to make money and their bankers want to earn interest to extricate themselves from their own crisis—it is not a matter of helping the Chinese people. The Communist Parties and progressive groups in these countries are urging their governments to establish trade and even diplomatic relations with us. This is goodwill, this is help, this cannot be mentioned in the same breath with the conduct of the bourgeoisie in the same countries. Throughout his life, Sun Yat-sen appealed countless times to the capitalist countries for help and got nothing but heartless rebuffs. Only once in his whole life did Sun Yat-sen receive foreign help, and that was Soviet help. Let readers refer to Dr. Sun Yat-sen's testament; his earnest advice was not to look for help from the imperialist countries but to "unite with those nations of the world which treat us as equals." Dr. Sun had experience; he had suffered, he had been deceived. We should remember his words and not allow ourselves to be deceived again. Internationally, we belong to the side of the anti-imperialist front headed by the Soviet Union, and so we can turn only to this side for genuine and friendly help, not to the side of the imperialist front . . .

[*Selected Works of Mao Tse-tung,* IV (Peking: Foreign Languages Press, 1961), pp. 413–15, 417.]

THE US ABANDONS CHIANG KAI-SHEK

2. Secretary of State Dean Acheson's "Letter of Transmittal" with China White Paper, July 30, 1949 (Extracts)

The historic policy of the United States of friendship and aid toward the people of China was . . . maintained in both peace and war. Since V-J Day, the United States Government has authorized aid to Nationalist China in the form of grants and credits totaling approximately 2 billion dollars, an amount equivalent in value to more than 50 percent of the monetary expenditures of the Chinese Government and of proportionately greater magnitude in relation to the budget of that Government than the United States has provided to any nation of Western Europe since the end of the war. In addition to these grants and credits, the United States Government has sold the Chinese Government large quantities of military and civilian war surplus property with a total procurement cost of over 1 billion dollars, for which the agreed realization to the United States was 232 million dollars. A large proportion of the military supplies furnished the Chinese armies by the United States since V-J Day has, however, fallen into the hands of the Chinese Communists through the military ineptitude of the Nationalist leaders, their defections and surrenders, and the absence among their forces of the will to fight.

It has been urged that relatively small amounts of additional aid—military and economic—to the National Government would have enabled it to destroy communism in China. The most trust-worthy military, economic, and political information available to our Government does not bear out this view.

A realistic appraisal of conditions in China, past and present, leads to the conclusion that the only alternative open to the United States was full-scale intervention in behalf of a Govern-ment which had lost the confidence of its own troops and its own people. Such intervention would have required the expenditure of even greater sums than have been fruitlessly spent thus far, the command of Nationalist armies by American officers, and the probable participation of American armed forces—land, sea, and air—in the resulting war. Intervention of such a scope and magni-tude would have been resented by the mass of the Chinese people, would have diametrically reversed our historic policy, and would have been condemned by the American people.

It must be admitted frankly that the American policy of assist-ing the Chinese people in resisting domination by any foreign power or powers is now confronted with the gravest difficulties. The heart of China is in Communist hands. The Communist leaders have foresworn their Chinese heritage and have publicly announced their subservience to a foreign power, Russia, which during the last 50 years, under czars and Communists alike, has been most assiduous in its efforts to extend its control in the Far East. In the recent past, attempts at foreign domination have appeared quite clearly to the Chinese people as external aggression and as such have been bitterly and in the long run successfully resisted. Our aid and encouragement have helped them to resist. In this case, however, the foreign domination has been masked behind the façade of a vast crusading movement which apparently has seemed to many Chinese to be wholly indigenous and national. Under these circumstances, our aid has been unavailing.

The unfortunate but inescapable fact is that the ominous result of the civil war in China was beyond the control of the government of the United States. Nothing that this country did or could have done within the reasonable limits of its capabilities could have changed that result; nothing that was left undone by this country has contributed to it. It was the product of internal Chinese forces, forces which this country tried to influence but could not. A decision was arrived at within China, if only a decision by default.

And now it is abundantly clear that we must face the situation as it exists in fact. We will not help the Chinese by basing our policy on wishful thinking. We continue to believe that, however tragic may be the immediate future of China and however ruthlessly a major portion of this great people may be exploited by a party in the interest of a foreign imperialism, ultimately the profound civilization and the democratic individualism of China will reassert themselves and she will throw off the foreign yoke. I consider that we should encourage all developments in China which now and in the future work toward this end.

In the immediate future, however, the implementation of our historic policy of friendship for China must be profoundly affected by current developments. It will necessarily be influenced by the degree to which the Chinese people come to recognize that the Communist regime serves not their interests but those of Soviet Russia and the manner in which, having become aware of the facts, they react to this foreign domination. One point, however, is clear. Should the Communist regime lend itself to the aims of Soviet Russian imperialism and attempt to engage in aggression against China's neighbors, we and the other members of the United Nations would be confronted by a situation violative of the principles of the United Nations Charter and threatening international peace and security.

Meanwhile our policy will continue to be based upon our own respect for the Charter, our friendship for China, and our traditional support for the Open Door and for China's independence and administrative and territorial integrity.

[*The China White Paper, August 1949* (Stanford, Calif.: Stanford University Press, 1967), I, pp. xv–xvii.]

3. President Truman's Statement on Status of Formosa, January 5, 1950 (Extract)

The United States Government has always stood for good faith in international relations. Traditional United States policy toward China, as exemplified in the open-door policy, called for international respect for the territorial integrity of China. This principle was recently reaffirmed in the United Nations General Assembly resolution of December 8, 1949, which, in part, calls on all states—

> To refrain from (a) seeking to acquire spheres of influence or to create foreign controlled regimes within the territory of China; (b) seeking to obtain special rights or privileges within the territory of China.

A specific application of the foregoing principles is seen in the present situation with respect to Formosa. In the joint declaration at Cairo on December 1, 1943, the President of the United States, the British Prime Minister, and the President of China stated that it was their purpose that territories Japan had stolen from China, such as Formosa, should be restored to the Republic of China. The United States was a signatory to the Potsdam declaration of July 26, 1945, which declared that the terms of the Cairo declaration should be carried out. The provisions of this declaration were accepted by Japan at the time of its surrender. In keeping with these declarations, Formosa was surrendered to Generalissimo Chiang Kai-shek, and for the past 4 years, the United States and the other Allied Powers have accepted the exercise of Chinese authority over the Island.

The United States has no predatory designs on Formosa or on any other Chinese territory. The United States has no desire to obtain special rights or privileges or to establish military bases on Formosa at this time. Nor does it have any intention of utilizing its armed forces to interfere in the present situation. The United States Government will not pursue a course which will lead to involvement in the civil conflict in China. Similarly, the United States Government will not provide military aid or advice to Chinese forces on Formosa. In the view of the United States Government, the resources on Formosa are adequate to enable them to obtain the items which they might consider necessary for the defense of the Island. The United States

Government proposes to continue under existing legislative authority the present ECA program of economic assistance.

[*American Foreign Policy* (hereafter *AFP*), *1950–1955* (Washington, D.C.: Department of State, 1957), II, pp. 2448–49]

4. Dean Acheson's Address to Special Press Conference, January 5, 1950 (Extract)

The Chinese have administered Formosa for 4 years. Neither the United States nor any other ally ever questioned that authority and that occupation. When Formosa was made a province of China nobody raised any lawyers' doubts about that. That was regarded as in accordance with the commitments.

Now, in the opinion of some, the situation is changed. They believe that the forces now in control of the mainland of China, the forces which undoubtedly will soon be recognized by some other countries, are not friendly to us, and therefore they want to say, "Well, we have to wait for a treaty." We did not wait for a treaty on Korea. We did not wait for a treaty on the Kuriles. We did not wait for a treaty on the islands over which we have trusteeship.

Whatever may be the legal situation, the United States of America, Mr. Truman said this morning, is not going to quibble on any lawyers' words about the integrity of its position. That is where we stand.

Therefore, the President says, we are not going to use our forces in connection with the present situation in Formosa. We are not going to attempt to seize the Island. We are not going to get involved militarily in any way on the Island of Formosa. So far as I know, no responsible person in the Government, no military man has ever believed that we should involve our forces in the island. . . .

[*AFP 1950–1955,* II, p. 2451.]

5. Dean Acheson's Speech to the National Press Club, Washington, D.C., on Relations Between the Peoples of the United States and Asia, January 12, 1950 (Extracts)

Nobody, I think, says that the Nationalist Government fell because it was confronted by overwhelming military force which it could not resist. Certainly no one in his right mind suggests that. Now, what I ask you to do is to stop looking for a moment under the bed and under the chair and under the rug to find out these reasons, but rather to look at the broad picture and see whether something doesn't suggest itself.

The broad picture is that after the war, Chiang Kai-shek emerged as the undisputed leader of the Chinese people. Only one faction, the Communists, up in the hills, ill-equipped, ragged, a very small military force, was determinedly opposed to his position. He had overwhelming military power, greater military power than any ruler had ever had in the entire history of China. He had tremendous economic and military support and backing from the United States. He had the acceptance of all other foreign countries, whether sincerely or insincerely in the case of the Soviet Union is not really material to this matter. Here he was in this position, and 4 years later what do we find? We find that his armies have melted away. His support in the country has melted away. His support largely outside the country has melted away, and he is a refugee on a small island off the coast of China with the remnants of his forces.

As I said, no one says that vast armies moved out of the hills and defeated him. To attribute this to the inadequacy of American aid is only to point out the depth and power of the forces which were miscalculated or ignored. What has happened in my judgment is that the almost inexhaustible patience of the Chinese people in their misery ended. They did not bother to overthrow this government. There was really nothing to overthrow. They simply ignored it throughout the country. They took the solution of their immediate village problems into their own hands. If there was any trouble or interference with the representatives of the government, they simply brushed them aside. They completely withdrew their support from this government, and when that support was withdrawn, the whole military establishment disintegrated. Added to the grossest incompetence ever experienced by any military command was this total lack of support both in the armies and in the country, and so the whole matter just simply disintegrated.

The Communists did not create this. The Communists did not create this condition. They did not create this revolutionary spirit. They did not create a great force which moved out from under Chiang Kai-shek. But they were shrewd and cunning to mount it, to ride this thing into victory and into power. . . .

U.S. Attitude Toward Asia

. . . What has our attitude been toward the peoples of Asia? It has been, I submit to you that we are interested—that Americans as individuals are interested in the peoples of Asia. We are not interested in them as pawns or as subjects for exploitation but just as people. . . . For 50 years, it has been the fundamental belief of the American people—and I am not talking about announcements of government but I mean a belief of people in little towns and villages and churches and missionary forces and labor unions throughout the United States—it has been their profound belief that the control of China by a foreign power was contrary to American interests. The interesting part about that is it was not contrary to the interests of the people of China. . . .

I hear almost every day someone say that the real interest of the United States is to stop the spread of communism. Nothing seems to me to put the cart before the horse more completely than that. Of course we are interested in stopping the spread of communism. But we are interested for a far deeper reason than any conflict between the Soviet Union and the United States. We are interested in stopping the spread of communism because communism is a doctrine that we don't happen to like. Communism is the most subtle instrument of Soviet foreign policy that has ever been devised, and it is really the spearhead of Russian imperialism which would, if it could, take from these people what they have won, what we want them to keep and develop, which is their own national independence, their own individual independence, their own development of their own resources for their own good and not as mere tributary states to this great Soviet Union. . . .

Soviet Attitude

Now, let me come to another underlying and important factor which determines our relations and, in turn, our policy with the peoples of Asia. That is the attitude of the Soviet Union toward Asia, and particularly toward those parts of Asia which are contiguous to the Soviet Union, and with great particularity this afternoon, to north China.

The attitude and interest of the Russians in north China, and in those other areas as well, long antedates communism. This is not something that has come out of communism at all. It long antedates it. But the Communist regime has added new methods, new skills, and new concepts to the thrust of Russian imperialism.

This [these] Communistic concept[s] and techniques have armed Russian imperialism with a new and most insidious weapon of penetration. Armed with these new powers, what is happening in China is that the Soviet Union is detaching the northern provinces [areas] of China from China and is attaching them to the Soviet Union. This process is complete in Outer Mongolia. It is nearly complete in Manchuria, and I am sure that in inner Mongolia and in Sinkiang there are very happy reports coming from Soviet agents to Moscow. This is what is going on. It is the detachment of these whole areas, vast areas—populated by Chinese—the detachment of these areas from China and their attachment to the Soviet Union.

I wish to state this and perhaps sin against my doctrine of non-dogmatism, but I should like to suggest at any rate that this fact that the Soviet Union is taking the four northern provinces of China is the single most significant, most important fact, in the relation of any foreign power with Asia.

Two Rules of U.S. Policy

What does that mean for us? It means something very, very significant. It means that nothing that we do and nothing that we say must be allowed to obscure the reality of this fact. All the efforts of propaganda will not be able to obscure it. The only thing that can obscure it is the folly of ill-conceived adventures on our part which easily could do so, and I urge all who are thinking about these foolish adventures to remember that we must not seize the unenviable position which the Russians have carved out for themselves. We must not undertake to deflect from the Russians to ourselves the righteous anger, and the wrath, and the hatred of the Chinese people which must develop. It would be folly to deflect it to ourselves. We must take the position we have always taken—that anyone who violates the integrity of China is the enemy of China and is acting contrary to our own interest. That, I suggest to you this afternoon, is the first and the greatest rule in regard to the formulation of American policy toward Asia.

I suggest that the second rule is very like the first. That is to keep our own purposes perfectly straight, perfectly pure, and perfectly aboveboard and do not get them mixed up with legal quibbles or the attempt to do one thing and really achieve another.

The consequences of this Russian attitude and this Russian action in China are perfectly enormous. They are saddling all those in China who are proclaiming their loyalty to Moscow, and who are allowing themselves to be used as puppets of Moscow, with the most awful responsibility which they must pay for. Furthermore, these actions of the Russians are making plainer than any speech, or any utterance, or any legislation can make throughout all of Asia, what the true purposes of the Soviet Union are and what the true function of communism as an agent of Russian imperialism is. These I suggest to you are the fundamental factors, fundamental realities of attitude out of which our relations and policies must grow.

Military Security in the Pacific

. . . What is the situation in regard to the military security of the Pacific area, and what is our policy in regard to it?

In the first place, the defeat and the disarmament of Japan has placed upon the United States the necessity of assuming the military defense of Japan so long as that is required, both in the interest of our security and in the interests of the security of the entire Pacific area and, in all honor, in the interest of Japanese security. We have American—and there are Australian—troops in Japan. I am not in a position to speak for the Australians, but I can assure you that there is no intention of any sort of abandoning or weakening the defenses of Japan and that whatever arrangements are to be made either through permanent settlement or otherwise, that defense must and shall be maintained.

This defensive perimeter runs along the Aleutians to Japan and then goes to the Ryukyus. We hold important defense positions in the Ryukyu Islands, and those we will continue to hold. . . .

The defensive perimeter runs from the Ryukyus to the Philippine Islands. . . .

So far as the military security of other areas in the Pacific is concerned, it must be clear that no person can guarantee these areas against military attack. But it must also be clear that such a guarantee is hardly sensible or necessary within the realm of practical relationship.

Should such an attack occur—one hesitates to say where such an armed attack could come from—the initial reliance must be on the people attacked to resist it and then upon the commitments of the entire civilized world under the Charter of the United Nations which so far has not proved a weak reed to lean on by any people who are determined to protect their independence against outside aggression. . . .

[*AFP 1950–1955,* II, pp. 2313–18]

6. State Department Replies to Questions in House Resolution: Review of US Policy in Relation to China, February 9, 1950 (Extract)

Question 1 (d)

Have the following been considered by the Executive as alternatives to the policy enunciated in said statement?

(1) *Insistence on the execution of the terms of the Cairo Declaration, which provided for the return of Formosa to the Republic of China.*

Comment.—This cannot properly be considered an alternative to the policy enunciated by the President. The President's statement of January 5, 1950 contained a reaffirmation of the Cairo Declaration on the part of the United States in respect to the disposition of Formosa. Formosa has been administered since 1945 by China, the surrender of Japanese forces on Formosa having been made to Generalissimo Chiang Kai-shek.

(2) *Consideration of Formosa as a possession of Japan to be administered by the victor powers until eventual disposition under a peace settlement with Japan.*

(3) *A plebiscite in Formosa, under the auspices of the Far Eastern Commission or a special commission of the UN, to determine whether the inhabitants desire—(a) to continue as a province of and the seat of government of the Republic of China; (b) to be placed under a United Nations trusteeship; or (c) to become an independent nation.*

Comment.—These alternatives were considered. As has been noted under (1) above, Formosa has been administered by China since 1945, when Japanese forces on the island surrendered to Generalissimo Chiang Kai-shek. It was incorporated into China as a province. It is now the seat of the Chinese Government. The Allied Powers associated in the war against Japan have not questioned these steps. The United States Government has not questioned these steps because they were clearly in line with its commitments made at Cairo and reaffirmed at Potsdam. In other words, the Allied Powers including the United States have for the past 4 years treated Formosa as a part of China.

For the United States Government, at this date, to seek to establish a non-Chinese administration on Formosa, either through SCAP or a United Nations or FEC-sponsored plebiscite, would be almost universally interpreted in mainland China and widely interpreted throughout Asia as an attempt by this Government to separate Formosa from China in violation of its pledges and contrary to its long-standing policy of respecting the territorial integrity of China. The important point from the standpoint of our interests in Asia, including mainland China, is not the technical justifications which we might urge for taking such steps but rather the way such action on our part would be viewed by the people of Asia. In this connection we do not wish to create a Formosa *irredenta* issue about which the Chinese Communists could rally support within China and with which they could divert attention from Soviet actions in the North. We must not place ourselves in the unenviable position of the U.S.S.R. with regard to the integrity of China and must remain free to take the position that anyone who violates the integrity of China is the enemy of China and is acting contrary to our own interests.

These are compelling reasons for rejecting the alternatives stated above. There are, of course, additional practical difficulties. The seat of the Chinese Government is now on Formosa and that island, with Hainan, is the only remaining substantial territory now under its control. There is no evidence that the Chinese Government would willingly accomplish its own demise by acquiescing in either of the proposed alternatives. There is likewise the question of military force to carry out the course of action proposed if the Chinese Government refuses its consent, and to defend the island if either proposal were effected. The United Nations, of course, has no forces and it seems clear that any defense of the island would finally rest upon the United States.

In any case the conduct of a plebiscite for the purpose of determining the wishes of the inhabitants on the future disposition of Formosa is beyond the competence of the Far Eastern Commission. The Far Eastern Commission by its terms of reference is "to formulate the policies, principles, and standards in conformity with which the fulfillment by Japan of its obligations under the terms of surrender may be accomplished." The terms of reference also provide that "the Commission shall not make recommendations with regard to the conduct of military operations nor with regard to territorial adjustments." . . .

[*AFP 1950–1955*, II, pp. 2457–58.]

II. The Impact of the Korean War

THE KOREAN WAR, though initiated neither by the People's Republic of China nor by the United States, embittered relations between those countries for two decades. American actions taken at that time still constituted the main issues in dispute between Peking and Washington when President Nixon's visit to China was arranged in July, 1971. In retrospect, those actions seem mistaken.

The large-scale North Korean attack across the 38th parallel frontier into South Korea took place at dawn on June 25, 1950. Two days later, President Truman ordered the US Seventh Fleet to defend Formosa against attack by "Communist forces" on the grounds that Communist occupation of the island would threaten US forces in the Pacific area (7). In the same announcement, Truman declared that the future status of Formosa must await determination. With a few brief sentences, the American administration had re-entered the Chinese civil war. The decisions to abandon Chiang Kai-shek to his fate and to eschew legal quibbling over Formosa had been reversed.

The justification for the order to the Seventh Fleet was plainly the ascription of the attack in Korea not just to North Korea, or even North Korea backed by the Soviet Union, but to "Communism." An attack by one Communist nation in one place was taken as meaning a general military threat from all Communist nations everywhere, presumably under the direction of Moscow. This analysis, while understandable in a European context, could only be applied to China if one assumed that its leaders, like those of Eastern Europe, were under Stalin's thumb. As we have seen, this was precisely what Dean Acheson did believe in January, 1950 (5), and presumably what he still believed when the Korean War broke out.

China's reactions in the early days of the Korean War indicated intense concern about American actions in the Formosa Strait and surprisingly little interest in the fighting in the Korean peninsula.[1] Chou En-lai immediately denounced Truman's action (8), and an article in the Chinese press indicated that Peking was well aware that its plans to liberate Formosa had sustained a major setback.[2]

In July, the Indian Government suggested that the PRC should be admitted to the United Nations as part of a move toward a Korean settlement. George Kennan has recorded that he was in a minority of one at the State Department supporting this initiative. The majority view was that this would confuse the American public who would look on it as a retreat.[3]

It was not until the third week of August that the Chinese began to indicate their direct concern about developments in Korea and to demand to be included in discussions on the war. The concern and the demand were expressed in a cable from Chou En-lai to the United Nations dated August 20. This *démarche* was clearly in response to a statement by the American ambassador in the Security Council on August 17 that the United Nations should aim for a united, free Korea.[4] If an American-dominated UN army was planning to drive to the Manchurian frontier, Peking could no longer consider the Korean War the exclusive concern of the North Koreans and the Russians.

As the North Korean forces retreated, the Chinese began to issue private and public warnings that they could not tolerate

[1] Allen S. Whiting, *China Crosses the Yalu: The Decision to Enter the Korean War* (New York: Macmillan, 1960), p. 53.

[2] *Ibid.*, pp. 63–64.

[3] George F. Kennan, *Memoirs, 1925–50* (London: Hutchinson, 1968), pp. 490–97.

[4] Whiting, *op. cit.*, pp. 78–79, 84–87.

American troops crossing the North Korean frontier [5] (9). The warnings were ignored. US troops crossed the 38th parallel on October 7. Chinese Communist forces moved secretly into Korea between October 14 and 16. The first clash between them and South Korean troops took place ten days later; on November 2, the Chinese attacked American units.[6]

The Chinese were cautious. Their insistence on the volunteer nature of their forces (10) indicated a desire to avert the spread of the war to China and, after their initial attack, they broke off contact from November 7 for almost three weeks. The motives for the pause are still unclear.[7] The Chinese may have hoped to achieve by a powerful but limited display of force—a sort of warning shot fired into rather than across the bows—what they had failed to obtain by diplomacy. Their behavior at this time invites comparison with their actions on the Indian frontier in 1962 when again they withdrew after a brief but powerful offensive.

However, the Americans were stronger and more self-confident than the Indians were to prove; and they were led by the fire-eating MacArthur. On November 24, the day a Chinese delegation arrived in the United States to take part in the Security Council's deliberations, MacArthur announced the start of an offensive to "end the war." Two days later, the Chinese launched a crushing

[5] *Ibid.*, pp. 106–9. The Indian ambassador to China was personally informed by Chou En-lai that the Chinese were concerned only about an American crossing of the 38th parallel; the actions of the South Koreans did not matter. See K. M. Panikkar, *In Two Chinas* (London: Allen & Unwin, 1955), p. 110.

[6] Whiting, *op. cit.*, pp. 116–17.

[7] *Ibid.*, pp. 160–62. It has been persuasively argued that the Chinese may have been interested in the British proposal for a buffer zone along the Korean frontier; see Edward Friedman, "Problems in Dealing with an Irrational Power: America Declares War on China," in Edward Friedman and Mark Selden (eds.), *America's Asia: Dissenting Essays on Asian-American Relations* (New York: Vintage, 1971), pp. 234–38. However, according to Panikkar, who put the British proposal to the Chinese, "The strange British idea of a neutralized zone, meaning thereby the annexation of the rest of Korea by Syngman Rhee, was naturally brushed aside as irrelevant by the Chinese" (Panikkar, *op. cit.*, p. 115).

counterattack that eventually forced the UN forces south of the 38th parallel again. On November 28, the head of the special Peking delegation to the United Nations, Wu Hsiu-ch'üan, made his major speech to the Security Council (11). He confined himself to the Formosa issue because he objected to the phrasing of the agenda item on Korea; it talked of aggression against South Korea and not of American armed intervention in Korea, as Chou En-lai had wished. Wu's tactic may have seemed strange when the Chinese were now committed to all-out war with the UN forces in the Korean peninsula, but it did accurately reflect fundamental Chinese interests. The fighting in Korea might be a threat to Chinese security, but the cordoning off of Formosa was effectively an invasion of Chinese territory. Wu Hsiu-ch'üan had a field day suggesting American analogies.

The Chinese presence at the United Nations did not result in a settlement in Korea. Wu Hsiu-ch'üan and his colleagues returned to China, and, in January, 1951, the US Senate passed resolutions calling for the United Nations to declare the PRC an aggressor and deny it the China seat (12). The UN did condemn China as an aggressor on February 1, 1951, and that resolution had not been annulled when the PRC, after twenty years of successful American-led obstruction, finally took over the representation of China in the autumn of 1971.

The failure of the two sides to find a peace formula also resulted in a tightening of the ties between the United States and the Chinese Nationalists. Truman dismissed MacArthur, who wanted to expand the war and attack China. Truman also decided against accepting Chiang's offer of troops for Korea.[8] But the decision to protect Formosa had an inescapable logic, and, in February, 1951, the Americans signed a Mutual Defense Assistance Agreement with the Nationalists (13). Moreover, official American attitudes toward the Chinese Communists became frozen in their early 1950 posture; the puppet stereotype became

[8] David Rees, *Korea: The Limited War* (London: Macmillan, 1964), p. 27.

dogma. Dean Rusk, than Assistant Secretary of State for Eastern Affairs, stated that the Communist regime was not the government of China because it was not Chinese (14).

Peace did not come to Korea until after the death of Stalin in March, 1953.[9] By the time the armistice agreement was signed on July 27, the United States had suffered more than 142,000 casualties, including 33,629 dead. The Chinese casualties were never disclosed but were estimated by the United Nations at 900,000;[10] Mao Tse-tung's son was among those killed.[11] The memory of all that bloodshed was another bitter barrier between China and America in the years ahead.

[9] *Ibid.*, p. 406. The argument that Stalin's death was the turning point in Korea is based on the fact that the UN commander did not receive a reply to his suggestion of an exchange of sick and wounded, made on February 22, until three weeks after Stalin's death on March 5. The Sino-Korean response, when it came on March 28, set in motion the discussions that led eventually to the armistice.

[10] *Ibid.*, p. 461.

[11] See the biography of Mao in Donald W. Klein and Anne B. Clark, *Biographic Dictionary of Chinese Communism, 1921–1965* (Cambridge, Mass.: Harvard University Press, 1971).

THE AMERICANS PROTECT FORMOSA

7. Truman's Statement on the Mission of the Seventh Fleet in the Formosa Area, June 27, 1950 (Extract)

The attack upon Korea makes it plain beyond all doubt that communism has passed beyond the use of subversion to conquer independent nations and will now use armed invasion and war. It has defied the orders of the Security Council of the United Nations issued to preserve international peace and security. In these circumstances, the occupation of Formosa by Communist forces would be a direct threat to the security of the Pacific area and to United States forces performing their lawful and necessary functions in that area.

Accordingly, I have ordered the Seventh Fleet to prevent any attack on Formosa. As a corollary of this action, I am calling upon the Chinese Government on Formosa to cease all air and sea operations against the mainland. The Seventh Fleet will see that this is done. The determination of the future status of Formosa must await the restoration of security in the Pacific, a peace settlement with Japan, or consideration by the United Nations. . . .

[*AFP 1950–1955,* II, p. 2468.]

8. Foreign Minister Chou En-lai's Statement on Truman's June 27th Statement, June 28, 1950 (Extract)

On behalf of the Central People's Government of the People's Republic of China, I declare that Truman's statement of June 27, and the actions of the American Navy, constitute aggression against the territory of China, and a total violation of the United Nations Charter. This violent, predatory action by the U.S. Government comes as no surprise to the Chinese people, but only increases their wrath because the Chinese people have, over a long period, constantly exposed all the conspiratorial schemes of the American imperialists for aggression against China and grabbing Asia by force.

All that Truman's statement does is openly expose his premeditated plan and put it into practice. In fact, the attack by the puppet Korean government of Syngman Rhee on the Korean Democratic People's Republic at the instigation of the U.S. Government was a premeditated move by the United States, designed to create a pretext for the United States to invade Taiwan, Korea, Viet Nam and the Philippines. It is precisely a further act of intervention by American imperialism in the affairs of Asia.

On behalf of the Central People's Government of the People's Republic of China, I declare that no matter what obstructive action the U.S. imperialists may take, the fact that Taiwan is part of China will remain unchanged forever. This is not only an historical fact—it has also been confirmed by the Cairo and Potsdam declarations and by the situation since the surrender of Japan.

All the people of our country will certainly fight to the end single-mindedly to liberate Taiwan from the grasp of the American aggressors. The Chinese people, who defeated Japanese imperialism and Chiang Kai-shek, the hireling of American imperialism, will surely be victorious in driving off the American aggressors and in recovering Taiwan and all other territories belonging to China. . . .

[New China News Agency, June 29, 1950.]

THE CHINESE INTERVENE IN KOREA

9. Premier Chou En-lai's Report to the Chinese People's Political Consultative Conference, September 30, 1950 (Extract)

It is obvious that the Chinese people, after liberating the whole territory of their own country, want to rehabilitate and develop their industrial and agricultural production and cultural and educational work in a peaceful environment, free from threats. But if the American aggressors take this as a sign of the weakness of the Chinese people, they will commit the same fatal blunder as the Kuomintang reactionaries.

The Chinese people enthusiastically love peace, but in order to defend peace they never have been and never will be afraid to oppose aggressive war. The Chinese people absolutely will not tolerate foreign aggression, nor will they supinely tolerate seeing their neighbors being savagely invaded by imperialists. Whoever attempt[s] to exclude the nearly 500 million Chinese people from the U.N. and whoever set at nought and violate the interests of this one fourth of mankind in the world and fancy vainly to solve any Eastern problems directly concerned with China arbitrarily, will certainly break their skulls. . . .

[New China News Agency, October 3, 1950.]

10. *People's Daily* Editorial, "Smash the Enemy's Slanders, Deceits, and Threats," November 11, 1950 (Extracts)

The enemy's attempts to slander the Chinese people's volunteers' actions in Korea as "intervention" or "invasion" are baseless and absurd. There have been many interventions and invasions, and also many examples of popular volunteers actions in history; and they have never been confused.

To cite some of the best known examples: Hitler's and Mussolini's troops intervened in the Spanish civil war and supported Franco's attack on the Spanish people. This was undoubtedly intervention. But, on the other hand, people from Britain, France, America, the Soviet Union and other countries took up arms and assisted the Spanish people to resist Franco. This was undoubtedly an example of action by people's volunteers.

Even the Americans have acknowledged that what happened in Korea was comparable to what happened then in Spain. The armed forces of America and Britain, Canada and other countries are interventionists like Hitler and Mussolini. The United States has absolutely no justification for sending its troops to Korea, because in Korea there is only an internal conflict. But, actually, American troops have not only been sent to Korea to support Syngman Rhee, the enemy of all the Korean people, in slaughtering the Korean people; they have also openly become the masters of Syngman Rhee's troops. Thus, the American Government has done what Hitler and Mussolini did not do for Franco. . . .

In an attempt to dupe the Chinese people, the enemy says that the US will not invade China, but will stop at a proper limit. This is intended to convince the Chinese people that the American invasion of Korea can be ignored. But if we use our memories, we can recall that in the bloody history of imperialist aggression against China during the past 100 years, there has been no limit. In every instance, the terminal point of their aggression was swiftly turned into a starting point for further aggression. In the imperialists' dictionary there are only such terms as "insatiable greed" and "give us an inch and we will take an ell"; there is absolutely no stopping at a proper limit, unless we check them with force and compel them to stop.

Today, the US has not only invaded Korea, China's close neighbor, and threatened China's border, but has moreover invaded our Taiwan with her navy and our Northeast with her air force. Why do such people as MacArthur and Austin avoid talking about such obvious facts? A man whose existence is threatened by a wolf cannot save himself by "appeasement" or "prayer." If he does not strike it down, the wolf will bite him. There is no alternative. . . .

[New China News Agency, November 11, 1950.]

11. Speech of PRC Delegate Wu Hsiu-ch'üan at Security Council, November 28, 1950 (Extracts)

Mr. President, members of the Security Council: on the instructions of the Central People's Government of the People's Republic of China, I am here in the name of the 475 million people of China to accuse the United States Government of the unlawful and criminal act of armed aggression against the territory of China, Taiwan—including the Penghu Islands. . . .

This charge of aggression against Taiwan by the United States Government brought by the Central People's Government of the People's Republic of China should have been lodged by the representative on the Security Council of the People's Republic of China as a permanent member of the Security Council. But, owing to the manipulation and obstruction by the United States Government, the lawful representatives of the People's Republic of China have been and are still excluded from the United Nations and, for that reason, I must first of all protest to the United Nations for allowing even to this day the so-called "representative" of the Chinese

Kuomintang reactionary remnant clique to sit unashamed here in our midst, professing to be representing the Chinese people and to arrogate to himself the right of representing the people of China. Members of the Security Council, this is a state of affairs that the Chinese people cannot possibly tolerate. . . .

I would like to remind the members of the Security Council that so long as the United Nations persists in denying admittance to a permanent member of the Security Council representing 475 million people, it cannot make lawful decisions on any major issues or solve any major problems, particularly those which concern Asia. Indeed, without the participation of the lawful delegates of the People's Republic of China, representing 475 million people, the United Nations cannot in practice be worthy of its name. Without the participation of the lawful representatives of the People's Republic of China, the people of China have no reason to recognize any resolutions or decisions of the United Nations.

Therefore, in the name of the Central People's Government of the People's Republic of China, I once more demand that the United Nations expel the so-called "delegates" of the Kuomintang reactionary remnant clique and admit the lawful delegates of the People's Republic of China.

The members of the Security Council will recall that on 24 August Foreign Minister Chou En-lai lodged a charge with the United Nations Security Council that the United States Government had committed armed aggression against China's territory, Taiwan. But the United States Government used every means to obstruct the discussion by the Security Council of this just accusation. It was only because of the righteous stand of the Soviet Union representative who was President of the Security Council during August, and the support of other countries, that the charge by the People's Republic of China against United States armed aggression in Taiwan has now been placed on the agenda of the Security Council, although because of the opposition of the United States, it was given its present imperfect form: "complaint of armed aggression against Taiwan (Formosa)." . . .

The case for the charge filed by the Central People's Government of the People's Republic of China against the United States Government is irrefutable.

People with any common sense know that Taiwan is an inseparable part of the territory of China. Long before Christopher Columbus discovered America, the Chinese people were already in Taiwan. Long before the United States achieved its own independence, Taiwan had already become an inseparable part of the territory of China. Precisely because of this irrevocable historical fact that Taiwan is part of China, civilized nations of the whole world have never conceded that the occupation of Taiwan by imperialist Japan during the fifty-year period from 1895 to 1945 was justifiable. Moreover, the people of Taiwan have always opposed the rule of Japanese imperialism. During the fifty years under Japanese imperialist rule, the people of Taiwan lived like beasts of burden and underwent all the sufferings of a subject people. But during these fifty years the people in Taiwan never ceased conducting a dauntless struggle against the alien rule of Japanese imperialism and for their return to the motherland. In their heroic struggle against Japanese imperialism, the people in Taiwan have written with blood and fire into the pages of history that they are a member, an integral part of the great family of the Chinese nation. Even the White Paper, *United States Relations with China* compiled by the United States Department of State, has to admit that:

> The native population for fifty years had been under the rule of a foreign invader and therefore welcomed the Chinese forces as liberators. During the Japanese occupation the principal hope of the people had been reunion with the mainland.*

Precisely because Taiwan is an inseparable part of China, the Cairo Declaration jointly signed on 1 December 1943 by the Governments of China, the United States of America and the United Kingdom explicitly stipulated that "it is their"—the three great Powers'—"purpose . . . that all territories Japan has stolen from the Chinese, such as Manchuria, Formosa and the Pescadores, shall be restored to the Republic of China."

Taiwan is an integral part of China. This is not only an unshakable historical fact, but also one of the main aims for which the Chinese people fought unitedly against imperialist Japan. The Cairo Declaration signed on 1 December 1943 by the United States, the United Kingdom and China clearly reflected this aim of the people of China. Moreover, the Cairo Declaration is a solemn international commitment which the United States Government has pledged itself to observe. As one of the principal provisions concerning the unconditional surrender of Japan, this

---

* *United States Relations with China*, Department of State Publication 3573, page 308.

solemn international commitment was again laid down in the Potsdam Declaration which was signed jointly on 26 July 1945 by China, the United States and the United Kingdom, and was subsequently adhered to by the Soviet Union. Section 8 of the Potsdam Declaration, which provides the terms of the unconditional surrender of Japan, states:

> The terms of the Cairo Declaration shall be carried out and Japanese sovereignty shall be limited to the islands of Honshu, Hokkaido, Kyushu, Shikoku and such minor islands as we determine.

On 2 September 1945, Japan signed the Instrument of Surrender, the first article of which explicitly provided that Japan accepts—I am quoting from the original wording—"the provisions set forth in the Declaration issued by the heads of the Governments of the United States, China and Great Britain on July 26, 1945, at Potsdam, and subsequently adhered to by the Union of Soviet Socialist Republics." When the Chinese Government accepted the surrender of the Japanese armed forces in Taiwan and exercised sovereignty over the island, Taiwan became, not only *de jure,* but also *de facto,* an inalienable part of Chinese territory, and this has been the situation as regards Taiwan since 1945. For this reason, during the five post-war years from 1945 to 27 June 1950, no one has ever questioned the fact that Taiwan is an inseparable part of Chinese territory, *de jure* or *de facto.*

This state of affairs was so clear that on 5 January 1950 . . . even President Truman admitted that Taiwan is Chinese territory.

Thus it can be seen that there is no room for the slightest doubt that Taiwan is an inseparable part of Chinese territory. Yet the United States Government had the audacity to declare its decision to use armed force to prevent the liberation of Taiwan by the Central People's Government of the People's Republic of China, and to dispatch its armed forces on a large-scale, open invasion of Taiwan. . . .

Having declared and put into operation the policy of armed aggression against Taiwan, President Truman sent General MacArthur, Commander-in-Chief of the United States Armed Forces in the Far East, to Taiwan to confer clandestinely with Chiang Kai-shek on concrete measures for using Taiwan as a base from which to wage war against the Chinese people. MacArthur and Chiang Kai-shek decided that the land, naval and air forces of the United States and those of Chiang Kai-shek should be placed under the unified command of MacArthur for the "joint defense" of Taiwan. On his departure from Taiwan for Japan on 1 August MacArthur openly declared:

> Arrangements have been completed for effective co-ordination between the American forces under my command and those of the Chinese Government (the Kuomintang reactionary remnant clique).

And this is what Chiang Kai-shek said:

> An agreement was reached between General MacArthur and myself on all the problems discussed in the series of conferences held in the past two days. The foundation for a joint defence of Formosa and for Sino-American military co-operation has thus been laid.

In league with its puppet, the Chiang Kai-shek reactionary clique, the United States Government, which has invaded and occupied Taiwan, thus cast the gauntlet of war before the Chinese people. . . .

Let us first of all deal with the question of the status of Taiwan and the peace treaty with Japan. Does it hold water to say that, since the status of Taiwan is not yet determined, the invasion of Taiwan by United States armed forces constitutes no aggression against China? No, it does not. Here we have in the first place the Truman of 5 January 1950 contradicting the Truman of 27 June 1950. On 5 January, this year Mr. Truman stated:

> The United States and the other Allied Powers have accepted the exercise of Chinese authority over the island.

Surely, at that time, Mr. Truman could not consider that a peace treaty with Japan had already been signed. Then, we have President Roosevelt contradicting President Truman. On 1 December 1943, President Roosevelt solemnly declared in the Cairo Declaration that

> All the territories Japan has stolen from the Chinese, such as Manchuria, Formosa and the Pescadores, shall be restored to the Republic of China.

Surely, neither President Roosevelt nor anyone else considered at that time that, in the absence of a peace treaty with Japan, the Cairo Declaration would be invalid and that Manchuria, Taiwan and the Penghu Islands would remain in the possession of Japan. . . .

President Truman declared that the so-called question of the status of Taiwan must await consideration by the United Nations. . . .

My government has protested in strong terms to the United Nations General Assembly, resolutely opposing the inclusion of the so-called "Question of Formosa"—concerning the status of Taiwan—in the agenda of the fifth session of the General Assembly. Whatever decision the United Nations General Assembly may take on the so-called question of the status of Taiwan, whether it be to hand over the island to the United States so that it might administer it openly under the disguise of "trusteeship," or "neutralization," or whether it be to procrastinate by way of "investigation," thereby maintaining the present state of actual United States occupation, it will, in substance, be stealing China's legitimate territory and supporting United States aggression against Taiwan in opposition to the Chinese people. Any such decision would in no way shake the resolve of the Chinese people to liberate Taiwan, nor would it prevent action by the Chinese people to liberate Taiwan. . . .

Next, I should like to say a few words about the absurd argument that United States aggression against Taiwan is aimed at safeguarding security in the Pacific. The United States Government has persistently circulated a fabrication to the effect that United States aggression against Taiwan is a "temporary measure" arising from the Korean war, and is intended to "localize" the Korean war and safeguard security in the Pacific. Therefore, according to the United States Government, "the determination of the future status of Formosa must await the restoration of security in the Pacific."

The civil war in Korea was created by the United States— but in no sense whatsoever can the civil war in Korea be used as a justification or pretext for United States aggression against Taiwan. I repeat: in no sense whatsoever can the civil war in Korea be used as a justification or pretext for United States aggression against Taiwan.

Members of the Security Council: is it conceivable that, because of the Spanish civil war, Italy would be entitled to occupy the French territory of Corsica? Is it conceivable that civil war in Mexico would confer upon the United Kingdom the right to occupy the State of Florida in the United States? This is utterly absurd and inconceivable.

In fact, the United States Government's policy of armed aggression against Taiwan, no less than its policy of armed aggression against Korea, had been decided upon long before the United States created the civil war in Korea. Six days before the outbreak of the Korean civil war—that is, on 19 June 1950— *The New York Times* wrote the following editorial:

> It would seem, then, that the retention of some sort of bases for defending Japan was an imperative. On the other hand, in modern warfare the old idea of three or four relatively isolated bases is, of course, nonsense. . . .
>
> It may well be for reasons such as these that General MacArthur is, according to recent reports, ready to urge a co-ordinated defense pattern for the whole of the Western Pacific, and not merely for Japan alone. This revives the question of what should or can be done about Formosa. There is a substantial body of opinion to the effect that the Island can be held and that, although it is late, it is not too late. . . .
>
> A vigorous defense program, on a regional basis, would therefore involve political decisions of the first order. It could require a reversal of our position on Formosa.

An item in the *New York Post* on 27 June went further to say:

> Before Johnson and Bradley went to Japan, the United States Joint Chiefs of Staff had agreed upon a Far Eastern policy including the following two points: (1) no peace treaty with Japan for the next five years, (2) adoption of all measures to prevent Formosa from falling into communist hands.

A dispatch from Tokyo in the *New York Herald Tribune* of 25 June vividly revealed the specific details of this decision:

> A firm stand by the United States on Formosa would, according to Supreme Headquarters, have a 90 per cent chance of deterring Communist invasion because the Chinese themselves are not ready for a head-on tilt with American power. . . .

In his message to the Veterans of Foreign Wars of the United States on 28 August, General MacArthur flagrantly admitted that the United States regarded Taiwan as "the center" of the United States Pacific front, "an unsinkable aircraft carrier," and that the United States must control Taiwan in order to be able to "dominate with air power every Asiatic port from Vladivostok to Singapore." . . .

Further, the United States Government perversely argues that the United States armed invasion and occupation of Taiwan was designed to effect the military "neutralization" of Taiwan. The United States Government has attempted to use this hypocritical slogan as its "justification" for armed aggression against Taiwan, in order to deceive people all over the world and particularly the

American people; but the people of the United States and of the whole world clearly understand that the liberation of Taiwan, which the Chinese people are determined to carry out, is entirely China's domestic affair, and that no deceptive slogans can conceal the fact that this action on the part of the United States Government constitutes armed intervention in China's domestic affairs. Let the American people pause to consider: if a country dispatches its naval fleet between Hawaii and the United States mainland, divides up American territory and prevents the United States Government from exercising sovereignty there, while at the same time alleging that such action has been taken for the military neutralization of Hawaii so as to safeguard security in the Pacific, would the American people tolerate that?

Let the American people further pause to consider the situation at the time when President Lincoln was mopping up the remnant forces of the southern slave owners.

If a foreign Power had suddenly stepped in and occupied the State of Virginia by armed force, while alleging that this was designed for the military neutralization of Virginia so as to safeguard the security of the American continent, would not the American people have considered this a flagrant intervention in the domestic affairs of the United States? Would not the American people have considered this armed occupation of the United States? . . .

In his letter of 25 August 1950, to Mr. Trygve Lie, Secretary-General of the United Nations, Mr. Austin, the United States representative to the United Nations, stated: "The United States has not encroached on the territory of China, nor has the United States taken aggressive action against China" (S/1716). Very well. Where then have the United States Seventh Fleet and the Thirteenth Air Force gone? Can it be that they have gone to the planet Mars? . . .

The armed aggression of the United States Government on our territory, Taiwan, is not accidental. It is the inevitable consequence of the United States Government's policy of aggression against China to interfere in China's internal affairs and to seek exclusive domination over China—a United States imperialist policy of long standing. . . .

The American imperialists have never been the friends of the Chinese people. They have always aligned themselves with the enemies of the Chinese people. They have always been the enemies of the Chinese people. However shamelessly the American imperialists claim to be friends of the Chinese people, the historical record which distinguishes friend from foe cannot be altered.

Before the Second World War, because of the advantage gained by other imperialists in China, the American imperialists adopted what was known as the "open door" and "equal opportunity" policy, which though ostensibly different from the policies of the other imperialist Powers, was in fact an aggressive policy aimed at sharing the spoils with other imperialists. . . .

After the surrender of imperialist Japan in 1945, the United States Government immediately adopted a policy of open intervention in China's internal affairs, using every means to smooth the way for the Kuomintang reactionary clique to launch a bloody civil war to slaughter the Chinese people. The United States Government mobilized 113,000 men of its naval, ground and air forces to make landings in the major ports of China, to grab important strategic points from which the Kuomintang reactionary clique could launch the civil war, and to assist the Kuomintang reactionary clique by transporting one million troops to the fronts on which the civil war was to be launched. Moreover, the United States Government equipped, at one time or another, 166 divisions of Chiang Kai-shek's reactionary army, as the main force for the invasion of the Chinese people's liberated areas; it helped Chiang to equip nine squadrons consisting of 1,720 aircraft; it supplied the Chiang navy with 757 vessels, it gave materials and financial aid to Chiang in the amount of over six thousand million U.S. dollars, although the United States Government admits only one-third of this figure. . . .

During Chiang Kai-shek's bloody civil war against the Chinese people, apart from the fact that the United States Government had sent over 1,000 military advisers to Chiang Kai-shek to plan the civil war, United States troops stationed in China in fact participated directly in the civil war, and invaded the Chinese people's liberated areas more than forty times. During this period, the United States Government and the Chiang Kai-shek Kuomintang reactionary clique signed all kinds of unequal treaties and agreements which reduced China to the status of a colony and military base of the United States. . . .

Furthermore, on the basis of these treaties and agreements, the United States Government secured many naval and air bases in Kuomintang China and gained control of the military, political, financial and economic branches of the Kuomintang Government. American goods flooded China's markets, causing China's national industries to fall into bankruptcy. The monopoly capitalists of the United States, through the four big families of Chiang, Soong, Kung and Chen, controlled the lifestream of China's economy. In fact the Chiang Kai-shek Kuomintang reactionary regime was nothing more than a puppet whereby American imperialism controlled China. The Chinese people are completely justified in entering all the tyrannical crimes of Chiang Kai-shek on the account of the American imperialists. The Chinese people will never forget their blood debt against the American imperialists. . . .

But the United States Government, still reluctant to admit that this is its final defeat, has converged for the time being all its activities of aggression against China on Taiwan Island, the lair of the Chiang Kai-shek remnant clique in its last desperate struggle. . . .

In the spring of 1948, Admiral Charles M. Cooke, Jr., arrived in Taiwan with the United States West Pacific Fleet under his command and compelled the Kuomintang regime—which had intended to cover up the fact that it had sold China's seaports—to declare officially that Keelung as well as Tsingtao were ports open to the United States Navy.

From that time onward, vessels of the United States Navy have continually violated the territorial waters of our country around Taiwan and have been stationed in the various ports of Taiwan. In the port of Kaohsiung alone, at one time there were stationed as many as twenty-seven United States naval vessels. In regard to land forces, the United States "Joint Military Advisory Group" long ago sent a large staff of officers in active service to be stationed permanently on Taiwan. In accordance with the joint war plans of the United States and Chiang Kai-shek, this military staff is responsible for organizing, equipping and training the so-called "new army" of the Kuomintang to be used to attack the Chinese people. Thus, the United States has, in reality, taken over the military role of Japan, put Taiwan under its control and converted it into a military base of the United States.

Economically, the United States Government and American monopolies such as the Westinghouse Electric Company, the Reynolds Metal Company, the American Express Company and others, have, through various devices, jointly dominated Taiwan's main industries—electric power, aluminum, cement, fertilizer, and others —controlled the economic life of Taiwan, and actually reduced it to a colony of the United States. Under such conditions, it is natural that the United States will not lightly give up Taiwan. Consequently, in order to realize its aim to dominate Taiwan, the

United States Government has long been engaged in a variety of vicious political conspiracies. The instigation by the United States of the "Taiwan Separation Movement" reached such a height of brazenness that an American government official in Taiwan openly declared that, if the people in Taiwan wanted to relieve themselves of China's rule, the United States was ready to help them. . . .

I must further point out that the armed aggression of the United States Government against the Chinese territory, Taiwan, is not an isolated affair. It is an integral part of the over-all plan of the United States Government to intensify its aggression, control and enslavement of Asian countries and the peoples of Korea, Viet-Nam, the Philippines, Japan, etc. It is a further step in the development of interference by American imperialism in the affairs of Asia. . . .

Since the Chinese people won their victory on the Chinese mainland, the United States Government has still more frantically carried out a policy of rearming Japan to oppose the Chinese people and the other Asian peoples. At present, the United States Government has not only turned Japan into its main base in the Far East in preparation for aggressive war, but it has already begun to use this base as a means to launch aggressive wars against a series of Asia countries. The headquarters of the United States Government for its aggression against Korea and Taiwan is in Japan.

Under the pretext of the Korean civil war, which was of its own making, the United States Government launched armed aggression simultaneously against Korea and Taiwan. From the very outset the United States armed aggression against Korea gravely threatened China's security. Korea is about 5,000 miles away from the boundaries of the United States. To say that the civil war in Korea would affect the security of the United States is a flagrant, deceitful absurdity. But there is only a narrow river between Korea and China. The United States armed aggression in Korea inevitably threatens China's security. That the United States aggression forces in Korea have directly threatened China's security is fully borne out by the facts.

From 27 August to 10 November 1950, the military aircraft of the United States aggression forces in Korea have violated the territorial air of North-East China ninety times; they have conducted reconnaissance activities, strafed and bombed Chinese cities, towns and villages, killed and wounded Chinese peaceful inhabitants and damaged Chinese properties. . . .

Now the United States forces of aggression in Korea are approaching our north-eastern frontiers. The flames of the war of aggression waged by the United States against Korea are swiftly sweeping towards China. Under such circumstances the United States armed aggression against Korea cannot be regarded as a matter which concerns the Korean people alone. No, decidedly not. The United States aggression against Korea gravely endangers the security of the People's Republic of China. The Korean People's Democratic Republic is a country bound by close ties of friendship to the People's Republic of China. Only a river separates the two countries geographically. The Chinese people cannot afford to stand idly by in the face of this serious situation brought about by the United States Government's aggression against Korea and the dangerous tendency towards the extension of the war. . . .

One of the master-planners of Japanese aggression, Tanaka, once said: to conquer the world, one must first conquer Asia; to conquer Asia, one must first conquer China; to conquer China, one must first conquer Manchuria and Mongolia; to conquer Manchuria and Mongolia, one must first conquer Korea and Taiwan.

Ever since 1895, the course of aggression taken by imperialist Japan has exactly corresponded to the Tanaka plan. In 1895, imperialist Japan invaded Korea and Taiwan. In 1931, imperialist Japan occupied the whole of North-East China. In 1937, imperialist Japan launched the war of aggression against the whole of China. In 1941, it started the war aimed at the conquest of the whole of Asia. Naturally, as everyone knows, before it had realized this design, Japanese imperialism collapsed. American imperialism, by its aggression against Taiwan and Korea, in practice plagiarizes Tanaka's memorandum and follows the beaten path of the Japanese imperialist aggressors. The Chinese people are maintaining a sharp vigilance over the progress of American imperialist aggression. They have already acquired the experience and learned the lesson from history as to how to defend themselves from aggression.

American imperialism has taken the place of Japanese imperialism. It is now following the old track of aggression against China and Asia on which Japanese imperialism set forth in 1894–95, only hoping to proceed with greater speed. But after all, 1950 is not 1895; the times have changed, and so have the circumstances. The Chinese people have arisen. The Chinese people who have victoriously overthrown the rule of Japanese imperialism and of American imperialism and its lackey, Chiang Kai-shek on China's mainland, will certainly succeed in driving out the United States aggressors and recover Taiwan and all other territories that belong to China. . . .

In order to safeguard international peace and security and to uphold the sanctity of the United Nations Charter, the United Nations Security Council has the inalienable duty to apply sanctions against the United States Government for its criminal acts of armed aggression upon the territory of China, Taiwan, and its armed intervention in Korea. In the name of the Central People's Government of the People's Republic of China, I therefore propose to the United Nations Security Council:

First, that the United Nations Security Council should openly condemn, and take concrete steps to apply severe sanctions against, the United States Government for its criminal acts of armed aggression against the territory of China, Taiwan, and armed intervention in Korea.

Second, that the United Nations Security Council should immediately adopt effective measures to bring about the complete withdrawal by the United States Government of its forces of armed aggression from Taiwan, in order that peace and security in the Pacific and in Asia may be ensured.

Third, that the United Nations Security Council should immediately adopt effective measures to bring about the withdrawal from Korea of the armed forces of the United States and all other countries and to leave it to the people of North and South Korea to settle the domestic affairs of Korea themselves, so that a peaceful solution of the Korean question may be achieved. . . .

[UN, *Security Council Official Records,* 5th year, 527 Meeting; November 28, 1950, No. 69, pp. 2–25.]

THE AMERICANS DENOUNCE THE PRC, FORGE NEW TIES WITH THE CHINESE NATIONALISTS

12. Senate Resolutions on China, January 23, 1951

Resolved, That it is the sense of the Senate that the United Nations should immediately declare Communist China an aggressor in Korea.

Resolved, That it is the sense of the Senate that the Communist Chinese Government should not be admitted to membership in the United Nations as the representative of China.

[Department of State *Bulletin,* XXIV, No. 605, February 5, 1951, p. 208.]

13. Mutual Defense Assistance Agreement Between the United States and the Republic of China, February 9, 1951 (Extracts)

The Government of the United States is prepared to make available to the Republic of China under the terms of P. L. 329, 81st Congress, as amended, certain military material for the defense of Taiwan against possible attack.

This material, and any other furnished under the authority of the law referred to, is transferred on the understanding that it will be used and disposed of pursuant to the following undertakings. . . .

1. The Chinese Government will use the material to maintain its internal security or its legitimate self-defense. . . .

3. The Chinese Government agrees to receive personnel of the United States Government who will discharge in the territory under the control of the Chinese Government the responsibilities of the United States Government under this agreement. . . .

[*AFP 1950–1955,* II, p. 2470]

14. Speech of Assistant Secretary of State for Far Eastern Affairs Dean Rusk, on "American Friendship for the Peoples of China," to the China Institute, New York, May 18, 1951 (Extracts)

The independence of China is gravely threatened. In the Communist world, there is room for only one master—a jealous and implacable master, whose price of friendship is complete submission. How many Chinese, in one community after another, are now being destroyed because they love China more than the Soviet Union? How many Chinese will remember in time the fates of Rajk, Kostov, Petkov, Clementis, and all those in other satellites who discovered that being Communist is not enough for the conspirators of the Kremlin?

The freedoms of the Chinese people are disappearing. Trial by mob, mass slaughter, banishment as forced labor to Manchuria, Siberia or Sinkiang, the arbitrary seizure of property, the destruction of loyalties within the family, the suppression of free speech—these are the facts behind the parades and celebrations and the empty promises.

The territorial integrity of China is now an ironic phrase. The movement of Soviet forces into Sinkiang, the realities of "joint exploitation" of that great province by Moscow and Peiping, the separation of Inner Mongolia from the body politic of China, and the continued inroads of Soviet power into Manchuria under the cloak of the Korean aggression mean in fact that China is losing its great northern areas to the European empire which has stretched out its greedy hands for them for at least a century. . . .

The peace and security of China are being sacrificed to the ambitions of the Communist conspiracy. China has been driven by foreign masters into an adventure of foreign aggression which cuts across the most fundamental national interests of the Chinese people. . . .

It is not my purpose, in these few moments this evening, to go into specific elements of our own national policy in the present situation. But we can tell our friends in China that the United States will not acquiesce in the degradation which is being forced upon them. We do not recognize the authorities in Peiping for what they pretend to be. The Peiping regime may be a colonial Russian government—a Slavic Manchukuo on a larger scale. It is not the Government of China. It does not pass the first test. It is not Chinese. . . .

[*AFP 1950–1955*, II, pp. 2473–74.]

III. The Dulles Era

AMERICAN ATTITUDES toward the People's Republic of China hardened after the election of General Eisenhower to the presidency in November, 1952, and the appointment of John Foster Dulles as his Secretary of State. Among the new President's first acts was the "unleashing" of Chiang Kai-shek. In his State of the Union Message to Congress on February 2, 1953, Eisenhower announced a modification of Truman's instructions to the Seventh Fleet: No longer would it have to prevent Nationalist attacks upon the Chinese mainland from Formosa (15). A major Nationalist attack was unlikely, but the gesture signposted the new administration's tougher posture.

One objective of "unleashing" Chiang, according to Eisenhower, was "to put the Chinese Communists on notice that the days of stalemate were numbered; that the Korean War would either end or extend beyond Korea." Eisenhower was convinced that his gesture helped bring the war to an end. But though Eisenhower was able to redeem his election pledge of peace in Korea six months after taking office, this made no appreciable difference to his China policy. This was presumably partly because he and Dulles believed that the Chinese Communists "like Communists everywhere—respect only force and hold fidelity to the pledged word in contempt." [1]

Another major factor in hardening the administration's attitude toward China was the continuing struggle between the French and

[1] Dwight D. Eisenhower, *The White House Years: I, Mandate for Change, 1953–1956* (Garden City, N.Y.: Doubleday, 1963), p. 123.

the Communist Viet Minh in Indochina. Eisenhower felt that a Communist victory would mean that all Southeast Asia would be threatened.[2] The United States participated, along with the People's Republic of China in the Geneva Conference that brought peace to Vietnam in the summer of 1954. But Washington did not like the result, and the administration's "domino" theory led the Americans to promote the formation of the South-East Asia Treaty Organization (SEATO) in the aftermath of the French defeat. It was an alliance that China saw as being motivated in part by hostility to itself (16).[3]

The SEATO treaty was signed on September 8, 1954. Five days earlier, the Chinese Communists had laid down a heavy artillery barrage against the offshore island of Quemoy, still occupied by the Nationalists although only 2 miles from the mainland port of Amoy. Tension had been rising in the Formosa Strait for some months. Now the Eisenhower administration was faced with the problem of defining its attitude toward the Nationalist-held offshore islands, the Quemoys, the Matsus, 12 miles off the port of Foochow, and the Tachens even further north. The Seventh Fleet had no orders to defend them, only Formosa.[4]

The crisis intensified in November as Chinese planes bombed the Tachen Islands, and the concentration of troops on the mainland opposite Formosa increased. The American response was to sign a Mutual Defense Treaty with the Nationalists on December 2, 1954 (17), something Chiang had requested a year earlier.[5] The treaty committed the Americans only to defending Taiwan[6] and the Pescadores and left open the question of the defense of "other territories" (i.e., the offshore islands). A clarificatory ex-

[2] *Ibid.*, p. 333.

[3] The SEATO states were the United States, the United Kingdom, France, Pakistan, the Philippines, Thailand, Australia, and New Zealand.

[4] Eisenhower, *op. cit.*, pp. 459–63.

[5] See Dulles's testimony on the treaty before the Senate, *American Foreign Policy, 1950–1955* (Washington, D.C.: Dept. of State, 1957), I, p. 953.

[6] Starting in late 1954, U.S. documents have increasingly used the term Taiwan, rather than Formosa. The term Formosa had been current during the Japanese occupation. Taiwan was also preferred by Peking and Taipei.

change of notes, kept secret for a month, extracted an agreement from the Nationalists not to attack the mainland unilaterally (18).[7] Chiang was leashed again. Dulles later justified the treaty by indicating that Taiwan was now considered part of America's island defense perimeter on the western rim of the Pacific. He argued, too, the need to demonstrate that America had no intention of trading Taiwan as part of a settlement with Peking (20). He thus injected into the American handling of the China problem an obligation of honor to defend Taiwan, a concept that came to override considerations of security and national interest.

The treaty did not solve the offshore islands issue. The problem became crucial in January, 1955, when Communist forces overwhelmed an island 7 miles north of the Tachens. The American administration decided to help evacuate the Tachens but to indicate publicly its intention of assisting in the defense of Quemoy and Matsu so long as the Chinese Communists professed an intention of attacking Taiwan.[8] To demonstrate national solidarity, President Eisenhower sought and obtained a Congressional resolution—it became known as the "Formosa resolution"—which authorized him to use his discretion in deciding what other islands to help defend in the interests of protecting Formosa (19).

The Chinese received a further warning when Eisenhower also told a press conference that he saw no reason why the United States could not use tactical nuclear weapons—"just exactly as you would use a bullet or anything else"—against strictly military targets in the event of war in the Far East.[9]

The tension was taken out of the Formosa Strait crisis by Chou En-lai. On April 23, 1955, during the course of the Afro-Asian Conference at Bandung, Indonesia, the Chinese Premier issued a press statement expressing China's willingness to negotiate with the United States (21). A somewhat negative instant response from the State Department was cautiously modified by Dulles

[7] Eisenhower, *op. cit.*, pp. 465–66.
[8] *Ibid.*, p. 467.
[9] *New York Times*, March 17, 1955.

three days later (**22**).[10] On July 25, it was agreed to raise the consular-level talks, initiated the previous year at the Geneva conference on Indochina and Korea, to ambassadorial level (**23**).[11]

The talks started on August 1 in Geneva. The only specific item on the agenda concerned the mutual return of civilians— several thousand Chinese students in the United States and forty Americans in China. Agreement on this item was reached in six weeks (**24**). Sixteen years later, when President Nixon's visit to China was arranged, this was still the only subject on which the two sides had ever reached agreement at the ambassadorial talks. And even this one agreement was soon followed by charge and countercharge of reneging (**25** and **26**).[12]

However, in the immediate aftermath of the agreement on the return of civilians, a certain mild optimism was expressed on both sides. The Chinese used the opportunity to press for a meeting at the foreign minister level, i.e., Chou En-lai and Dulles, and for a lifting of the trade embargo imposed during the Korean War. But the Americans preferred to maintain negotiations at ambassadorial level and, at Geneva, discussions turned to the crucial issue of Taiwan.

The Americans were determined to sustain Chiang Kai-shek's regime and were anxious to get the Chinese to agree to renounce force in the Taiwan area. The Chinese were not prepared to surrender their right to use force in the settlement of an internal dispute, i.e., the civil war between themselves and the Nationalists. They were prepared to agree on mutual renunciation of force between themselves and the Americans, clearly with the ultimate objective of securing the removal of the Seventh Fleet and Ameri-

[10] The State Department's initial response had specified that Nationalist China would have to participate in "*any* discussions concerning the area" (see *American Foreign Policy, 1950–1955*, II, p. 2496; emphasis added); Dulles modified this to mean any discussions concerning the rights and claims of the Chinese Nationalists in the area. See Kenneth T. Young, *Negotiating with the Chinese Communists: The United States Experience, 1953–1967* (New York: McGraw-Hill for the Council on Foreign Relations, 1968), pp. 45–46.

[11] *Ibid.*, pp. 36–40, for a description of the origins of the consular talks.

[12] *Ibid.*, Chapter III, for a description of the origins, negotiations, and aftermath of this agreement.

can military support for the Nationalists. A series of draft proposals and counterproposals were produced (27), but with the two sides sticking adamantly to their basic position, an agreement was never in the cards.

The dangers inherent in this stalemate appeared to be underlined by a candid discussion by Secretary of State Dulles of what came to be known as "brinkmanship." Elaborating on an article about him in *Life* magazine at his press conference on January 17, 1956, Dulles confirmed that the "ability to get to the verge without getting into the war is the necessary art" (28).

For the moment, however, there seemed to be no need for brinkmanship in the Formosa Strait. At the Chinese National People's Congress session in June, 1956, Chou En-lai formally offered to negotiate with the Nationalists "on specific steps and terms for the peaceful liberation of Taiwan."[13] Though rumors of deals being made between Peking and Taipei could always be picked up in Hong Kong, there is no evidence that the Nationalists responded to this offer, or even thought of doing so. A few weeks later, the Chinese Government offered to allow US correspondents into China (29), but the State Department refused to validate the correspondents' passports for travel to China on the grounds that the Chinese were still holding American citizens and using them as political hostages (30).

At the Eighth Congress of the CCP in September, 1956, Marshal Ch'en Yi, who was to become Foreign Minister in 1958, delivered the main speech on Chinese foreign policy (31). Although toughly worded, the speech indicated that the Chinese still hoped that their current "softer" line toward the Americans had a chance of success. In a major address on China policy nine months later, Dulles uncompromisingly reaffirmed the American position and stated his belief that Communism was, in China as elsewhere, "a passing and not a perpetual phase" (32). A quotation in the speech showed that Dulles had been confirmed in this conviction by the

[13] See the text of his speech in BBC, *Summary of World Broadcasts,* Supplement to Part V (July 5, 1956), "3rd Session of Chinese National People's Congress," No. 5, June 28–30, p. 13.

recent upsurge of criticism of the Peking regime during the CCP's rectification campaign.[14] It was probably the turmoil among the Chinese intelligentsia and students produced by this campaign, coupled with pressure from American news media, that decided the State Department to rescind its ban on American correspondents going to China (33). However, the United States was not prepared to admit Chinese correspondents, and the Chinese Government therefore refused to grant visas to the newsmen, alleging also that Washington wanted to use the correspondents to collect intelligence.[15]

The final document in this section is a State Department memorandum dated August 12, 1958, which restated for the benefit of American missions overseas the justification of Washington's refusal to recognize the People's Republic of China (34).

[14] The rectification campaign, launched at the end of April, 1957, was an attempt by Mao to correct the errors and misdeeds of CCP members by encouraging non-Communists to criticize them. When by early June the critics seemed to be getting carried away—see the remark of a university lecturer cited by Dulles—Mao agreed to counterattack them.

[15] Young, *op. cit.,* p. 130.

CHIANG KAI-SHEK "UNLEASHED"; US-ROC RELATIONS STRENGTHENED

15. President Eisenhower's State of the Union Message, February 2, 1953 (Extract)

In June 1950, following the aggressive attack on the Republic of Korea, the United States Seventh Fleet was instructed both to prevent attack upon Formosa and also to insure that Formosa should not be used as a base of operations against the Chinese Communist mainland.

This has meant, in effect, that the United States Navy was required to serve as a defensive arm of Communist China. Regardless of the situation of 1950, since the date of that order the Chinese Communists have invaded Korea to attack the United Nations forces there. They have consistently rejected the proposals of the United Nations Command for an armistice. They recently joined with Soviet Russia in rejecting the armistice proposal sponsored in the United Nations by the Government of India. This proposal had been accepted by the United States and 53 other nations.

Consequently there is no longer any logic or sense in a condition that required the United States Navy to assume defensive responsibilities on behalf of the Chinese Communists. This permitted those Communists, with greater impunity, to kill our soldiers and those of our United Nations allies in Korea.

I am therefore issuing instructions that the Seventh Fleet no longer be employed to shield Communist China. Permit me to make this crystal clear: This order implies no aggressive intent on our part. But we certainly have no obligation to protect a nation fighting us in Korea . . .

[*AFP 1950–1955*, II, p. 2475.]

16. Chou En-lai's Report on Government Work to the National People's Congress, September 23, 1954 (Extracts)

In Asia, the United States aggressive group recently pulled together a conference of eight countries in Manila which concluded a so-called Southeast Asia collective defence treaty. This treaty shows that the purpose of the United States is the destruction of the Geneva Conference agreements, the organisation of a military alliance to split Asia, hostility to the People's Republic of China, interference in the internal affairs of the Asian countries and the creation of new tension. In my report on foreign affairs made on August 11, 1954, to the Central People's Government Council, I have indicated to all the states concerned that the Chinese Government firmly opposes the formation of the so-called Southeast Asia treaty organisation by the United States aggressive group . . .

The Ministry of Foreign Affairs of the Soviet Government on September 14, 1954, issued a statement on the question of the "Southeast Asia collective defence treaty", pointing out that the states participating on this military alliance should assume the entire responsibility for their actions, which are in violent contradiction to the tasks of strengthening peace. This view is identical with that of the Chinese Government. . . .

The Chinese people must liberate Taiwan. So long as Taiwan is not liberated, China's territory is not intact, China cannot have a tranquil environment for peaceful construction and peace in the Far East and throughout the world is not secure. On August 11, 1954, the Central People's Government Council passed a resolution urging all Chinese people and the Chinese People's Liberation Army to redouble their efforts in all fields of work and strive for the liberation of Taiwan and the elimination of the traitorous Chiang Kai-shek group, so as to complete our people's sacred task of liberation. On August 22, all the democratic parties and groups and people's organisations of China issued a joint declaration on the liberation of Taiwan in response to this call of the Central People's Government. This is a manifestation of the unshakable common will of the 600 million people of China. . . .

[New China News Agency, Supplement No. 218, October 14, 1954.]

17. Mutual Defense Treaty Between the US and the ROC, December 2, 1954 (Extract)

The Parties to this Treaty,
Reaffirming their faith in the purposes and principles of the Charter of the United Nations and their desire to live in peace

with all peoples and all Governments, and desiring to strengthen the fabric of peace in the West Pacific Area,

Recalling with mutual pride the relationship which brought their two peoples together in a common bond of sympathy and mutual ideals to fight side by side against imperialist aggression during the last war,

Desiring to declare publicly and formally their sense of unity and their common determination to defend themselves against external armed attack, so that no potential aggressor could be under the illusion that either of them stands alone in the West Pacific Area, and

Desiring further to strengthen their present efforts for collective defense for the preservation of peace and security pending the development of a more comprehensive system of regional security in the West Pacific Area,

Have agreed as follows:

Article I

The Parties undertake, as set forth in the Charter of the United Nations, to settle any international dispute in which they may be involved by peaceful means in such a manner that international peace, security and justice are not endangered and to refrain in their international relations from the threat or use of force in any manner inconsistent with the purposes of the United Nations.

Article II

In order more effectively to achieve the objective of this Treaty, the Parties separately and jointly by self-help and mutual aid will maintain and develop their individual and collective capacity to resist armed attack and communist subversive activities directed from without against their territorial integrity and political stability.

Article III

The Parties undertake to strengthen their free institutions and to cooperate with each other in the development of economic progress and social well-being and to further their individual and collective efforts toward these ends.

Article IV

The Parties, through their Foreign Ministers or their deputies, will consult together from time to time regarding the implementation of this Treaty.

Article V

Each Party recognizes that an armed attack in the West Pacific Area directed against the territories of either of the Parties would be dangerous to its own peace and safety and declares that it would act to meet the common danger in accordance with its constitutional processes.

Any such armed attack and all measures taken as a result thereof shall be immediately reported to the Security Council of the United Nations. Such measures shall be terminated when the Security Council has taken the measures necessary to restore and maintain international peace and security.

Article VI

For the purposes of Articles II and V, the terms "territorial" and "territories" shall mean in respect of the Republic of China, Taiwan and the Pescadores; and in respect to the United States of America, the island territories in the West Pacific under its jurisdiction. The provisions of Articles II and V will be applicable to such other territories as may be determined by mutual agreement.

Article VII

The Government of the Republic of China grants, and the Government of the United States of America accepts, the right to dispose such United States land, air and sea forces in and about Taiwan and the Pescadores as may be required for their defense, as determined by mutual agreement.

Article VIII

This Treaty does not affect and shall not be interpreted as affecting in any way the rights and obligations of the Parties under the Charter of the United Nations or the responsibility of the United Nations for the maintenance of international peace and security.

Article IX

This Treaty shall be ratified by the United States of America and the Republic of China in accordance with their respective constitutional processes and will come into force when instruments of ratification thereof have been exchanged by them at Taipei.

Article X

This Treaty shall remain in force indefinitely. Either Party may terminate it one year after notice has been given to the other Party. . . .

18. Note to Secretary of State Dulles from the ROC Foreign Minister, December 10, 1954

Excellency:

I have the honor to acknowledge the receipt of Your Excellency's Note of today's date, which reads as follows:

I have the honor to refer to recent conversations between representatives of our two Governments and to confirm the understandings reached as a result of those conversations, as follows:

The Republic of China effectively controls both the territory described in Article VI of the Treaty of Mutual Defense between the Republic of China and the United States of America signed on December 2, 1954, at Washington and other territory. It possesses with respect to all territory now and hereafter under its control the inherent right of self-defense. In view of the obligations of the two Parties under the said Treaty and of the fact that the use of force from either of these areas by either of the Parties affects the other, it is agreed that such use of force will be a matter of joint agreement, subject to action of an emergency character which is clearly an exercise of the inherent right of self-defense. Military elements which are a product of joint effort and contribution by the two Parties will not be removed from the territories described in Article VI to a degree which would substantially diminish the defensibility of such territories without mutual agreement.

I have the honor to confirm on behalf of my Government, the understanding set forth in Your Excellency's Note under reply.

I avail myself of this opportunity to convey to Your Excellency the assurances of my highest consideration.

George K C Yeh
Minister for Foreign Affairs
of the Republic of China

19. House Joint Resolution Authorizing the President to Use American Forces for the Protection of Formosa and Related Territories, January 29, 1955

Whereas, the primary purpose of the United States, in its relations with all other nations, is to develop and sustain a just and enduring peace for all; and

Whereas certain territories in the West Pacific under the jurisdiction of the Republic of China are now under armed attack, and threats and declarations have been and are being made by the Chinese Communists that such armed attack is in aid of and in preparation for armed attack on Formosa and the Pescadores;

Whereas such armed attack if continued would gravely endanger the peace and security of the West Pacific Area and particularly of Formosa and the Pescadores; and

Whereas the secure possession by friendly governments of the Western Pacific Island chain, of which Formosa is a part, is essential to the vital interests of the United States and all friendly nations in or bordering ùpon the Pacific Ocean; and

Whereas the President of the United States on January 6, 1955, submitted to the Senate for its advice and consent to ratification a Mutual Defense Treaty between the United States of America and the Republic of China, which recognizes that an armed attack in the West Pacific area directed against territories, therein described, in the region of Formosa and the Pescadores, would be dangerous to the peace and safety of the parties to the treaty: Therefore be it

Resolved by the Senate and House of Representatives of the United States of America in Congress assembled, That the President of the United States be and he hereby is authorized to employ the Armed Forces of the United States as he deems necessary for the specific purpose of securing and protecting Formosa and the Pescadores against armed attack, this authority to include the securing and protection of such related positions and territories of that area now in friendly hands and the taking of such other measures as he judges to be required or appropriate in assuring the defense of Formosa and the Pescadores.

This resolution shall expire, when the President shall determine that the peace and security of the area is reasonably assured by international conditions created by action of the United Nations or otherwise, and shall so report to the Congress.

[*AFP 1950–1955,* II, pp. 2486–87.]

20. Dulles's Testimony Before the Senate Committee on Foreign Relations on the US-ROC Treaty, February 7, 1955 (Extract)

To summarize—what the treaty would accomplish is this:

It would give the Chinese Communists notice, beyond any possibility of misinterpretation, that the United States would regard an armed attack directed against Taiwan (Formosa) and the Pescadores as a danger to its own peace and safety and would act to meet the danger—such action to be in accordance with our constitutional processes.

It would provide firm reassurance to the Republic of China and to the world that Taiwan (Formosa) and the Pescadores are not a subject for barter as part of some Far Eastern "deal" with the Chinese Communists.

Taken in conjunction with the treaties which have already been concluded by the United States and to which I have referred above, this treaty rounds out the Western Pacific security system. It would be theoretically preferable if that rounding out were accomplished by a multilateral regional pact. This may come as a future development. However, that is not practical at the present time, and, in the meantime, we need to act within the limits of the practical.

After the treaty was signed, there took place an exchange of notes, dated December 10, 1954, between the Chinese Minister for Foreign Affairs and myself. These were designed to insure that our two Governments will act in harmony and concert in relation to the present troubled state of affairs in that area. It was agreed that offensive military operations by either party from the territories held by the Republic of China would be undertaken only as a matter of joint agreement. This is obviously a reasonable and prudent understanding, because unilateral action of an offensive character by one party might throw heavy burdens upon the other party. Therefore, neither will act in disregard of the other.

It is furthermore agreed that military elements which are a product of joint effort and contribution will not be removed from the treaty area to a degree which would substantially diminish its defensibility unless by mutual agreement. This means, for example, that, if the United States has granted supplies and equipment for the forces on Formosa or has aided in the training, support and equipment of armed forces, the resultant strength will not be removed from Formosa to other areas without our consent. Otherwise, the United States might be required continuously to replace what we had designed for the defense of Formosa. . . .

[*AFP 1950–1955,* I, p. 955.]

US-PRC AMBASSADORIAL TALKS BEGIN

21. Chou En-lai's Press Statement at Bandung, Indonesia, April 23, 1955

The Chinese Government is willing to sit down and enter into negotiations with the United States Government to discuss the question of relaxing tension in the Far East and especially the question of relaxing tension in the Taiwan area.

[Quoted in George McTurnan Kahin, *The Asian-African Conference: Bandung, Indonesia, April 1955* (Ithaca, NY: Cornell University Press, 1956), pp. 28–29.]

22. Dulles Answers Questions on Chou En-lai's Offer at His Press Conference, April 26, 1955 (Extracts)

Q. Mr. Secretary, in the Chou En-lai proposal he spoke not only of the specific Formosa problem but of the general Far East problem. Is it your view that our position is that we should settle the Formosan problem before we get into a larger discussion with Communist China, or is it possible to have a larger discussion in which Formosa can be a part of it?

A. The first thing, it seems to me, that requires to be determined is whether there is apt to be a cease-fire in the area. One cannot very well settle matters under the threat of a gun. So far there has been nothing but war threats in the area. There has been and there is still continuing a very large buildup, particularly of Chinese Communist air capabilities, in the Formosa Straits area. There has been until quite recently a very violent propaganda campaign to the effect that they were going to take Formosa by force and that the islands, such as Tachen, were useful to carry out their program of force. As I say, you do not negotiate—at least, the United States does not negotiate—with a pistol aimed at its head.

The first thing is to find out whether there is a possibility of a cease-fire in the area. That is a matter which can be discussed perhaps bilaterally, or at the United Nations, or possibly under other circumstances. But I regard a cease-fire as the indispensable prerequisite to anything further. When you get into further matters, then the interests of the Chinese Nationalists would naturally come to play a very large part.

Q. Mr. Secretary, have the Nationalist Chinese accepted the concept of a cease-fire? Are they prepared to accept a cease-fire in that area?

A. They have indicated opposition to a cease-fire in the area, and in that respect our views do not wholly coincide. At the time when New Zealand put this matter on the agenda of the Security Council, there was, as I recall, a statement issued by the Chinese Nationalists indicating they did not favor a cease-fire in the area.

Q. Mr. Secretary, you said that, after discussing the cease-fire, in other matters the interests of the Chinese Nationalists would play a part. Do I understand correctly from what you said that the presence of the Chinese Nationalists would not be indispensable for the discussion of a cease-fire?

A. Not as far as concerns a cease-fire which involved the possible interests of the United States, which has undertaken to react to an attack against Formosa. If we could get assurances there was to be no attack against Formosa, we would accept those.

Q. Mr. Secretary, it has been suggested that the move by the Chinese Communists—by Chou En-lai at Bandung—did not come as a complete surprise but in fact you had some information, or at least expectations of it—that it figured in your discussions with the President in Augusta and it may perhaps have played some part in the mission of Assistant Secretary of State Robertson and Admiral Radford at Formosa.

A. I would say this: It is no secret that we have hoped that the Bandung conference would result in a more peaceful attitude on the part of the Chinese Communists. I have sometimes said that

I felt that a great deal would depend, as far as the future is concerned, on whether the Chinese Communists came away from Bandung feeling that they had a green light to go ahead and take Formosa by force or whether they felt that to do so would antagonize the good will of the free Asian countries which they were seeking. . . .

I don't think that there occurred any moral or spiritual conversion on the part of the Chinese Communists. But I do think that there may have been a realization of the fact that a real peacefulness, instead of just talk about peace while carrying on war, was from their standpoint the best policy. If that has happened, it is something which we can be very glad about. . . .

[*AFP 1950–1955*, II, pp. 2499–2501.]

23. US-PRC Joint Communiqué on Ambassadorial-Level Talks, July 25, 1955

As a result of communication between the United States and the People's Republic of China through the diplomatic channels of the United Kingdom, it has been agreed that the talks held in the last year between consular representatives of both sides at Geneva should be conducted on ambassadorial level in order to aid in settling the matter of repatriation of civilians who desire to return to their respective countries and to facilitate further discussions and settlements of certain other practical matters now at issue between both sides. The first meeting of ambassadorial representatives of both sides will take place on August 1, 1955 at Geneva.

[*AFP 1950–1955*, II, p. 2516.]

24. US-PRC Agreement on the Return of Civilians, September 10, 1955

The Ambassadors of the United States of America and the People's Republic of China have agreed to announce measures which their respective governments have adopted concerning the return of civilians to their respective countries.

With respect to Chinese in the United States, Ambassador U. Alexis Johnson, on behalf of the United States, has informed Ambassador Wang Ping-nan that:

1. The United States recognizes that Chinese in the United States who desire to return to the People's Republic of China are entitled to do so and declares that it has adopted and will further adopt appropriate measures so that they can expeditiously exercise their right to return.

2. The Government of the Republic of India will be invited to assist in the return to the People's Republic of China of those who desire to do so as follows:

A. If any Chinese in the United States believes that contrary to the declared policy of the United States he is encountering obstruction in departure, he may so inform the Embassy of the Republic of India in the United States and request it to make representations on his behalf to the United States Government. If desired by the People's Republic of China, the Government of the Republic of India may also investigate the facts in any such case.

B. If any Chinese in the United States who desires to return to the People's Republic of China has difficulty in paying his return expenses, the Government of the Republic of India may render him financial assistance needed to permit his return.

3. The United States Government will give wide publicity to the foregoing arrangements and the Embassy of the Republic of India in the United States may also do so.

With respect to Americans in the People's Republic of China, Ambassador Wang Ping-nan, on behalf of the People's Republic of China, has informed Ambassador U. Alexis Johnson that:

1. The People's Republic of China recognizes that Americans in the People's Republic of China who desire to return to the United States are entitled to do so, and declares that it has adopted and will further adopt appropriate measures so that they can expeditiously exercise their right to return.

2. The Government of the United Kingdom will be invited to assist in the return to the United States of those Americans who desire to do so as follows:

A. If any American in the People's Republic of China believes that contrary to the declared policy of the People's Republic of China he is encountering obstruction in departure, he may so inform the Office of the Chargé d'Affaires of the United Kingdom in the People's Republic of China and request it to make representations on his behalf to the Government of the People's Republic of China. If desired by the United States, the Government of the United Kingdom may also investigate the facts in any such case.

B. If any American in the People's Republic of China who desires to return to the United States has difficulty in paying his return expenses, the Government of the United Kingdom may render him financial assistance needed to permit his return.

3. The Government of the People's Republic of China will give wide publicity to the foregoing arrangements and the Office of the Chargé d'Affaires of the United Kingdom in the People's Republic of China may also do so.

[*AFP 1950–1955,* II, pp. 2516–17.]

25. PRC Foreign Ministry Statement on Implementation of Agreement on Return of Civilians, December 15, 1955

Recently, United States Secretary of State, Mr. John Foster Dulles, and other official spokesmen of the United States repeatedly charged, without any foundation, that the Chinese side had not fully complied with the agreement on the return of civilians reached at the Sino-American Ambassadorial ta!ks. The Chinese Government deems it necessary to issue the following statement to set forth the truth:

The Chinese side has consistently been carrying out faithfully the agreement on the return of civilians reached by both sides at the Sino-American talks. It is precisely the American side which has not fully complied with the agreement and has acted in violation of it.

(1) At the very start of the Sino-American Ambassadorial talks, the Chinese side furnished the American side with a name list and information concerning all the Americans in China and gave it a clear accounting. But the American side has failed, up to now, to furnish our side with a name list and information concerning all the Chinese in the United States. Consequently, after agreement was reached at the Sino-American talks on the return of civilians, the Government of the Republic of India, entrusted by China to assist in the return to China of the Chinese in the United States, did not possess adequate data required for the full execution in the task. Our side is fully entitled to request the Gov-

ernment of the Republic of India, through its Embassy in the United States, to investigate the facts of their encountering obstruction in the departure and to assist in their return. But the United States Government again indicated that it could not give the Indian Embassy in the United States any assistance in this respect. The American side stated that the Indian Embassy in the United States could contact the Chinese residents only if the latter themselves had asked for it. Our side does not agree with the interpretation of the agreement made by the American side, yet since the American side persists in such an attitude, our side naturally cannot give the office of the British Chargé d'Affaires in China, as entrusted by the United States, more than reciprocal rights. Our side is not satisfied with the present situation where the third countries invited by China and the United States are unable to take the initiative to contact the civilians or the side concerned, but the American side has no right at all to complain, in this connection against the Chinese side, as the situation is of its own making. Should the American side wish to change the situation, it should first of all furnish our side with a name list and information concerning all the Chinese in the United States, and agree to assist the Indian Embassy in taking the initiative to contact them.

(2) The American side has repeatedly raised the question of the Americans imprisoned in China. It should be pointed out that the Americans imprisoned in China are Americans who have committed offences against the Chinese law. When they are serving their sentences, there can be no question of their returning to the United States and still less can there be any question of their encountering obstruction in departure. In the Sino-American talks our side has stated that the Chinese Government will examine their cases individually and take measures of leniency on the basis of their behavior in accordance with Chinese legal procedures. Since August 1 when the Sino-American talks started, 26 out of the 40 Americans who committed offences against the law have been released. That is to say, during this period of a little more than 4 months, two-thirds of the Americans who committed offences against the law have already been released. As for the remaining Americans who committed offences against the law, the Chinese Government is also continuing with the work of examining their cases individually.

On the other hand, the American side has never informed us how many Chinese are imprisoned in the United States, nor has it provided us with a list of their names. Consequently, our side is in no position to check the facts, and the Indian Embassy is in no position to offer them any assistance.

(3) The American side has also raised repeatedly the question of the speed with which China has released those Americans who committed offences against the Chinese law. The Chinese side has explicitly stated, even before the agreement on the return of civilians was reached at the Sino-American talks, that the Americans who had committed offences against the law in China must be dealt with in accordance with Chinese legal procedures and that no time limit could be set to the release of these Americans. This is a matter of Chinese sovereignty. The American side also repeatedly stated in the Sino-American talks that it respects the Chinese legal procedures and has no intention of impairing Chinese sovereignty. Therefore, after the conclusion of the agreement, there is no justification at all for the American side to ask, or to ask in a disguised form, for setting a time-limit to the release of American criminals, and, in fact, our side is precisely releasing expeditiously those Americans who committed offences against law. On the other hand, however, the American side has not taken any corresponding measures in regard of any Chinese imprisoned in the United States.

(4) As to the ordinary American residents in China, their departure has never been obstructed. Since the start of the Sino-American talks, China has assisted all those Americans who desire to return to their country in tidying up expeditiously their unsettled affairs so that they can return to their country at an early date. Since August 1, out of 59 ordinary Americans in China all 16 who applied have been permitted to depart. Among these 16, there are 3 who have not left China, but that is because they themselves have some affairs to be settled, and China is doing its best to help them. As for the other American residents, they can leave at any time when they desire to return to their country, and they will receive similar assistance. On the other hand, however, even among those 103 Chinese admitted by the American side, who had long ago applied for permission to depart but were long prevented by the United States Government from leaving, there are still 38 who have not yet returned to China. The American side declared that their departure has been approved, but it has never given an accounting of their addresses nor of the reason why they have not yet returned. What is more, the American side

has refused to assist the Indian Embassy in learning about their conditions.

(5) The American side not only has failed to furnish our side with a name list of all the Chinese in the United States and has refused to give due assistance to the Indian Embassy, but has recently issued a regulation that the Chinese students continuing to reside in the United States must secure an entrance permit for Taiwan. This is obviously a further threat directed against those Chinese students who are unable for the time being to return to China, so that they would not dare to apply for returning to the Chinese mainland in the future; as early as on April 2 this year the United States Department of State admitted in an open statement that "some Chinese students may refrain from applying to the Immigration and Naturalisation Service for permission to depart from the United States for fear of being refused". The American side has not taken any appropriate measures to dispel their apprehensions resulting from the prolonged obstruction and threat to which they have been subjected; on the contrary, it has now taken additional measures of threat against them. This is an outright violation of the letter and spirit of the agreement on the return of civilians reached between the two sides.

The charge of the American side that China has not fully complied with the agreement is completely untenable. The Chinese Government firmly asks that the American side put a stop to all its acts in violation of the agreement and fully comply with the agreement between both sides.

[New China News Agency, December 16, 1955.]

26. State Department Reply to PRC's December 15th Statement, December 16, 1955

The Chinese Communists on December 15 issued a statement defending their continued detention of U.S. civilians in China. At the same time they accused the United States of not complying with the agreed announcement of September 10 regarding the repatriation of civilians to Communist China.

Because the Communist statement contains many errors, this statement is being made. The facts show that the United States has scrupulously complied with its agreement and that Chinese in the United States are now and have at all times since the announcement been free to leave.

Unfortunately, the same is not true with respect to the Chinese Communist performance of its agreement to permit U.S. civilians to "expeditiously" return to the United States. Of the 19 U.S. citizens in Communist China who were being prevented from returning on September 10, the date of the Chinese Communist agreement, only 5 have been released.

U.S. Ambassador Johnson has repeatedly protested to Communist Ambassador Wang, in the Geneva talks, the failure of the Communists to permit U.S. citizens to leave China. He has also protested the cruel and inhuman treatment of those concerning whom facts are available.

The answer to these protests has been the public statement by the Communists charging that the United States has not permitted Chinese to leave the United States.

In the agreed announcement of September 10, the Chinese Communist Ambassador declared:

> The People's Republic of China recognizes that Americans in the People's Republic of China who desire to return to the United States are entitled to do so, and declares that it has adopted and will further adopt appropriate measures so that they can expeditiously exercise their right to return.

This declaration is simple, clear, and positive. It says that any U.S. citizen has the right to leave China and that the Communists have taken or will take the necessary steps so that those who wish may leave "expeditiously." No distinction is made as between those in prison and those out of prison. All U.S. citizens who wish to leave should have been out of Communist China long before this. The continued holding of these U.S. citizens by the Communists is a violation of their agreed announcement, for which the United States must continue to protest.

As for the Communist charge that the United States is preventing Chinese from leaving the United States, it is sufficient to point out that not a single Chinese has been refused exit. If anyone knows of any Chinese who wishes to leave and who claims he is being prevented, he should communicate at once with the Department of State or the Indian Embassy at Washington D.C., which the United States has agreed may render assistance. The Indian Embassy has made no representation that any Chinese is being prevented from leaving.

It is unfortunate that the Chinese Communists have seen fit to make a public announcement containing charges which are without foundation. This cannot conceal the fact that U.S. citizens continue to be held in prison by the Communists in violation of their public announcement of September 10. It is hoped that these U.S. citizens will be permitted promptly to leave Chinese prisons and return to their homes.

[*AFP 1950–1955,* II, pp. 2517–19.]

THE DANGERS IN THE TAIWAN STRAIT

27. US and PRC Proposals and Counterproposals on the Renunciation of Force, October, 1955–May, 1956

US Statement and Proposal on Renunciation of Force,
October 8, 1955

One of the practical matters for discussion between us is that each of us should renounce the use of force to achieve our policies when they conflict. The United States and the PRC confront each other with policies which are in certain respects incompatible. This fact need not, however, mean armed conflict, and the most important single thing we can do is first of all to be sure that it will not lead to armed conflict.

Then and only then can other matters causing tension between the parties in the Taiwan area and the Far East be hopefully discussed.

It is not suggested that either of us should renounce any policy objectives which we consider we are legitimately entitled to achieve, but only that we renounce the use of force to implement these policies.

Neither of us wants to negotiate under the threat of force. The free discussion of differences, and their fair and equitable solution, become impossible under the overhanging threat that force may be resorted to when one party does not agree with the other.

The United States as a member of the United Nations has agreed to refrain in its international relations from the threat or use of force. This has been its policy for many years and is its guiding principle of conduct in the Far East, as throughout the world.

The use of force to achieve national objectives does not accord with accepted standards of conduct under international law.

The Covenant of the League of Nations, the Kellogg-Briand Treaties, and the Charter of the United Nations reflect the universal view of the civilized community of nations that the use of force as an instrument of national policy violates international law, constitutes a threat to international peace, and prejudices the interests of the entire world community.

There are in the world today many situations which tempt those who have force to use it to achieve what they believe to be legitimate policy objectives. Many countries are abnormally divided or contain what some consider to be abnormal intrusions. Nevertheless, the responsible governments of the world have in each of these cases renounced the use of force to achieve what they believe to be legitimate and even urgent goals.

It is an essential foundation and preliminary to the success of the discussions under Item 2 that it first be made clear that the parties to these discussions renounce the use of force to make the policies of either prevail over those of the other. That particularly applies to the Taiwan area.

The acceptance of this principle does not involve third parties, or the justice or injustice of conflicting claims. It only involves recognizing and agreeing to abide by accepted standards of international conduct.

We ask, therefore, as a first matter for discussion under Item 2, a declaration that your side will not resort to the use of force in the Taiwan area except defensively. The United States would be prepared to make a corresponding declaration. These declarations will make it appropriate for us to pass on to the discussion of other matters with a better hope of coming to constructive conclusions.

PRC Draft Declaration on Renunciation of Force,
October 27, 1955

1. Ambassador Wang Ping-nan on behalf of the Government of the People's Republic of China and Ambassador U. Alexis Johnson on behalf of the Government of the United States of America jointly declare that,

2. In accordance with Article 2, Paragraph 3, of the Charter of the United Nations, "All members shall settle their international

disputes by peaceful means in such a manner that international peace and security, and justice, are not endangered"; and

3. In accordance with Article 2, Paragraph 4 of the Charter of the United Nations, "All members shall refrain in their international relations from the threat or use of force against the territorial integrity or political independence of any state, or in any other manner inconsistent with the purposes of the United Nations";

4. The People's Republic of China and the United States of America agree that they should settle disputes between their two countries by peaceful means without resorting to the threat or use of force.

5. In order to realize their common desire, the People's Republic of China and the United States of America decide to hold a conference of Foreign Ministers to settle through negotiations the question of relaxing and eliminating the tension in Taiwan area.

US Draft Declaration on Renunciation of Force,
November 10, 1955

1. The Ambassador of the United States of America and the Ambassador of the People's Republic of China during the course of the discussions of practical matters at issue have expressed the determination that the differences between the two sides shall not lead to armed conflict.

2. They recognize that the use of force to achieve national objectives does not accord with the principles and purposes of the United Nations Charter or with generally accepted standards of international conduct.

3. They furthermore recognize that the renunciation of the threat or use of force is essential to the just settlement of disputes or situations which might lead to a breach of the peace.

4. Therefore, without prejudice to the pursuit by each side of its policies by peaceful means, they have agreed to announce the following declarations:

5. Ambassador Wang Ping-nan informed Ambassador U. Alexis Johnson that:

6. In general, and with particular reference to the Taiwan area, the People's Republic of China renounces the use of force except in individual and collective self-defense.

7. Ambassador U. Alexis Johnson informed Ambassador Wang Ping-nan that:

8. In general, and with particular reference to the Taiwan area, the United States renounces the use of force, except in individual and collective self-defense.

PRC Draft Counterproposal for an Agreed Announcement, December 1, 1955

1. Ambassador Wang Ping-nan, on behalf of the Government of the People's Republic of China, and Ambassador Alexis Johnson on behalf of the Government of the United States of America, agree to announce:

2. The People's Republic of China and the United States of America are determined that they should settle disputes between their two countries through peaceful negotiations without resorting to the threat or use of force.

3. The two Ambassadors should continue their talks to seek practical and feasible means for the realization of this common desire.

US Revision of PRC December 1 Counterproposal, January 12, 1956

1. Ambassador Wang Ping-nan, on behalf of the Government of the People's Republic of China, and Ambassador U. Alexis Johnson, on behalf of the Government of the United States of America, agree to announce:

2. The People's Republic of China and the United States of America are determined that they will settle disputes between them through peaceful means and that, without prejudice to the inherent right of individual and collective self-defense, they will not resort to the threat or use of force in the Taiwan area or elsewhere.

3. The two Ambassadors should continue their talks to seek practical and feasible means for the realization of this common desire.

US Draft Agreed Announcement, April 19, 1956

Ambassador U. Alexis Johnson, on behalf of the Government of the United States of America, and Ambassador Wang Ping-nan, on behalf of the Government of the People's Republic of China, agree, without prejudice to the pursuit by each side of its policies by peaceful means or its inherent right of individual or collective self-defense, to announce:

The United States of America and the People's Republic of

China are determined that they should settle disputes between their two countries through peaceful negotiations without resorting to the threat or use of force in the Taiwan area or elsewhere.

The two Ambassadors should continue their talks to seek practical and feasible means for the realization of this common desire.

PRC Draft Agreed Announcement, May 11, 1956

Ambassador Wang Ping-nan, on behalf of the Government of the People's Republic of China, and Ambassador U. Alexis Johnson, on behalf of the Government of the United States of America, agree, without prejudice to the principles of mutual respect for territorial integrity and sovereignty and non-interference in each other's internal affairs, to announce:

The People's Republic of China and the United States of America are determined that they should settle disputes between their two countries in the Taiwan area through peaceful negotiations without resorting to the threat or use of force against each other;

The two Ambassadors should continue their talks to seek and to ascertain within two months practical and feasible means for the realization of this common desire, including the holding of a Sino-American conference of the foreign ministers, and to make specific arrangements.

[*AFP 1956*, pp. 795–98; New China News Agency, June 12, 1956.]

28. Dulles Answers Questions on "Brinkmanship" at His Press Conference, January 17, 1956 (Extracts)

An article in *Life* Magazine has attracted much comment. Let me say this. . . . Most of the statements specifically attributed to me are quotations or close paraphrases of what I had already said elsewhere. One is somewhat ambiguously phrased, but the ambiguity can easily be resolved if read in context and with reference to the many public statements which I have made.

I believe that the United States should adopt every honorable course to avoid engagement in the war. Indeed, I have devoted my whole life to the pursuit of a just and durable peace. I believe, however, that there are basic moral values and vital interests for which we stand, and that the surest way to avoid war is to let it be known in advance that we are prepared to defend these principles, if need be by life itself.

This policy of seeking to prevent war by preventing miscalculation by a potential aggressor is not a personal policy; it is not a partisan policy; it is a national policy. It is expressed in mutual security treaties which we now have with 42 nations and which the United States Senate has overwhelmingly approved. It is expressed in Public Law 4, whereby the Congress, by an almost unanimous bipartisan vote, authorized the President to use the armed forces of the United States in the Formosa area, if he deemed it necessary for the protection of Formosa and the Penghus.

This policy of making clear our position in advance, of course, involves risks. As Senator Vandenberg said about the North Atlantic Treaty, it is a calulated risk for peace. But as we have learned by hard experience, failure to make our position known in advance makes war more likely because then an aggressor may miscalculate. The policy of deterrence is only one aspect of the task of maintaining a just and durable peace. It is necessary to be patient; it is necessary to be conciliatory; it is necessary to make our peace a vital force for justice and human welfare so that all men will aspire to share that kind of peace. . . .

Q. *Mr. Secretary, is this the sentence that you considered ambiguous: "The ability to get to the verge without getting into the war is the necessary art"?*

A. Will you read the preceding sentence, I think.

Q. *The preceding sentence is—it is two sentences: "You have to take chances for peace, just as you must take chances in war. Some say that we were brought to the verge of war. Of course we were brought to the verge of war. The ability to get to the verge without getting into the war is the necessary art."*

A. Yes, that second sentence if read out of context does, I think, give an incorrect impression. The important thing is that we were "brought" to the verge of war by threats which were uttered in relation to Korea, in relation to Indochina, and in relation to Formosa. . . .

[Department of State, *Bulletin*, XXIV, No. 866, January 30, 1956, pp. 155, 157.]

A CHINESE OLIVE BRANCH REJECTED

29. *New York Times* **Report by Anthony Lewis on PRC Foreign Ministry's Offer of Visas to US Correspondents, August 6, 1956 (Extracts)**

Washington, Aug. 6—Communist China lifted today a seven-year ban on visits by American correspondents. However, whether any American news man would actually enter Communist China remained a question tonight.

The State Department promptly expressed its disapproval of the idea. Lincoln White, department press officer, said no exceptions would be made in the long-standing policy of forbidding use of United States passports for travel into Communist China.

The Peiping Government, in a surprise move, cabled offers of visas to fifteen United States newspapers, news agency, magazine and radio-television reporters. The cablegrams invited the correspondents for a month's visit beginning at the end of August.

The possibility remained that one or more of the news organizations concerned would ignore the State Department position and assign correspondents to accept the invitation. This would theoretically subject the reporters to prosecution, but the actual chance of any legal action against them was considered slight.

Until last year United States passports were stamped "not valid" for travel in the Soviet Union, Communist China, and all the Soviet satellites. A special passport validation had to be obtained from the State Department to visit any Communist country.

Last Oct. 31, at the Geneva Conference of the Big Four Foreign Ministers, Secretary of State Dulles announced that this restriction would be eased. Since then no special permission has been needed for travel to the Soviet Union, Poland, Czechoslovakia, Hungary or Rumania.

However, an absolute ban has remained on travel to countries with which the United States has no diplomatic relations—Communist China, Albania, Bulgaria, North Korea, and North Vietnam. . . .

A criminal statute provides a maximum five-year prison term and $2,000 fine for anyone who violates the "conditions or restrictions" on a passport. The provision is in Title 18, Section

1544, United States Code. But officials today could recall no recent case in which the law was involved. United States correspondents have visited Bulgaria and North Vietnam in the last year and heard nothing about it from the State Department. Senator George W. Malone, Republican of Nevada, made a highly publicized trip to Bulgaria last year with an ordinary non-validated passport. . . .

Some of the correspondents invited had applied for Chinese visas in recent years and received no reply. At least one had never applied. The cablegram to him nevertheless said that his request for a visa had been "granted."

The cablegrams said visas could be picked up between Aug. 20 and 30 at the Chinese Communist Embassy in Moscow or at Sumchon across the border from Hong Kong. The correspondents were asked to "contact Intourist Canton for travel and accommodations here."

The cablegrams were signed by Chu Lieh, secretary of the Information Department of the Foreign Ministry in Peiping.

Indications were that the invitations were timed for the Eighth Congress of the Chinese Communist party, which is to meet in Peiping Sept. 15. . . .

The argument of news organizations for permitting the visits would be that sending a correspondent in no way expressed approval of the Chinese Communist regime but would simply be a proper and important move to keep the American public informed.

No United States correspondents have been allowed into China since the Communists completed their victory over the Nationalists in 1949. Other Western countries have sent reporters on lengthy trips, and permanent correspondents are now maintained in Peiping by the British agency Reuters and Agence France Presse.

Whatever the outcome of today's invitations, Peiping seemed certain to reap a propaganda harvest. It could accuse the State Department of erecting information barriers between Americans and the Communist regime.

[*New York Times,* August 7, 1956. Reprinted by permission.]

30. State Department Statement on Nonissuance of Passports for Travel to the PRC, August 7, 1956

The Department of State has taken note of the fact that the Chinese Communist regime has announced that it has invited certain United States newspaper correspondents and commentators to visit Communist China.

The State Department has taken the occasion to review carefully its policy with respect to the nonissuance of passports validated for travel to Communist China. After such review, it continues to be the policy of the State Department not to issue such passports.

The United States welcomes the free exchange of information between different countries irrespective of political and social differences. But the Chinese Communist regime has created a special impediment. It adopted the practice of taking American citizens into captivity and holding them in effect as political hostages. It continues to do so despite the fact that on September 10, 1955, at Geneva, it promised that all Americans in Communist China would be allowed expeditiously to exercise their right to return to the United States.

So long as these conditions continue it is not considered to be in the best interests of the United States that Americans should accept the Chinese Communist invitation to travel in Communist China.

[*AFP 1956*, pp. 805–6.]

CHINA'S AMERICA POLICY; AMERICA'S CHINA POLICY

31. Vice-Premier Ch'en Yi's Report on "The International Situation and Our Foreign Policy" to the CCP's Eighth Congress, September 25, 1956 (Extracts)

Within the United States itself, the war policy of the monopoly circles has also aroused widespread dissatisfaction and opposition. The policy of the arms drive and war preparations has imposed a heavy burden of military expenditure on the broad masses of the working people as well as on the small enterprises, but brought unprecedented, huge profits to the monopoly circles. The production of and experimenting on weapons of vast destructive power has also made the American people realize what colossal calamities will be brought them by the war policy of the US monopoly circles. For this reason the American people are unceasingly struggling for the safeguarding of their personal interests and for peace. In the latest election campaign in the United States, the two bourgeois political parties have been obliged to put forward slogans of peace. Within the US ruling circles, a more clear-sighted section of people have also begun to realize that to continue to carry out the policy of the arms drive and war preparations will not only result in the greater isolation of the United States, but also bring serious consequences to the economy of the United States itself. Very recently, a section of the ruling circles in the US have begun to advocate the reduction of armed forces, the lifting of embargo, and the adoption of a more realistic attitude towards international affairs. They demand an agonizing reappraisal of US foreign policy. Much as these suggestions are not thorough going, much as they have not become dominant within the US ruling circles, the very fact that they have been made indicates the sorry plight in which the policy of war pursued by the monopoly cliques now finds itself.

Working for the common objective of striving for peace and opposing war, all the peace-loving forces in the world are now merging into a mighty stream. The present international situation is favourable to world peace, and unfavorable to the war schemes of the monopoly circles in their attempt to establish world domination. There is no doubt whatsoever that the possibilities for winning peace and averting war have greatly increased.

But it is certain that the US aggressive bloc will not of itself give up its plots for war and aggression. The struggle between the international forces of peace and the forces of war will still be a prolonged and unremitting one. It would be a serious mistake if, in this struggle, we were to lose our vigilance against the danger of war. In order to win consolidated and lasting peace, we still have to make unremitting and greater efforts together with all the peace-loving countries and peoples throughout the world. . . .

Our policy of peaceful co-existence excludes no one, not even the United States of America.

The United States has all along taken a hostile attitude towards the People's Republic of China. The People's Republic of China was established in circumstances where the American armed intervention had come to naught. Not long after the founding of the People's Republic of China, the United States began menacing China and embarked upon its aggression against our country from Korea, Indo-China and Taiwan, on what they called a "three-pronged front." Up to the present, the United States is still occupying our territory, Taiwan, and trying to interfere in the liberation of our off-shore islands.

China has put up resolute resistance to the armed intervention and acts of aggression on the part of the United States. For we know full well that only by putting up determined resistance to aggression can we preserve peace. Facts have proved that only by making a determined effort to protect our national independence and the security of our country will the aggressors gradually come to their senses and will they be impelled to settle international disputes through peaceful consultation. Meanwhile, we have not let slip any possibility of relaxing tensions, and China has made contributions to bringing about armistice in Korea and the restoration of peace in Indochina. Even with regard to the dispute between China and the United States in the Taiwan area, China has put forward concrete proposals to hold a meeting between China and the United States on the foreign minister level for peaceful consultation.

The encroachment upon Taiwan and the interference in the internal affairs of China by the United States is meeting with the opposition of increasing numbers of countries and the broad masses of the people of the world. American penetration in the political, economic and cultural fields in Taiwan and the domination it is trying to establish there, have further aroused our compatriots in Taiwan, including the military and political personnel of the Kuomintang, to more and more intensified discontent and resistance. Our great motherland is growing stronger and stronger with each passing day. The possibility of bringing about a peaceful liberation of Taiwan is increasing too. Nevertheless, whatever form the liberation of Taiwan will take, Taiwan is sure to return to the bosom of our motherland. Nothing can stop the Chinese people from liberating Taiwan. If the United States does not abandon its policy of encroaching upon Taiwan and interfering with the internal affairs of our country, then it will only find itself sinking deeper and deeper into the quagmire from which it can never hope to extricate itself.

Comrades! The international situation is favorable to the socialist construction in our country and to the accomplishment of our task of liberating Taiwan. . . .

[New China News Agency, September 25, 1956, reproduced in *Current Background* (Hong Kong: U.S. Consulate General), No. 414, October 6, 1956, pp. 5, 8.]

32. Dulles's Speech on China Policy to Lions International, San Francisco, June 28, 1957

It is appropriate that in this great city of San Francisco, which faces the Far East, we should consider our polices toward communism in China.

On the China mainland 600 million people are ruled by the Chinese Communist Party. That party came to power by violence and, so far, has lived by violence.

It retains power not by will of the Chinese people but by massive, forcible repression. It fought the United Nations in Korea; it supported the Communist war in Indochina; it took Tibet by force. It fomented the Communist Huk rebellion in the Philippines and the Communists' insurrection in Malaya. It does not disguise its expansionist ambitions. It is bitterly hateful of the United States, which it considers a principal obstacle in the way of its path of conquest.

In the face of this condition the United States has supported, morally and materially, the free nations of the Western Pacific and Southeast Asia. Our security treaties make clear that the violation of these nations by international communism would be considered as endangering our own peace and safety and that we would act accordingly.

Together we constitute a goodly company and a stout bulwark against aggression.

As regards China, we have abstained from any act to encourage the Communist regime—morally, politically or materially. Thus:

We have not extended diplomatic recognition to the Chinese Communist regime;

We have opposed its seating in the United Nations;

We have not traded with Communist China or sanctioned cultural interchanges with it.

These have been, and are, our policies. Like all our policies, they are under periodic review.

As we review our China policy, we naturally and properly recall our recognition policy as regards Communist Russia.

The Bolsheviks seized power from Kerensky in 1917. Nevertheless, we continued for 16 years to treat the Kerensky representatives in exile as representing the lawful government of Russia. By 1933 it seemed that the Communist regime might be considered as a peaceful member of society. For more than a decade it had committed no act of armed aggression. It had accepted the independence of Estonia, Latvia, and Lithuania, and of Poland. It was not demonstrably maltreating American citizens. It promised to ease subversive activities in the United States, to respect American rights in Russia, and to settle Russia's public and private debts to the United States.

Also, by 1933, we desired to encourage the Soviet regime to resist Japanese aggressive policies in the Far East. The Republic of China, inspired by this same notion, had recognized the Soviet Government in December 1932, and we shortly followed suit.

We need not question that act of recognition under the circumstances which then prevailed. Recognition seemed indicated by many tests, and we did not read the future.

However, it can, I think, be said with confidence that recognition would not have been accorded to the Soviet Union even in 1933 had there been clear warning that the Soviet promises given in that connection were totally unreliable, that aggressive war would soon become an instrumentality of Soviet policy, and that it would be neutral toward Japanese aggression in Asia.

In the case of Communist China we are forewarned. That regime fails to pass even those tests which, after 16 years, the Soviet regime seemed to pass.

(1) Soviet Russia, in 1933, had had a decade of peaceful and non-aggressive relations with neighboring states; Communist China's past record is one of armed aggression.

(2) The Soviet regime seemed to want peace for the future. In the case of Communist China the situation is quite the reverse. Mr. Chou En-lai, at the time of the Bandung conference, said that, "The Chinese people do not want to have war with the United States and are willing to settle international disputes by peaceful means." But when the United States took him up and sought explicit reciprocal renunciations of force, his ambassador, after presenting various evasive formulas, finally stated frankly that his regime did intend to use armed force to take Taiwan (Formosa) unless they could get it in some other way.

(3) The Soviet Union in 1933 was not flagrantly violating its international engagements. The Chinese Communist regime is violating the 1953 Korean armistice and the 1954 Indochina armistice.

(4) There was reason to hope that the Soviet regime would treat our nationals with respect. The Chinese Communist regime violates the persons of our citizens in defiance of the elementary

code of international decency, and it breaches its 1955 pledge to release them.

(5) It seemed, in 1933, that the Soviet regime and the United States had parallel interests in resisting Japanese aggression in the Far East. Today the political purposes of Communist China clash everywhere with our own.

United States diplomatic recognition of Communist China would have the following consequences:

(1) The many mainland Chinese, who by Mao Tse-tung's own recent admission seek to change the nature of their government, would be immensely discouraged.

(2) The millions of overseas Chinese would feel that they had no Free China to which to look. Today increasing numbers of these overseas Chinese go to Free China to study. Six years ago there were less than 100 Chinese students from Southeast Asia and Hong Kong studying in Taiwan. Now there are nearly 5,000.

The number of Chinese students from overseas communities coming to Free China has increased year by year; the number going to Communist China has declined, and hundreds of disillusioned students have made their way out of mainland China in the past 2 years.

If the United States recognized the Chinese Communist regime, many of the millions of overseas Chinese in free Asian countries would, reluctantly, turn to acceptance of the guiding direction of the Communist regime. This would be a tragedy for them; and it would imperil friendly governments already menaced by Chinese Communist subversion.

(3) The Republic of China, now on Taiwan, would feel betrayed by its friend. That Government was our ally in the Second World War and for long bore alone the main burden of the Far Eastern war. It had many tempting opportunities to compromise with the Japanese on terms which would have been gravely detrimental to the United States. It never did so. We condemn the Soviets for having dishonored their 20-year treaty pledge of 1945 to support the Chinese National Government as the central government of China. We are honorbound to give our ally, to whom we are pledged by a mutual defense treaty, a full measure of loyalty.

(4) The free Asian governments of the Pacific and Southeast Asia would be gravely perplexed. They are not only close to the

vast Chinese land mass, but geographically and, to some extent, politically, they are separated as among themselves. The unifying and fortifying influence is, above all, the spirit and resolution of the United States. If we seemed to waver and to compromise with communism in China, that would in turn weaken free Asia resistance to the Chinese Communist regime and assist international communism to score a great success in its program to encircle us.

United States recognition of Communist China would make it probable that the Communist regime would obtain the seat of China in the United Nations. That would not be in the interest either of the United States or of the United Nations.

The United Nations is not a reformatory for bad governments. It is supposedly an association of those who are already "peace-loving" and who are "able and willing to carry out" the charter obligations. The basic obligation is not to use force, except in defense against armed attack.

The Chinese Communist regime has a record of successive armed aggressions, including war against the United Nations itself, a war not yet politically settled but discontinued by an armistice. The regime asserts not only its right but its purpose to use force if need be to bring Taiwan under its rule.

The Republic of China is entitled to a permanent seat and veto power in the Security Council. Should a regime which in 7 years has promoted five foreign civil wars—Korea, Indochina, Tibet, the Philippines, and Malaya; which itself has fought the United Nations and which today stands condemned by the United Nations as an aggressor; which defies the United Nations' decision to reunify Korea; and which openly proclaims its continuing purpose to use force—should that regime be given a permanent seat, with veto power, in the body which under the charter has "primary responsibility for the maintenance of international peace and security"?

Communist Russia, with its veto power, already seriously limits the ability of the United Nations to serve its intended purposes. Were Communist China also to become a permanent, veto-wielding member of the Security Council, that would, I fear, implant in the United Nations the seeds of its own destruction.

Let me turn now to the matter of trade and cultural relations, which could exist, to a limited degree, without recognition.

Normal peacetime trade with China, from which the American and Chinese peoples would benefit, could be in the common interest. But it seems that that kind of trade is not to be had in any appreciable volume.

Trade with Communist China is not a normal trade. It does not provide one country with what its people want but cannot well produce for themselves, in exchange for what other people want but cannot well produce for themselves. Trade with Communist China is wholly controlled by an official apparatus, and its limited amounts of foreign exchange are 'used to develop as rapidly as possible a formidable military establishment and a heavy industry to support it. The primary desire of that regime is for machine tools, electronic equipment, and, in general, what will help it produce tanks, trucks, planes, ammunition, and such military items.

Whatever others may do, surely the United States, which has heavy security commitments in the China area, ought not build up the military power of its potential enemy.

We also doubt the value of cultural exchanges, which the Chinese Communists are eager to develop. They want this relationship with the United States primarily because, once that example were given, it would be difficult for China's close neighbors not to follow it. These free nations, already exposed to intense Communist subversive activities, could not have the cultural exchanges that the Communists want without adding greatly to their danger.

These are the considerations which argue for a continuance of our present policies. What are the arguments on the other side?

There are some who say that we should accord diplomatic recognition to the Communist regime because it has now been in power so long that it has the *right* to that.

That is not sound international law. Diplomatic recognition is always a privilege, never a right.

Of course, the United States knows that the Chinese Communist regime exists. We know that very well, for it has fought us in Korea. Also, we admit of dealing with the Chinese Communists in particular cases where that may serve our interests. We have dealt with it in relation to the Korean and Indochina armistices. For nearly 2 years we have been, and still are, dealing with it in an effort to free our citizens and to obtain reciprocal renunciations of force.

But diplomatic recognition gives the recognized regime valuable rights and privileges, and, in the world of today, recognition by the United States gives the recipient much added prestige and influence at home and abroad.

Of course, diplomatic recognition is not to be withheld capriciously. In this matter, as others, the United States seeks to act in accordance with principles which contribute to a world society of order under law.

A test often applied is the ability of a regime actually to govern. But that is by no means a controlling factor. Nations often maintain diplomatic relations with governments-in-exile. And they frequently deny recognition to those in actual power.

Other customary tests are whether, as Thomas Jefferson put it, the recognized government reflects "the will of the nation, substantially declared"; whether the government conforms to the code of civilized nations, lives peacefully, and honors its international obligations.

Always, however, recognition is admitted to be an instrument of national policy, to serve enlightened self-interest.

One thing is established beyond a doubt. There is nothing automatic about recognition. It is never compelled by the mere lapse of time.

Another argument beginning to be heard is that diplomatic recognition is inevitable, so why not now?

First, let me say emphatically that the United States need never succumb to the argument of "inevitability." We, with our friends, can fashion our own destiny. We do not accept the mastery of Communist forces.

And let me go on to say: Communist-type despotisms are not so immutable as they sometimes appear. Time and circumstances work also upon them.

There is often an optical illusion which results from the fact that police states, suppressing differences, give an external appearance of hard permanency, whereas the democracies, with their opposition parties and often speaking through different and discordant voices, seem the unstable, pliable members of the world society.

The reality is that a governmental system which tolerates diversity has a long life expectancy, whereas a system which seeks to impose conformity is always in danger. That results from the basic nature of human beings. Of all the arguments advanced for recognition of the Communist regime in China, the least cogent is the argument of "inevitability."

There are some who suggest that, if we assist the Chinese Communists to wax strong, then they will eventually break with Soviet Russia and that is our best hope for the future.

No doubt there are basic power rivalries between Russia and China in Asia. But also the Russian and Chinese Communist parties are bound together by close ideological ties.

Perhaps, if the ambitions of Chinese Communists are inflated by successes, they might eventually clash with Soviet Russia. Perhaps, too, if the Axis Powers had won the Second World War, they would have fallen out among themselves. But no one suggested that we should tolerate and even assist an Axis victory because in the end they would quarrel over the booty—of which we would be part.

We seek to appraise our China policies with an open mind and without emotion, except for a certain indignation at the prolonged and cruel abuse of American citizens in China. We have no feeling whatsoever that change is to be avoided merely in the interest of consistency or because change might be interpreted as admitting past error.

We always take into account the possibility of influencing the Communist regime to better ways if we had diplomatic relations with it, or if, without that, we had commercial and cultural contacts with it. But the experience of those who now recognize and deal with the Chinese Communist regime convinces us that, under present conditions, neither recognition, nor trade, nor cultural relations, nor all three, would favorably influence the evolution of affairs in China. The probable result, internally, would be the opposite of what we hope for.

Internationally the Chinese Communist regime does not conform to the practices of civilized nations; does not live up to international obligations; has not been peaceful in the past and gives no evidence of being peaceful in the future. Its foreign policies are hostile to us and our Asian allies. Under these circumstances it would be folly for us to establish relations with the Chinese Communists which would enhance their ability to hurt us and our friends.

You may ask, "What of the future?" Are our policies merely negative? Do we see any prospect of resuming the many friendly ties which, for many generations, the American people have had with the Chinese people and which we want to have again? Do we see any chance that the potentially great Chinese nation, with its rich and ancient culture and wisdom, will again be able to play a constructive part in the councils of the nations?

We confidently answer these questions in the affirmative. Our confidence is based on certain fundamental beliefs. One is a belief in the future of human freedom. We know that the materialistic rule of international communism will never permanently serve the aspirations with which human beings are endowed by their Creator.

Within the Soviet Union the rulers have had to disavow Stalin's brand of communism. Within the Soviet satellites even 12 years of indoctrination do not persuade the people that the Soviet system satisfies either their national or their individual desires.

Communism is repugnant to the Chinese people. They are, above all, individualists. We read the recent brave words uttered within Red China by the university lecturer: "To overthrow you cannot be called unpatriotic, because you Communists no longer serve the people."

We can confidently assume that international communism's rule of strict conformity is, in China as elsewhere, a passing and not a perpetual phase.* We owe it to ourselves, our allies and the Chinese people to do all that we can to contribute to that passing.

---

* At his July 2, 1957, news conference, in reply to questions asked by news correspondents, the Secretary of State amplified this phrase, saying:

I meant primarily the type of communism that is now reflected by what we call international communism. I do not think that it is by any means safe to predict that in every country in the world there may not be some form of socialism, because Communist regimes practice what they call socialism, really. They do not claim in Russia to practice communism; they practice socialism. They say the time for communism has not arrived as a practicing doctrine. One cannot predict for all the world that there may not be different forms of socialism. But I do believe that the type of rule which is reflected by the doctrine of strict conformity and the elimination of any difference of opinion—and that does not necessarily go with socialism or communism and it may go with a type of Fascist dictatorship equally—I do not believe that that kind of government or regime will anywhere prevail in the long run.

What it presupposes is this, that we accept, as a working hypothesis, the view that that type of despotism will never prevail and that the kind of a government which is responsive to the will of the people, which admits of diversity and freedom of thought and expression, is the government which has the future ahead of it.

Now that, as I say, is a working hypothesis that we assume. It underlies all our actions, all our conduct in these matters. I say it's a working hypothesis, but I don't know how it's going to work out. These matters work out in an infinite variety of ways. All that I mean is that we do not assume that that type of despotism represents the wave of the future in China or anywhere else. American policy is conducted on the assumption, as a working hypothesis, that free governments in the long run are going to prevail and despotic governments in the long run are going to go under. (Department of State, *Bulletin,* July 22, 1957, pp. 139, 143–44.)

If we believed that this passing would be promoted by trade and cultural relations, then we would have such relations.

If we believed that this passing would be promoted by our having diplomatic relations with the present regime, then we would have such relations.

If we believed that this passing would be promoted by some participation of the present regime in the activities of the United Nations, then we would not oppose that.

We should be, and we are, constantly testing our policies, to be as certain as we can be that, in the light of conditions as they from time to time are, our policies shall serve the great purposes to which our Nation has been dedicated since its foundation— the cause of peace, justice, and human liberty.

Our policies are readily adjustable to meet the requirements of changing conditions. But there are occasions when not we but others should provide the change. Nothing could be more dangerous than for the United States to operate on the theory that, if hostile and evil forces do not quickly or readily change, then it is we who must change to meet them.

The United States exerts an immense influence in the world today, not only because it is powerful but because we stand for peace, for national independence, and personal liberty. Many free nations seek to coordinate their foreign policies with ours. Such coordination is indeed indispensable if the free world is to have the cohesion needed to make it safe. But United States policies will never serve as rallying points for free peoples if the impression is created that our policies are subject to change to meet Communist wishes for no reason other than that communism does not want to change. If communism is stubborn for the wrong, let us be steadfast for the right.

The capacity to change is an indispensable capacity. Equally indispensable is the capacity to hold fast that which is good. Given those qualities, we can hopefully look forward to the day when those in Asia who are yet free can confidently remain free and when the people of China and the people of America can resume their long history of cooperative friendship.

[*AFP 1957*, pp. 1124–32.]

33. State Department Statement Lifting Ban on US Correspondents Going to China, August 22, 1957 (Extract)

Heretofore it has been the policy of the U.S. Government to authorize no travel by U.S. citizens to the Communist-ruled mainland of China. That regime has not honored its undertaking to permit U.S. citizens jailed by them to return to their homes. The Chinese Communist regime has, however, continued to persist in its refusal to comply with its undertaking or to follow the practices of civilized governments.

During this period new factors have come into the picture, making it desirable that additional information be made available to the American people respecting current conditions within China. The Secretary of State has accordingly determined that it may prove consistent with the foreign policy of the United States that there be travel by a limited number of American news representatives to the mainland of China in order to permit direct reporting by them to the American people about conditions in the area under Chinese Communist control. It is hoped, among other things, that they may be able to report on the Americans illegally held in Chinese prisons as to whose fate there is deep concern on the part of the American nation.*

In view of this determination, the Department of State has asked each of the newsgathering organizations, which has demonstrated sufficient interest in foreign news coverage to maintain at least one full-time American correspondent overseas, whether it wishes to send a full-time American correspondent to the China mainland to be stationed there on a resident basis for 6 months or longer. Twenty-four affirmative replies have been received from the organizations identified on the attached list.

The Department of State is of the view that this number comes within the intent of the Secretary's determination and it is therefore prepared, on an experimental basis, to issue to one such correspondent representing each of the listed news gathering organizations a passport not restricted as regards travel to and on the mainland of China. The Department of State is asking the Treasury Department to issue licenses under the Trading with the Enemy Act—limited to authorizing such transactions as may be necessary to allow these correspondents to carry out their functions.

* Of the 10 Americans held in Chinese prisons in January 1957, 4 have been released—the Rev. Fulgence Gross and Paul Mackinsen in March 1957 and the Rev. John Alexander Houle and the Rev. Charles Joseph McCarthy in June 1957. The six Americans still held are as follows: John Thomas Downey, Richard Fecteau, Robert McCann, the Rev. Joseph Patrick McCormack, H. F. Redmond, and the Rev. John Paul Wagner.

The present validation of passports will be for a period of 7 months after the date hereof.

Those traveling to mainland China do so knowing that they face abnormal personal risks due to the failure of the Chinese Communist regime to treat American citizens in accordance with the accepted code of civilized nations.

It is to be understood that the United States will not accord reciprocal visas to Chinese bearing passports issued by the Chinese Communist regime.

It is emphasized that this experiment is founded upon the desire to have the American people better informed through their own representatives about actual conditions in the areas under Chinese Communist control. It does not change the basic policy of the United States toward communism in China which was recently restated by the Secretary of State in his address of June 28, 1957, at San Francisco. Generally speaking, it is still not consistent with United States policy, or lawful, that there be travel by Americans to areas of China now under Communist control.

[*AFP 1957*, pp. 1134–35.]

34. State Department Memorandum, Circulated to Overseas Missions, on Question of Recognition of the PRC, August 12, 1958

Policy toward Communist China has been an important issue since the Communists came to power there, and it is of critical significance to the United States and the free world today. In the United States the issue is a very real one to the vast majority of the people. As a result of Korean and Chinese Communist aggression in Korea, the United States suffered 142,000 casualties, bringing tragedy to communities all over the country. Nevertheless, despite the emotions thus engendered and the abhorrence of the American people for the brutality and utter lack of morality of Communist systems, the policy of the United States Government toward China has necessarily been based on objective considerations of national interest. It also reflects a continuing appraisal of all available facts.

Basically the United States policy of not extending diplomatic recognition to the Communist regime in China proceeds from the conviction that such recognition would produce no tangible benefits to the United States or to the free world as a whole and would be of material assistance to Chinese Communist attempts to extend Communist dominion throughout Asia. It is not an "inflexible" policy which cannot be altered to meet changed conditions. If the situation in the Far East were so to change in its basic elements as to call for a radically different evaluation of the threat Chinese Communist policies pose to United States and free-world security interests, the United States would of course readjust its present policies. However, the course of events in the Far East since the establishment of the Chinese Communist regime in 1949 has thus far confirmed the United States view that its interests and those of the free world are best served by withholding diplomatic recognition from the regime in Peiping.

The basic considerations on which United States policy toward China rests are twofold. First, the Soviet bloc, of which Communist China is an important part, is engaged in a long-range struggle to destroy the way of life of the free countries of the world and bring about the global dominion of communism. The Chinese Communist regime has made no secret of its fundamental hostility to the United States and the free world as a whole nor of its avowed intention to effect their downfall. Today its defiance of and attacks on the non-Communist world have reached a level of intensity that has not been witnessed since the Korean war. The second basic factor is that East Asia is peculiarly vulnerable to the Communist offensive because of the proximity of the free countries of that area to Communist China, the inexperience in self-government of those which have recently won their independence, their suspicions of the West inherited from their colonial past, and the social, political, and economic changes which inevitably accompany their drive toward modernization.

The Chinese Communists see the victory of communism in Asia as inevitable; and now that they control the vast population and territory of mainland China they are utilizing the advantages these give to encompass their ends. Chinese Communist leaders have shown by their words and their acts that they are not primarily interested in promoting the welfare of their people while living at peace with their neighbors. Their primary purpose is to extend the Communist revolution beyond their borders to the rest of Asia and thence to the rest of the world. Liu Shao-chi, the second-ranking member of the Chinese Communist Party, has said: "The most fundamental and common duty of Communist

Party members is to establish communism and transform the present world into a Communist world." Mao Tse-tung himself has said that his regime's policy is "to give active support to the national independence and liberation movements in countries in Asia, Africa, and Latin America." That these are not empty words was shown by Chinese Communist aggression in Korea and provision of arms and other assistance to the Communist rebels in Indochina.

United States policy in Asia, as elsewhere in the world, is to promote the domestic welfare and to strengthen the independence of free nations. Because of the proximity of many Asian nations to mainland China and the disparity in size and power between them and Communist China, this can be done only if the Communist threat is neutralized. The first need of United States policy in the Far East is to deter Communist aggression, else the free nations would be in grave danger of succumbing to Communist pressures before they had gathered the strength with which to resist them. The United States has sought to accomplish this by military assistance to the nations directly in the path of Chinese Communist expansion—Korea, Taiwan, and Viet-Nam—and by a system of mutual defense arrangements with other nations of the area. We have been successful in this effort, and since 1954 the Chinese Communists have not been able to make further gains through the open use of military force.

The measures the United States and its allies in Asia have taken to preserve the security of the free nations of the area are of vital interest to the other free nations of the world. Loss of the rest of East Asia to communism could have a disastrous effect on the free world's ability to resist effectively the encroachments of communism elsewhere. The consequences for Australia and New Zealand would be especially serious. Loss of the islands of the West Pacific and of the Southeast Asian peninsula would isolate these countries and place them in a strategically exposed and dangerous position.

Efforts to halt further Communist expansion cannot be confined to military deterrence alone. Countermeasures against Chinese Communist subversion and political infiltration are equally necessary. This is especially so as, since 1955, Peiping has increasingly resorted to propaganda, subversion, "people's diplomacy," and political maneuvering in its dealings with its Asian neighbors. Peiping seeks to win by this means what it apparently does not dare attempt through military conquest. The United

States therefore considers that in preserving the peace and security of Asia, it is as important to be alert to the threat of subversion as to that of open military attack.

In the effort to block Peiping's attempts to extend Communist rule in Asia the withholding of diplomatic recognition is an important factor. The extension of diplomatic recognition by a great power normally carries with it not only increased access to international councils but enhanced international standing and prestige as well. Denial of recognition on the other hand is a positive handicap to the regime affected and one which makes it that much the more difficult for it to pursue its foreign policies with success. One basic purpose of United States nonrecognition of Communist China is to deny it these advantages and to that extent limit its ability to threaten the security of the area.

In the case of China there are special considerations which influence United States policy with regard to recognition. For one thing, although the Chinese Communists have seized the preponderant bulk of China, they have not completed their conquest of the country. The generally recognized legitimate Government of China continues to exist and in Taiwan is steadily developing its political, economic, and military strength. The Government of the Republic of China controls the strategic island of Taiwan and through its possession of a sizable military force—one of the largest on the side of the free world in Asia—presents a significant deterrent to renewed Chinese Communist aggression. Recognition of Communist China by the United States would seriously cripple, if not destroy altogether, that Government. On the other hand, continued United States recognition and support of the Republic of China enables it to challenge the claim of the Chinese Communists to represent the Chinese people and keeps alive the hopes of those Chinese who are determined eventually to free their country of Communist rule.

Recognition of Communist China by the United States would have an adverse effect on the other free governments of Asia which could be disastrous to the cause of the free world in that part of the world. Those nations which are closely allied to the United States and are striving to maintain their independence on the perimeter of Chinese Communist power, especially Korea and Viet-Nam, would be profoundly confused and demoralized. They would interpret such action as abandonment of their cause by the United States. They might reason that their only hope for survival lay in desperate measures, not caring whether these threatened the peace of the area and the world. Governments further removed from the borders of China would see in American recognition of Communist China the first step in the withdrawal of the United States from the Far East. Without the support of the United States they would be unable long to defy the will of Peiping, and some would probably conclude that their wisest course would be speedily to seek the best terms obtainable from Peiping. Needless to say, these developments would place the entire free world position in Asia in the gravest peril.

Another special consideration in the case of China is that large and influential "overseas" Chinese communities exist in most of the countries of Southeast Asia. The efforts of these countries to build healthy free societies and to develop their economies would be seriously retarded if these communities were to fall under the sway of the Chinese Communists, and a grave threat of Communist subversion through these overseas communities would arise. Recognition of Communist China by the United States and the decline in the fortunes of the Republic of China which would inevitably result would have such a profound psychological effect on the overseas Chinese that it would make inevitable the transfer of loyalties of large numbers to the Communist side. This in turn would undermine the ability of the host countries to resist the pressures tending to promote the expansion of Chinese Communist influence and power.

Still another factor which must be considered in the case of China is the effect which recognition of the Communist regime would have on the United Nations. Recognition of Peiping by the United States would inevitably lead to the seating of Peiping in that body. In the view of the United States this would vitiate, if not destroy, the United Nations as an instrument for the maintenance of international peace. The Korean war was the first and most important effort to ha't aggression through collective action in the United Nations. For Communist China, one of the parties against which the effort of the United Nations was directed, to be seated in the United Nations while still unpurged of its aggression and defying the will of the United Nations in Korea would amount to a confession of failure on the part of the United Nations and would greatly reduce the prospects for future successful action by the United Nations against aggression. Moreover, the Republic of China is a charter member in good standing of the United Nations, and its representatives there have contributed importantly to the constructive work of that organization. If the representatives of the Chinese Communist regime were to be seated in their place and given China's veto in the Security Council, the ability of that body in the future to discharge the responsibility it has under the charter for the maintaining of international peace and security would be seriously impaired.

Those who advocate recognition of the Chinese Communists often assume that by the standards of international law applied to such cases the Peiping regime is "entitled" to diplomatic recognition. In the view of the United States diplomatic recognition is a privilege and not a right. Moreover, the United States considers that diplomatic recognition is an instrument of national policy which it is both its right and its duty to use in the enlightened self-interest of the nation. However, there is reason to doubt that even by the tests often cited in international law the Chinese Communist regime qualifies for diplomatic recognition. It does not rule all China, and there is a substantial force in being which contests its claim to do so. The Chinese Communist Party, which holds mainland China in its grip, is a tiny minority comprising less than 2 percent of the Chinese people, and the regimentation, brutal repression, and forced sacrifices that have characterized its rule have resulted in extensive popular unrest. To paraphrase Thomas Jefferson's dictum, this regime certain'y does not represent "the will of the populace, substantially declared." Finally, it has shown no intention to honor its international obligations. One of its first acts was to abrogate the treaties of the Republic of China, except those it chose to continue. On assuming power it carried out a virtual confiscation without compensation of the properties of foreign nationals, including immense British investments notwithstanding the United Kingdom's prompt recognition of it. It has failed to honor various commitments entered into since, including various provisions of the Korean armistice and the Geneva accord on Viet-Nam and Laos as well as the agreed announcement of September 1955 by which it pledged itself to permit all Americans in China to return home "expeditiously."

The United States policy toward recognition of Communist China is then based on a carefully considered judgment of the national interest. Nonrecognition of Peiping coupled with continued recognition and support of the Republic of China facilitates the accomplishment of United States policy objectives in the Far East. Recognition of Peiping would seriously hinder accomplishment of these objectives and would facilitate the advance of Communist power in Asia.

In the process of determining its policy toward China the United States has taken into account the various statements and arguments advanced by proponents of extending diplomatic recognition to Peiping. One of the most commonly advanced reasons for recognition is that reality must be "recognized" and 600 million people cannot be "ignored." While superficially appealing, both statements themselves overlook the realities of the situation. United States policy is, of course, based on full appreciation of the fact that the Chinese Communist regime is currently in control of mainland China. However, it is not necessary to have diplomatic relations with a regime in order to deal with it. Without extending diplomatic recognition the United States has participated in extended negotiations with Chinese Communist representatives in the Korean and Indochina armistice negotiations, and more recently in the ambassadorial talks in Geneva. Similarly, United States policy in no sense "ignores" the existence and the aspirations of the Chinese people. Its attitude toward the people remains what it historically has been, one of friendship and sympathetic understanding. It is nonetheless clear that our friendship for the Chinese people must not be permitted to blind us to the threat to our security which the Communist regime in China now presents. Moreover, the United States is convinced that the Chinese Communist regime does not represent the true will or aspirations of the Chinese people and that our policy of withholding recognition from it is in actuality in their ultimate interest.

It is sometimes contended that by recognition of Communist China it would be possible to exert leverage on the Peiping regime which might ultimately be successful in weakening or even breaking the bond with Moscow. Unfortunately there is no evidence to support this belief, and there are important reasons why it is unlikely. The alliance between Moscow and Peiping is one of long standing; it traces its origin to the very founding of the Chinese Communist Party in 1921, in which representatives of the Comintern played an important role. It is based on a common ideology and on mutually held objectives with respect to the non-Communist world. All recent evidence points to the closeness of the tie between the Chinese Communists and the U.S.S.R. rather than in the other direction. The Chinese Communists were outspoken in championing the armed intervention of the Soviets in Hungary and have given unqualified endorsement to the execution of Nagy and the other leaders of the Hungarian revolt. They were also leaders in the recent Communist-bloc attack on Yugoslavia for its attempts to pursue national policies independent of Kremlin control. These and other facts make it apparent that the two partners in the Sino-Soviet alliance clearly realize their mutual dependence and attach great importance to bloc unity vis-à-vis the free world.

Furthermore, the alliance with the U.S.S.R. has a special importance for the Chinese Communists since it provides them with a dependable source of arms and military supplies. The Chinese Communist leaders, including Mao Tse-tung himself, came to power through their command of military force. They are therefore keenly conscious of the importance of military force to keep themselves in power against domestic and external opposition and to achieve the goals of their foreign policy. It is scarcely credible that they would dare risk any course of action which could lead to loss of their source of military supplies. For this reason alone it would seem unrealistic to believe that recognition of Peiping by the United States or any other leading nation would have the effect of tempting the Chinese Communists to play a "Titoist" role.

In fact, the opposite is quite likely to be the result. Were the United States to grant diplomatic recognition to Peiping—with all that this would entail by way of enhanced international prestige—its leaders would most likely feel confirmed in the correctness of their policies and the advantages of continued close cooperation with Moscow.

It is often alleged that recognition of Communist China is a necessary step in expanding trade relations with that country. For the United States this is of course not a consideration, since the United States embargoes trade with Peiping under the Trading With the Enemy Act as a result of the Korean war.* But even for countries which do desire to expand trade with mainland China the facts do not support the contention that trade is dependent on recognition. To the contrary, Great Britain, which recognized Communist China in 1950, has found that she buys more goods from Communist China than Communist China buys from her. West Germany on the other hand does not recognize Peiping and enjoys a favorable trade balance with mainland China. In any case, trade opportunities with Communist China are severely limited by a shortage of foreign exchange which is likely to persist

* The embargo went into effect Dec. 7, 1950; see *American Foreign Policy: Current Documents, 1956*, p. 1085.

for many years to come. Moreover, such trade would always be at the mercy of Communist policies. Peiping uses trade as a means of exerting pressure on the trading partner whenever it deems this to be expedient. A striking example is the case of Japan, where the Chinese Communists recently retaliated against [the] Japanese refusal to make certain political concessions by cutting off all trade and even canceling contracts which had already been entered into. It would therefore seem that over the long run the advantages of trade with Peiping will prove more ephemeral than real.

An argument often heard is that the Chinese Communists are here "to stay," that they will have to be recognized sooner or later, and that it would be the course of wisdom to bow to the inevitable now rather than be forced to do so ungracefully at a later date. It is true that there is no reason to believe that the Chinese Communist regime is on the verge of collapse, but there is equally no reason to accept its present rule in mainland China as permanent. In fact, unmistakable signs of dissatisfaction and unrest in Communist China have appeared in the "ideological remodeling" and the mass campaign against "rightists" which have been in progress during the past year. Dictatorships often create an illusion of permanence from the very fact that they suppress and still all opposition, and that of the Chinese Communists is no exception to this rule. The United States holds the view that communism's rule in China is not permanent and that it one day will pass. By withholding diplomatic recognition from Peiping it seeks to hasten that passing.

In public discussions of China policy one of the proposals that has attracted widest attention is that known as the "two Chinas solution." Briefly, advocates of this arrangement propose that the Chinese Communist regime be recognized as the government of mainland China while the Government of Taipei remains as the legal government of Taiwan. They argue that this approach to the Chinese problem has the merit of granting the Communists only what they already control while retaining for the free world the militarily strategic bastion of Taiwan. However, it overlooks or ignores certain facts of basic importance. The Republic of China would not accept any diminution of its sovereignty over China and could be expected to resist such an arrangement with all the means at its disposal. If a "two Chinas solution" were to be forcefully imposed against its will, that Government's effectiveness as a loyal ally to the free-world cause would be destroyed.

Peiping, too, would reject such an arrangement. In fact, over the past year Chinese Communist propaganda has repeatedly and stridently denounced the "two Chinas" concept and, ironically, has been accusing the United States Government of attempting to put it into effect. Peiping attaches great importance to the eventual acquisition of Taiwan and has consistently reserved what it calls its "right" to seize Taiwan by force if other means fail. There is no prospect that it would ever acquiesce in any arrangement which would lead to the permanent detachment of Taiwan from China.

The "two Chinas" concept is bitterly opposed by both Peiping and Taipei. Hence, even if such a solution could be imposed by outside authority, it would not be a stable one. Constant policing would be required to avert its violent overthrow by one side or the other.

It is sometimes said that nonrecognition of Peiping tends to martyrize the Chinese Communists, thereby enabling them to pose, especially before Asian neutralists, as an innocent and injured party. It would be impossible to deny that there is some truth in this. But this disadvantage is far outweighed by the disadvantages that would result from following the opposite course. It is surely better that some neutralists, who are either unable or unwilling to comprehend the threat inherent in Chinese Communist policies, mistakenly consider Peiping unjustly treated than that the allies of the United States in Asia, who are the first line of defense against Chinese Communist expansion, should be confused and demoralized by what to them could only appear to be a betrayal of the common cause.

[*AFP 1958*, pp. 1136–43.]

IV. The Taiwan Strait Crisis of 1958

THE AMBASSADORIAL talks were broken off for about nine months after the departure of the American representative U. Alexis Johnson from Czechoslovakia to take up a new post in Bangkok early in 1958. Demands by the Chinese that the talks should be resumed were accompanied by denunciations of American dilatoriness on the matter. Eventually, Dulles revealed that the State Department was going to propose a shift of location of the talks from Geneva to Warsaw (where the Chinese representative, Wang Ping-nan, was ambassador). But when the American ambassador in Warsaw, Jacob Beam, approached his opposite number on August 4, he was informed that the matter was being considered in Peking.[1] Meanwhile a crisis was brewing in the Taiwan Strait.

The Chinese posture in foreign affairs had become harder during the autumn of 1957, a change signified by a dictum pronounced by Mao in Moscow in November that the east wind was now prevailing over the west wind. Encouraged by the achievements of Soviet rocket technology—the most spectacular being the launching of the first sputnik—the Chinese stressed the desirability of exploiting diplomatically what they believed to be the growing military superiority of the Communist bloc, even if this resulted in local tension from time to time.[2]

The Russians were, however, well aware that their military

[1] Young, *op. cit.*, pp. 132–40.
[2] Donald S. Zagoria, *The Sino-Soviet Conflict, 1956–1961* (London: Oxford University Press, 1962), pp. 160–76, 187–88.

position vis-à-vis the Americans was weaker than the Chinese supposed. They were therefore more inclined to caution. The differences in the approaches of Moscow and Peking were illustrated when a Middle Eastern crisis broke out in July, 1958. A coup against the pro-Western government in Iraq was followed by the dispatch of US troops to Lebanon and British troops to Jordan. Though it was widely believed that an Anglo-American invasion of Iraq would be the next move, Khrushchev was not prepared to put Soviet troops into the Middle East as a countermeasure. The Chinese were evidently sharply critical of his cautiousness.[3] This was the background to Khrushchev's visit to Peking from July 31 to August 3, a visit only revealed to the world on the day the Soviet leader was returning home.

The communiqué issued at the end of Khrushchev's visit made no mention of China's determination to liberate Taiwan, although Chinese propaganda on this score had been stepped up considerably over the previous week.[4] Then, on August 23, the Chinese laid down a heavy artillery barrage on Quemoy and started to harass shipping in the vicinity and around Matsu.

On the same day, Dulles directed a letter to the acting chairman of the House Committee on Foreign Affairs alluding to the PRC's military build-up opposite the offshore islands and hinting at likely American support for the Nationalists in the event of an attack on them (35). Despite this warning, on August 27, Chinese coastal radio stations began to threaten the Nationalist troops on Quemoy with an imminent attack and called on them to surrender.[5] Significantly, this threat was not broadcast generally on the national radio network. On September 4, the Chinese stated that their territorial waters extended for 12 miles offshore. This was a clear threat to American ships convoying Nationalist supply vessels to Quemoy, and the Americans rejected the 12-mile claim.

On the same day, Dulles issued a far clearer warning that the administration regarded the bombardment of the offshore islands

---

[3] *Ibid.*, pp. 195–99.
[4] *Ibid.*, p. 209.
[5] *Ibid.*, p. 210.

as part of an attempt to take Taiwan and therefore would feel free, under the terms of the "Formosa resolution," to help defend them (36). In a private briefing to correspondents, Dulles made the warning even more explicit.[6] Two days later, Chou En-lai replied, reaffirming China's right to liberate the offshore islands and Taiwan, but agreeing to a resumption of the ambassadorial talks (37). The worst of the crisis was past.

If the Chinese had been trying to prove to the Russians—who had been most reticent in their comments up till this point—that the Americans could be outfaced by threats and the judicious use of force, they had failed.[7] By late September, the Quemoy blockade was no longer effective; supplies were getting through despite the intense artillery barrage. On October 7, a Chinese Foreign Ministry spokesman confirmed a seven-day suspension of the bombardment of Quemoy announced the previous day in a broadcast to the offshore islands by the Defense Minister (40). Although the spokesman indicated two days later that this suspension was not to be taken as a first step to a permanent cease-fire (41), the crisis was effectively over.

The Americans, too, had their difficulties. The Taiwan Strait crisis had caused much alarm throughout the world, and there was pressure on the US Government to abandon the defense of the offshore islands.[8] Eisenhower had never been happy about the large number of troops—100,000 men, about a third of his forces —that Chiang Kai-shek had stationed there.[9] At his press conference on September 30, Dulles indicated that once there was a cease-fire, the Americans might put pressure on the Nationalists to reduce their garrisons (38). At the same time, Dulles threw cold water on ideas that the Nationalists might reconquer the

[6] Young, *op. cit.*, pp. 148–49.
[7] Zagoria, *op. cit.*, pp. 206–9; Alice Langley Hsieh, *Communist China's Strategy in the Nuclear Era* (Englewood Cliffs, N.J.: Prentice-Hall, 1962), p. 129.
[8] Dwight D. Eisenhower, *The White House Years: II. Waging Peace, 1956–1961* (Garden City, N.Y.: Doubleday, 1965), pp. 300, 301–2.
[9] *Ibid.*, pp. 293–94.

mainland, unless there were something like a Hungarian revolt in China (39). He even hinted that if there were some "give" on the Chinese side there would be a chance of important changes in American policy.

The Chinese did not respond favorably to Dulles's remarks on the offshore islands. They seem to have become concerned lest, if the Americans did force the Nationalists to evacuate the islands and concede them to the PRC, international support for China's recovery of Taiwan would wane. No one could reasonably maintain that Quemoy and Matsu were not an integral part of the mainland; but such a position could be maintained with respect to Taiwan if its umbilical cord to the mainland, the offshore islands, were cut. Then the Americans might secure wide acceptance for a "two-Chinas" solution to the Chinese civil war.[10] Fear of a "two-Chinas" plot was evident in Chinese statements from early October, for instance in the Foreign Ministry statement of October 9 (41).

If that was the Chinese worry, they did not have to live long with it. The negative response in Peking and Taipei to his remarks on the offshore islands led Dulles to return to supporting the Nationalist position. In a communiqué after talks between him and Chiang Kai-shek in Taipei, the two allies agreed that the defense of the offshore islands was closely related to the defense of Taiwan, albeit with the qualification "under the present conditions" (42). Dulles did, however, get Chiang to agree that force would not be the principal means of liberating the mainland. Chinese comments on the communiqué tried to exploit possible resentment among Nationalist leaders at this concession, which was depicted as part of an American attempt to make them "completely subservient" (43).

Ill health forced Dulles to resign in April, 1959. The new Secretary of State, Christian Herter, quickly took a fresh initiative on the correspondents' issue. He expressed himself ready to encourage a reciprocal exchange of newsmen, but the Chinese ob-

[10] Hsieh, *op. cit.,* pp. 127–28; Young, *op. cit.,* pp. 190–93.

jected to the method in which the admission of their correspondents would have to be arranged in accordance with American law.[11]

At some point in late 1959 or early 1960, the Chinese made a decision to struggle against Khrushchev's foreign policy, especially the manner in which he worked for peaceful coexistence with America (44).[12] Thereafter, China's attitude on its own negotiations with the United States also hardened. A new principle was injected into the Warsaw talks. There could be no progress on subsidiary issues until the Taiwan issue was settled, and to settle it two points would have to be agreed: no use or threat of force in disputes between the United States and the Chinese People's Republic, including in the Taiwan area; the United States must agree to withdraw its armed forces from the Taiwan area—when and how could be agreed later.[13] The Taiwan issue was injected into the question of exchanging correspondents (45). As a result, from the 100th ambassadorial meeting on September 6, 1960, according to the historian of Sino-American negotiations, the talks changed from "the diplomacy of negotiation to that of stalemate." [14]

[11] Young, *op. cit.*, pp. 221–23.
[12] Zagoria, *op. cit.*, p. 299.
[13] Young, *op. cit.*, pp. 230–32.
[14] *Ibid.*, p. 232.

35. Dulles's Letter on the Offshore Islands to the Acting Chairman of the House Committee on Foreign Affairs, August 23, 1958

DEAR MR. CHAIRMAN:
I have received your letter of August 22.*
We are, indeed, disturbed by the evidence of Chinese Communist buildup, to which you refer. It suggests that they might be tempted to try to seize forcibly the Quemoy or Matsu Islands.

As you know, these islands have been continuously in the hands of the Republic of China, and over the last four years the ties between these islands and Formosa have been closer and their interdependence has increased.

I think it would be highly hazardous for anyone to assume that if the Chinese Communists were to attempt to change this situation by force and now to attack and seek to conquer these islands, that could be a limited operation. It would, I fear, constitute a threat to the peace of the area. Therefore, I hope and believe that it will not happen.

Sincerely yours,
JOHN FOSTER DULLES

[*AFP 1958*, p. 1144.]

36. Dulles's Statement on the Taiwan Strait Situation, Released by the White House, Newport, Rhode Island, September 4, 1958

I have reviewed in detail with the President the serious situation which has resulted from aggressive Chinese Communist mili-

* Representative Morgan's letter read: "I have noted with concern the recent reports of the Chinese Communist build-up of air power on the mainland opposite the Islands of Quemoy and Matsu. I would appreciate having any comment you may wish to make regarding the situation."

tary actions in the Taiwan (Formosa) Straits area. The President has authorized me to make the following statement.

1. Neither Taiwan (Formosa) nor the islands of Quemoy and Matsu have ever been under the authority of the Chinese Communists. Since the end of the Second World War, a period of over 13 years, they have continuously been under the authority of Free China, that is, the Republic of China.

2. The United States is bound by treaty to help defend Taiwan (Formosa) from armed attack; and the President is authorized by Joint Resolution of the Congress to employ the armed forces of the United States for the securing and protecting of related positions such as Quemoy and Matsu.

3. Any attempt on the part of the Chinese Communists now to seize these positions or any of them would be a crude violation of the principles upon which world order is based, namely, that no country should use armed force to seize new territory.

4. The Chinese Communists have, for about 2 weeks, been subjecting Quemoy to heavy artillery bombardment and, by artillery fire and use of small naval craft, they have been harassing the regular supply of the civilian and military population of the Quemoys, which totals some 125 thousand persons. The official Peiping radio repeatedly announces the purpose of these military operations to be to take by armed force Taiwan (Formosa), as well as Quemoy and Matsu. In virtually every Peiping broadcast Taiwan (Formosa) and the offshore islands are linked as the objectives of what is called the "Chinese Peoples Liberation Army."

5. Despite, however, what the Chinese Communists say, and so far have done, it is not yet certain that their purpose is in fact to make an all-out effort to conquer by force Taiwan (Formosa) and the offshore islands. Neither is it apparent that such efforts as are being made, or may be made, cannot be contained by the courageous, and purely defensive, efforts of the forces of the Republic of China, with such substantial logistical support as the United States is providing.

6. The Joint Resolution of Congress, above referred to, includes a finding to the effect that "the secure possession by friendly governments of the Western Pacific Island chain, of which Formosa is a part, is essential to the vital interests of the United States and all friendly nations in and bordering upon the Pacific Ocean." It further authorizes the President to employ the Armed Forces of the United States for the protection not only of Formosa but for "the securing and protection of such related positions and

territories of that area now in friendly hands and the taking of such other measures as he judges to be required or appropriate in assuring the defense of Formosa." In view of the situation outlined in the preceding paragraph, the President has not yet made any finding under the Resolution that the employment of the Armed Forces of the United States is required or appropriate in insuring the defense of Formosa. The President would not, however, hesitate to make such a finding if he judged that the circumstances made this necessary to accomplish the purposes of the Joint Resolution. In this connection, we have recognized that the securing and protecting of Quemoy and Matsu have increasingly become related to the defense of Taiwan (Formosa). This is indeed also recognized by the Chinese Communists. Military dispositions have been made by the United States so that a Presidential determination, if made, would be followed by action both timely and effective.

7. The President and I earnestly hope that the Chinese Communist regime will not again, as in the case of Korea, defy the basic principle upon which world order depends, namely, that armed force should not be used to achieve territorial ambitions. Any such naked use of force would pose an issue far transcending the offshore islands and even the security of Taiwan (Formosa). It would forecast a widespread use of force in the Far East which would endanger vital free world positions and the security of the United States. Acquiescence therein would threaten peace everywhere. We believe that the civilized world community will never condone overt military conquest as a legitimate instrument of policy.

8. The United States has not, however, abandoned hope that Peiping will stop short of defying the will of mankind for peace. This would not require it to abandon its claims, however illfounded we may deem them to be. I recall that in the extended negotiations which the representatives of the United States and Chinese Communist regime conducted at Geneva between 1955 and 1958, a sustained effort was made by the United States to secure, with particular reference to the Taiwan area, a declaration of mutual and reciprocal renunciation of force, except in selfdefense, which, however, would be without prejudice to the pursuit of policies by peaceful means. The Chinese Communists rejected any such declaration. We believe, however, that such a course of conduct constitutes the only civilized and acceptable procedure. The United States intends to follow that course, so

far as it is concerned, unless and until the Chinese Communists, by their acts, leave us no choice but to react in defense of the principles to which all peace-loving governments are dedicated.

[*AFP 1958*, pp. 1146–47.]

37. Chou En-lai's Statement on the Taiwan Strait Situation, September 6, 1958

On September 4, 1958, United States Secretary of State Dulles, authorized by United States President Eisenhower, issued a statement openly threatening to extend United States aggression in the Taiwan Straits area against the People's Republic of China and carrying out war provocation, thereby aggravating the tension in this area created by the United States and seriously jeopardizing the peace of the Far East and the world. Regarding this, I have been authorized by the Government of the People's Republic of China to make the following statement.

(1) Taiwan and the Penghu Islands have been China's territories from ancient times. Following the Second World War, they were restored to China after being occupied by Japan for a period of time. It is entirely China's internal affair for the Chinese people to exercise their sovereign right to liberate these areas. This is the Chinese people's sacred and inviolable right. The United States Government itself also declared formally that it would not get involved in China's civil conflict in the Taiwan area. Were it not for the fact that the United States Government later went back on its own statement and carried out armed intervention, Taiwan and the Penghu Islands would have long been liberated and placed under the jurisdiction of the Government of the People's Republic of China. These are undeniable facts unanimously recognized by fair-minded world public opinion.

(2) United States support of the Chiang Kai-shek clique entrenched on Taiwan and the Penghu Islands, which has long been repudiated by all the Chinese people, and its direct armed occupation of Taiwan and the Penghu Islands constitute unlawful interference in China's internal affairs and infringement on China's territorial integrity and sovereignty, and are in direct conflict with the United Nations Charter and all codes of international law. All

so-called treaties concluded between the United States and the Chiang Kai-shek clique and all related resolutions adopted by the United States Congress are null and void as far as the Chinese people are concerned. They can never legalize United States aggression. Much less can they be used as pretexts by the United States for extending its aggression in the Taiwan Straits area.

(3) Supported by the United States, the Chiang Kai-shek clique has for long been using coastal islands such as Quemoy, which is close by Amoy, and Matsu, which is close by Foochow, as advance bases for conducting all sorts of harassing and disruptive activities against the Chinese mainland. Recently, since the United States launched armed intervention against the Arab states, the harassing and disruptive activities of the Chiang Kai-shek clique against the Chinese mainland have become more unbridled. The Chinese Government has every right to deal resolute blows and take necessary military action against Chiang Kai-shek's troops entrenched on the coastal islands; any outside intervention would be a criminal infringement on China's sovereignty. But the United States, in order to divert the attention of the people of the world from continued United States aggression in the Middle East and procrastination in withdrawing its troops from the Lebanon, attempts to take advantage of this situation and is amassing large numbers of armed forces in the Taiwan Straits area and openly threatening to extend its aggression in the Taiwan Straits area to Quemoy, Matsu, and other coastal islands. This is a grave war provocation against 600 million Chinese people and a serious menace to the peace of the Far East and the world.

(4) The Chinese people's determination to liberate their own territory of Taiwan and the Penghu Islands is unshakable. In particular the Chinese people cannot tolerate the presence in their inland waters along the mainland of an immediate threat posed by such coastal islands as Quemoy and Matsu. No amount of U.S. war provocations can cow the Chinese people; on the contrary, they will only arouse even greater indignation among our 600 million people, and make them even more determined to fight American aggressors to the very end. The fact that the United States, while not yet withdrawing its forces of aggression from the Lebanon, has hastened to create a new danger of war in the Taiwan Straits area, has made the peace-loving countries and people of the world see even more clearly the brutish features of the United States aggressors bent on sabotaging peace and that the United States imperialists are the most vicious enemy of all

national independence movements in Asia, Africa and Latin America and the world peace movement.

(5) In pursuance of its foreign policy of peace, the Chinese Government has always stood for peaceful coexistence of countries with different social systems in accordance with the Five Principles and for the settlement of all international disputes by the peaceful means of negotiation. Despite the fact that the United States has invaded and occupied China's territory of Taiwan and the Penghu Islands by armed force and crudely violated the minimum codes in international relations, the Chinese Government proposed to sit down to negotiate with the U.S. Government to seek relaxation and elimination of the tension in the Taiwan area. In the Sino-American ambassadorial talks which started in August 1955 the Chinese side time and again proposed that the two parties should, in accordance with the principles of mutual respect for sovereignty and territorial integrity and non-interference in each other's internal affairs, issue a statement declaring their intention to settle the dispute between China and the United States in the Taiwan area through peaceful negotiation and without resorting to the threat or use of force against each other. But, contrary to Dulles' assertion in his September 4 statement it is precisely the United States that has refused to issue such a statement and, moreover, has later suspended unilaterally the talks themselves. After the Chinese Government demanded in July this year that the talks be resumed within a set time-limit, the U.S. Government did not make a timely reply, but it has ultimately designated a representative of ambassadorial rank. Now, the U.S. Government again indicates its desire to settle the Sino-American dispute in the Taiwan area through peaceful negotiation. To make a further effort to safeguard peace, the Chinese Government is prepared to resume the ambassadorial talks between the two countries. But the danger of war created by the United States in China's Taiwan area has not been reduced thereby. In view of the fact that the U.S. Government often acts differently from what it says and often uses peaceful negotiation as a smokescreen to cover up its actual deed of continuously expanding aggression, the entire Chinese people and the peace-loving people all over the world must not relax in the least their struggle against U.S. interference in China's internal affairs and against [the] U.S. threat to the peace of the Far East and the world.

(6) The Sino-American dispute in the Taiwan Straits area and the Chinese people's internal matter of liberating their own territory are two matters entirely different in nature. The United States has all along tried to confuse these two matters so as to cover up its aggression and intervention in China. This is absolutely not to be allowed. The Chinese people have every right to liberate their own territory by all suitable means at suitable time, and will not tolerate any foreign interference. Should the U.S. Government, brazenly disregarding the Chinese people's repeated warnings and the desire of the people of the world for peace, persist in their aggression and intervention against China and impose war on the Chinese people, it must bear the responsibility for all the serious consequences.

[*Peking Review,* No. 28, September 9, 1958, pp. 15–16.]

DULLES'S PRESS CONFERENCE OF SEPTEMBER 30, 1958

38. Dulles Answers Questions on the Advisability of Holding the Offshore Islands, September 30, 1958 (Extract)

Q. Mr. Secretary, inasmuch as you say you do not think it was sound for the Nationalist Chinese to have built up their forces on Quemoy and Matsu, I would like to ask you if you now think it would be sound to work out some arrangement for the withdrawal of those forces from those two islands?

A. It all depends upon the circumstances under which they would be withdrawn. I think to withdraw as a retreat under fire would not be a wise step to take because of the probable impact of that upon other peoples, other countries, and upon the morale, indeed, on Formosa itself.

Q. Would you state, sir, the circumstances under which you think a withdrawal could be achieved?

A. If there were a cease-fire in the area which seemed to be reasonably dependable, I think it would be foolish to keep these large forces on these islands. We thought that it was rather foolish to put them there, and, as I say, if there were a cease-fire it would be our judgment, military judgment even, that it would not be wise or prudent to keep them there.

Q. Mr. Secretary, you seem to emphasize the need for a dependable cease-fire. Could you tell us how you can get a dependable cease-fire with the Communists, whose promises you don't like to accept?

A. That is certainly a fair question and a difficult one to answer. I believe that promises of the Communists are never dependable merely because they are promises. They are only dependable if there are unpleasant consequences in case the Communists break their promises. And I believe that circumstances could be created where it would be felt that the consequences of breaking this promise would be so undesirable to the Communists that we could assume that they would probably live up to their promise, not because of the sanctity of the given word— which they do not believe in—but because of expediency . . .

[Department of State, *Bulletin,* XXXIX, No. 1008, October 20, 1958, p. 602.]

39. Dulles Answers Questions on the Possibility of a Nationalist Return to the Mainland, September 30, 1958 (Extracts)

Q. Mr. Secretary, in referring to the previous question on the renunciation of force, is it the position of this Government that the United States expects or supports the idea that the Nationalist Chinese Government is someday going to return to the mainland either by force or some other means?

A. Well, that is a highly hypothetical matter. I think it all depends upon what happens on the mainland. I don't think that just by their own steam they are going to get there. If you had on the mainland a sort of unrest and revolt, like, for example, what broke out in Hungary, then the presence of a free China with considerable power a few miles away could be a very important element in the situation. I think that we would all feel that, if there had been a free government of Hungary at the time when that revolt took place, the situation might have developed in a different way from what it did.

So I wouldn't want to exclude any possibility of a situation developing on the mainland of China, or on parts of the mainland of China, which might not lead to reunification of some sort between mainland China, or that part of mainland China, and the free Government of China, the Republic of China, now on Formosa. I do not exclude it.

Q. Would that have to be entirely on the strength of the Government on Formosa, or is there any American commitment, explicit or implied, to aid in the kind of situation that you have described?

A. No. There is no commitment of any kind to aid in that. As I think you know, the only commitment that there is in this connection is the agreement involved in the exchange of letters between the Chinese Foreign Minister and myself which says that no force will be used from the treaty areas except in agreement between us. So neither of us is free to use force from the areas of the treaty against the mainland except, I think it says, in the case of emergency requirements of self-defense. But that exception would not cover the kind of a situation that you are speaking of.

Q. Mr. Secretary, if there were a rebellion or revolt in China, would you expect its leaders to, if they wanted to, turn over their mandate to Chiang Kai-shek?

A. Well, I really don't think that is a question that I can answer very well. It all—it depends upon the nature of the revolution. I would think that it would probably be primarily under local auspices and local leadership. And while outside cooperation and assistance might be sought, it would be hypothetical and problematical as to whether or not it would involve the going back of Chiang as the head of the government. I don't exclude that as a possibility. On the other hand, the situation is so hypothetical at the present time that it is almost unwise, I think, to try to guess about it. . . .

Q. Mr. Secretary, it is fair to say that, while United States policy has not changed as of now, there is a possibility of some important changes, provided there is some give on the Chinese Communist side?

A. Yes, I would say so. Our policy in these respects is flexible and adapted to the situation that we have to meet. If the situation we have to meet changes, our policy changes with it.

[Department of State, *Bulletin,* XXXIX, No. 1008, October 20, 1958, pp. 599, 604.]

THE PRC RELAXES THE PRESSURE ON THE
OFFSHORE ISLANDS

40. PRC Foreign Ministry Spokesman's Remarks, October 7, 1958

Between 01:00 hour on October 6, when our armed forces stopped shelling Quemoy, and the early morning of the 7th, US warships and aircraft continued to intrude into our country's territorial waters and the air space above them. This is impermissible. After 06:00 hours on October 7, however, no intrusions by US warships and aircraft into territorial waters and the air space above them in the Amoy area were evident for a whole day. As a reaction to the demand to the US to cease its escorting, this is worthy of note. China is willing to settle the international disputes between China and the US in the Taiwan area with the US by peaceful negotiation. If the US is not bent on interfering in China's internal affairs, and has the same desire to engage in peaceful negotiation, then it should first of all completely stop its so-called escort activities, stop intruding into China's territorial waters and air space and cease all military provocations and war threats against China.

Starting from October 6, our armed forces stopped shelling Quemoy. As shown by the response from all sides, the military and civilian compatriots in Taiwan, Penghu, Quemoy and Matsu have expressed their warm support for this. Yet the Taiwan authorities said that they would rather risk shelling than have the United States withdraw its escort. The Taiwan authorities, because they are long obsessed by prejudice and lean on the United States as their prop, have such ideas. This is understandable. We hope that the Taiwan authorities will esteem peace and patriotism. The shipping of supplies to Quemoy can be solved by themselves and should not be under American escort. The affairs of the Chinese people should be solved by the Chinese people themselves and should not be subject to intervention by the Americans. The Americans have their own intentions. At any rate problems among the Chinese people can be reasonably solved through negotiation.

[*Peking Review,* No. 33, October 14, 1958, p. 12.]

41. PRC Foreign Ministry Spokesman's Remarks, October 9, 1958

The temporary suspension of the shelling of Quemoy by our forces, which is a humanitarian act, is warmly welcomed by the troops and civilians in Taiwan, Penghu, Quemoy and Matsu and world public opinion. But U.S. Secretary of State Dulles and Under-Secretary of State Herter and others have shown great panic and arbitrarily tried to confuse this measure taken by our forces with the U.S. cease-fire plot. They have also demanded a so-called permanent cease-fire and employed resumption of the so-called escort operations as a threat. This has further exposed the imperialist face of the United States in persisting to interfere in China's internal affairs and deliberately creating tension.

Whether our troops do or do not stop their shelling of Quemoy and whether they stop it for a short or a long period, are purely internal affairs of our country which the Americans have no right whatsoever to butt into. Even the Americans cannot but admit that there is no fighting between China and the United States, and of course the question of cease-fire does not arise at all. As for the question between the Chinese Government and the Taiwan local authorities, the Americans have no right to speak on it for the Taiwan authorities. This is not only because the Taiwan authorities have not appointed the Americans to be their representatives, but even if they did so we would never recognize it. Any Chinese with national self-respect would certainly not have foreigners as their representatives in settling their domestic problems. In a word, the Chinese are fully capable of settling their own business by themselves, and US interference will by no means be tolerated. The US cease-fire plot can deceive no one.

Whatever the circumstances, the so-called escort operations by the US Department of State, that "the necessity for US China's internal affairs. Therefore, the point is not, as claimed by the US Department of State, that "the necessity for U.S. escort operations suspends," but that the United States, from the very start, has no right to provide any escort. The attempt of the United States to coerce the Chinese people into accepting their cease-fire plot by threatening to resume escort operations is a total miscalculation.

The reason the United States has haggled about a cease-fire

is because it attempts, under the cover of a cease-fire, to seize Taiwan and Penghu forever and further to interpose in Quemoy and Matsu so as to realize its plot to create "two Chinas." Interference in China's internal affairs will not be tolerated. The United States not only has no right to butt into Quemoy and Matsu, it also has absolutely no right to butt into Taiwan and Penghu. There is only one China, and even the Taiwan authorities do not dare to support the United States plot to create "two Chinas." No patriotic Chinese will allow the United States to carve Taiwan out of China's territory.

The matter gets clearer and clearer all the time. The tension in the Taiwan Straits is created entirely by the United States, single-handedly. Beginning on June 27, 1950, the United States seized Taiwan by force. In order to extend its aggression against China from Taiwan and Penghu to Quemoy and Matsu, the United States has, in the past month and more, amassed unprecedentedly huge armed forces in the Taiwan Straits and has continuously conducted armed provocations and war threats against China, infringing China's territorial sea and air space more than 20 times in succession. These have not yet ceased up to now. In the last two days alone, the United States dispatched a "Nike-Hercules" guided missile unit to be stationed in Taiwan and has used resumption of the so-called escort operations as a threat.

It is better for the doer to undo what he has done. The key to eliminating the tension in the Taiwan Straits is for the United States to withdraw all its armed forces from Taiwan and the Taiwan Straits. The Americans should go back where they came from. The days are gone when the imperialists could bluster at their will. Have not the Americans had to agree to withdraw their armed forces from the Lebanon? How can they perpetuate their stay in Taiwan and refuse to go?

If the Americans want to prove to the world that they have no intention to interfere in China's internal affairs or use war threats against China, then they should completely stop their so-called escort operations, stop intruding into the territorial sea and air space of the Chinese mainland and stop concentrating armed forces in the Taiwan Straits; and instead of haggling about a so-called cease-fire, their ambassador should sit down to negotiate seriously in Warsaw, consulting with our representative on concrete ways and steps to withdraw all US armed forces from Taiwan and the Taiwan Straits. Otherwise, they will meet with even stronger condemnation by the people of the world, and put themselves in an even more helpless position.

[*Peking Review,* No. 33, October 14, 1958, pp. 12–13.]

DULLES CONFERS WITH CHIANG KAI-SHEK

42. US-ROC Communiqué After Chiang-Dulles Consultations, Taipei, October 23, 1958 (Extracts)

The consultations had been arranged to be held during the two weeks when the Chinese Communists had declared they would cease fire upon Quemoy. It had been hoped that, under these circumstances, primary consideration could have been given to measures which would have contributed to stabilizing an actual situation of nonmilitancy. However, on the eve of the consultations, the Chinese Communists, in violation of their declaration, resumed artillery fire against the Quemoys. It was recognized that under the present conditions the defense of the Quemoys, together with the Matsus, is closely related to the defense of Taiwan and Penghu. . . .

The two Governments reaffirmed their solidarity in the face of the new Chinese Communist aggression now manifesting itself in the bombardment of the Quemoys. This aggression and the accompanying Chinese Communist propaganda have not divided them, as the Communists have hoped. On the contrary, it has drawn them closer together. They believe that by unitedly opposing aggression they serve not only themselves but the cause of peace. As President Eisenhower said on September 11, the position of opposing aggression by force is the only position consistent with the peace of the world.

The two Governments took note of the fact that the Chinese Communists, with the backing of the Soviet Union, avowedly seek to conquer Taiwan, to eliminate Free China and to expel the United States from the Western Pacific generally, compelling the United States to abandon its collective security arrangements with free countries of that area. This policy cannot possibly succeed. It is hoped and believed that the Communists, faced by the proven unity, resolution and strength of the Governments of the United States and the Republic of China, will not put their policy to the test of general war and that they will abandon the military steps which they have already taken to initiate their futile and dangerous policy. . . .

The United States recognizes that the Republic of China is the authentic spokesman for Free China and of the hopes and aspirations entertained by the great mass of the Chinese people. . . .

The two Governments reaffirmed their dedication to the principles of the Charter of the United Nations. They recalled that the treaty under which they are acting is defensive in character. The Government of the Republic of China considers that the restoration of freedom to its people on the mainland is its sacred mission. It believes that the foundation of this mission resides in the minds and the hearts of the Chinese people and that the principal means of successfully achieving its mission is the implementation of Dr. Sun Yat-sen's three people's principles (nationalism, democracy and social well-being) and not the use of force. . . .

[*AFP 1958,* pp. 1184–85.]

43. *People's Daily* Editorial on the Chiang Kai-shek–Dulles Talks, October 30, 1958 (Extracts)

Not long ago, US Secretary of State Dulles went to Taiwan and held talks with Chiang Kai-shek. Now the United States is ballyhooing these talks as marking a change in US policy towards China, as having strengthened the unity between the United States and Chiang Kai-shek and as a manifestation of US peaceful intentions. There is indeed a change in US policy towards China—its plot to create "two Chinas" is coming out into the open. This change, however, merely amounts to the implementation in another form of its policy of aggression and war against China. There are no peaceful intentions whatsoever about it. Dulles' aim in these talks was to force Chiang to accept the "two Chinas" scheme. He has actually made some gains in this respect. However, his dream is far from being realized. As to the lip service paid to greater unity, that is just so much eyewash. . . .

The plot to create "two Chinas" was hatched by the United States a long time ago. In the past, the US mostly stayed behind the scenes, spinning the plot while other countries that took their cue from it put the scheme into action. Now, it has openly come forward on its own. On the eve of publication of the communiqué on the Chiang-Dulles talks, US Vice-President Richard Nixon declared publicly that there was a "need for an independent Chinese government to which both the twelve million people on Formosa and the millions more of overseas Chinese can owe allegiance." In the Chiang-Dulles joint communiqué of October 23, Dulles forced the Taiwan authorities to accept the so-called principle of no recourse to the use of force, and granted the Chiang Kai-shek clique the right to represent only "free China." This appeared to be an agreement between Chiang Kai-shek and Dulles. In fact, as early as October 16, in his interview with the correspondent of the British Independent Television Service, Dulles had already taken Chiang Kai-shek's acceptance of this US decision for granted. In that interview, Dulles conferred upon the Chiang Kai-shek clique the title of a small China while declaring that he saw that Communist China actually existed and was willing to deal with it. This was obviously a public bid for "two Chinas."

The creation of "two Chinas," it must be pointed out, is merely a matter of expediency for the United States. The United States wants first to separate Taiwan from China and isolate it completely, so as to facilitate its control over the Chiang Kai-shek clique and strengthen its occupation of Taiwan. But this is only a first step. Once Taiwan should become a "de facto political unit" independent of China, the United States could then use some pretext or other to place it under trusteeship. In this way, the United States would make a double gain: on the one hand, it would legalize its seizure of Taiwan and turn that island into a US colony; at the same time, by involving certain other countries, it would get them to share its responsibility for aggression. The Chiang Kai-shek clique clearly has no place in this sinister US scheme. Nixon declared that the aim of the United States in the Far East was to make Taiwan an "island of freedom" rather than "to tie the United States policy to Chiang Kai-shek." Isn't the meaning of these words clear enough?

It is very absurd for the United States to abuse the principle of no recourse to the use of force in international relations, by trying to apply it to China's internal affairs. By so doing, the

United States aims to tie the hands of the Taiwan authorities and make them completely subservient to the US. The Taiwan authorities are not unaware of this. That is why, after the release of the Chiang-Dulles joint communiqué, they made such a hullabaloo about there being reservations to their declaration on renunciation of the use of force. However, the United States featured this same declaration as its major victory. Both parties are clinging to their own interpretation and making a big fuss about it. It was in these circumstances that, at his press conference on October 28, Dulles, as if handing down a verdict, came out bluntly with the remark that, despite all their reservations, the Taiwan authorities "didn't have much chance of winning by force." Coming from Dulles, isn't this a deliberate attempt to make it difficult for the Taiwan authorities even to drag on their miserable existence?

We stated long ago that it is absolutely impossible for the US to carry through its plot of creating "two Chinas" so as to occupy Taiwan indefinitely. The Chinese people who have stood up are confident that they can smash this US plot. There is only one China in the world, not two. Every patriotic Chinese opposes the "two Chinas" scheme. The masses of overseas Chinese oppose it. Even the Taiwan authorities do not agree to it. On October 24 Chiang Kai-shek said that Taiwan and the mainland were part of the same entity, with a flesh and blood relationship, sharing the common weal and woe. We believe that the US will be utterly defeated if the whole Chinese people unite and face the foreign foe. . . .

[*Peking Review,* No. 36, November 4, 1958, pp. 9–10.]

THE CHINESE POSITION HARDENS

**44. *Red Flag* Article, "Long Live Leninism!" April 16, 1960
(Extracts)**

Tito's speech at the end of last year referred repeatedly to the so-called "new epoch" of the modern revisionists. He said, "Today the world has entered an epoch in which nations can relax and tranquilly devote themselves to their internal construction tasks." . . .

But how do things really stand in the world?

Can the exploited and oppressed people in the imperialist countries "relax"? Can the peoples of all the colonies and semicolonies still under imperialist oppression "relax"?

Has the armed intervention led by the US imperialists in Asia, Africa and Latin America become "tranquil"? Is there "tranquillity" in our Taiwan Straits when the US imperialists are still occupying our country's Taiwan? Is there "tranquillity" on the African continent when the people of Algeria and many other parts of Africa are subjected to armed repressions by the French, British and other imperialists? Is there any "tranquillity" in Latin America when the US imperialists are trying to wreck the people's revolution in Cuba by means of bombing, assassination and subversion? . . .

Is Tito referring to the "internal construction tasks" of arms expansion which the imperialists are carrying out in order to oppress the peoples of their own countries and oppress the whole world? Or is it the "internal construction" carried out by socialism for the promotion of the people's happiness and in the pursuit of lasting world peace?

Is the question of war and peace no longer an issue? Is it that imperialism no longer exists, the system of exploitation no longer exists, and therefore the question of war no longer exists? Or is it that there can be no question of war even if imperialism and the system of exploitation are allowed to survive forever? The fact is that since the Second World War there has been continuous and unbroken warfare. Do not the imperialist wars to suppress national liberation movements and the imperialist wars of armed intervention against revolutions in various countries count as wars? Even though these wars have not developed into world wars, still do not these local wars count as wars? Even though these wars were not fought with nuclear weapons, still do not wars using so-called conventional weapons count as wars? Does not the US imperialists' allocation of nearly 60 per cent of the 1960 budget outlay to arms expansion and war preparations count as a bellicose policy on the part of US imperialism? Will the revival of West German and Japanese militarisms not confront mankind with the danger of a new big war? . . . .

Of course, whether or not the imperialists will unleash war is not determined by us: we are, after all, not chiefs-of-staff to the imperialists. As long as the people of all countries enhance their awareness and are fully prepared, with the socialist camp also mastering modern weapons, it is certain that if the US or other imperialists refuse to reach an agreement on the banning of atomic and nuclear weapons and should dare to fly in the face of the will of all humanity by launching a war using atomic and nuclear weapons, the result will be the very speedy destruction of these monsters encircled by the peoples of the world, and the result will certainly not be the annihilation of mankind. We consistently oppose the launching of criminal wars by imperialism, because imperialist war would impose enormous sacrifices upon the peoples of various countries (including the peoples of the United States and other imperialist countries). But should the imperialists impose such sacrifices on the peoples of various countries, we believe that, just as the experience of the Russian revolution and the Chinese revolution shows, those sacrifices would be repaid. On the débris of a dead imperialism, the victorious people would create very swiftly a civilization thousands of times higher than the capitalist system and a truly beautiful future for themselves. . . .

[*Peking Review,* No. 17, 1960, as reproduced in G. F. Hudson, Richard Lowenthal, and Roderick MacFarquhar, *The Sino-Soviet Dispute* (New York: Praeger, 1961), pp. 87–88, 93–94.]

45. US-PRC Exchanges on the Question of Correspondents, June–September, 1960 (Extracts)

The US Draft Proposal, June 7, 1960

Since August 1957 the United States has been endeavoring to obtain Chinese Communist agreement to the entry of U.S. newsmen into Communist China. On June 7, 1960, at Warsaw, in the 98th meeting of the ambassadorial talks with the Chinese Communists, United States Ambassador Jacob D. Beam proposed to Chinese Communist Ambassador Wang Ping-nan the issuance of an agreed announcement on the admission of newsmen into their respective countries. Ambassador Beam proposed that this announcement contain the following explicit statement of the position made known by the United States since August 1957 on admission of Chinese Communist newsmen. The announcement was to be conditioned on a parallel statement by the Chinese Communists:

> Ambassador Beam has explained to Ambassador Wang that the position of the United States with respect to the admission and treatment of newsmen of the People's Republic of China to the United States is:
>
> The Government of the United States of America, subject to the Constitution and applicable laws and regulations in force in the United States and in accordance with the principles of equality and reciprocity, will admit to the United States newsmen of the People's Republic of China in order to permit direct reporting about conditions in the United States. Newsmen of the People's Republic of China who are admitted to the United States will be accorded the same facilities for news reporting as are generally accorded newsmen from foreign countries in the United States.

At the 100th meeting of the two Ambassadors at Warsaw on September 6, 1960, Ambassador Wang rejected this proposal and refused to issue a parallel statement. From this it is clear that, while the United States stands prepared to engage in an exchange of newsmen in accordance with the principles of equality and reciprocity with Communist China, the Chinese Communist regime is not willing to enter into such an exchange. . . .

[State Department Press Release, September 8, 1960, in Department of State, *Bulletin,* XLIII, No. 1109, September 26, 1960, pp. 497–98.]

Why the PRC Rejected the US Draft and Made Its Own Proposal, September 6, 1960

Superficially, this American draft seems to have accepted the principles of equality and reciprocity put forward by the Chinese side. However, a little analysis of this draft will show that the U.S. Government has not in the least abandoned its consistent stand of refusing to observe the principles of equality and reciprocity. In this draft the U.S. side says in the first place that admittance of Chinese correspondents into the United States by the U.S. Government will be "subject to the Constitution and applicable laws and regulations in force in the United States." This is obviously done with ulterior motives. The U.S. Government repeatedly made clear in the past that according to U.S. immigration laws, the United States could not guarantee such reciprocity as suggested by the Chinese side. It can thus be seen that the

U.S. side, by introducing into its draft the phrase "subject to the Constitution and applicable laws and regulations in force in the United States," not only has nullified the "principles of equality and reciprocity" mentioned simultaneously in the draft, but has exactly left a pretext for future refusal to observe these principles so that it can at any time obstruct the entry of Chinese correspondents. This has its proof too in the September 8 statement of the U.S. State Department.

The American draft does not mention a single word about the purpose of exchanging correspondents between China and the United States. This is by no means an accidental slip. The Chinese Government has always held that the aim of exchanging correspondents between China and the United States on an equal and reciprocal basis can only be to help promote mutual understanding between the two peoples and improve relations between the two countries. It is essential to fix this aim in the agreement between the two sides, and all the more necessary to do so particularly in view of the consistent policy of hostility towards China pursued by the U.S. Government. Yet the American draft does not mention at all the aim of exchanging correspondents between the two countries. This cannot but make one suspect the actual intent of the United States in asking to exchange correspondents with China.

The American draft takes the form of statements to be issued by the ambassadors of the two countries separately. We remember that the agreement of the two sides on the return of civilians to their countries also took this form. But the fact that the U.S. side has so far failed to seriously implement this agreement shows that this form does not have enough binding force on the U.S. side. To prevent the U.S. side from again violating [an] agreement, the Chinese side resolutely maintains that all agreements between the two sides must take the form of joint announcements of both sides, and no longer take that of statements issued by the two sides separately.

For the above reasons, the Chinese side rejected the American draft at the 100th meeting of the Sino-American talks held on September 7 [*sic;* in fact the meeting was held on the 6th] and put forward a new draft of [an] agreed announcement, which reads in full as follows:

Ambassador Wang Ping-nan, on behalf of the Government of the People's Republic of China, and Ambassador Jacob D. Beam, on behalf of the Government of the United States of America, agree to announce:

In order to seek to eliminate estrangement between the Chinese and American peoples, to make a preliminary improvement in the present relations between the two countries and furthermore to impel the two countries to settle peacefully in accordance with the Five Principles of mutual respect for sovereignty and territorial integrity, mutual non-aggression, non-interference in each other's internal affairs, equality and mutual benefit and peaceful coexistence the question of withdrawal of all U.S. armed forces from China's territory Taiwan and the Taiwan Straits area, the Governments of the two countries have agreed on the following provisions to enable correspondents of each country to enter the other for news coverage on an equal and reciprocal basis.

(1) The two Governments agree that correspondents of their own countries who desire to enter the other country for news coverage must apply to the Government of the other country for approval, and that the number of correspondents of the other side whose entry is approved by the two Governments must be equal each time.

(2) The two Governments agree that neither of them will obstruct the entry of approved correspondents of the other side by any laws and regulations now in force or promulgated in the future.

(3) The two Governments agree that correspondents of the other side whose entry has been approved will enjoy the same facilities for news coverage as enjoyed by correspondents of their own countries in the other country.

(4) The two Governments guarantee that correspondents of their own countries entering the other country for news coverage will not engage in activities contrary to the aims mentioned in the preamble of the present agreement.

After the Chinese side put forward this draft, the U.S. side rejected it right away without giving it a thought. This thoroughly disclosed the real attitude of the U.S. Government on the question of exchanging correspondents between China and the United States. . . .

The fact that the U.S. Government refuses to agree to the aims set by the Chinese Government for the exchange of correspondents between the two countries shows exactly that the U.S. Government does not wish to eliminate estrangement between the two peoples, is not willing to improve relations between the two countries, and will continue to occupy by armed force China's territory Taiwan. . . .

The Chinese Government assumed in the past that, although a radical improvement in Sino-American relations would depend on the settlement of the fundamental issues between China and the United States, and first of all on U.S. agreement to withdraw all its armed forces from China's territory Taiwan and the Taiwan Straits area, the two sides might as well first discuss some comparatively minor questions and reach fair and reasonable agreements on them so as to create favourable conditions for the settlement of the fundamental issues between China and the United States. To this end, the Chinese side has, in the past 100 meetings of the Sino-American talks, put forward successively a series of reasonable proposals for the elimination of obstacles to trade between the two countries, the elimination of obstacles to cultural interflow and travel of personnel between the two countries and the exchange of correspondents on an equal and reciprocal basis. It is very much to be regretted that these proposals have all been unreasonably rejected by the U.S. Government one after another. Facts prove that so long as the U.S. Government still persists in its policy of hostility and aggression against China, still persists in occupying China's territory Taiwan by armed force, and continues its scheme to create "two Chinas," all efforts made by the Chinese side for first settling individual questions are of no avail. From the experience of the 100 meetings of the Sino-American talks in the past five years, the Chinese side cannot but draw the conclusion that there is no need in future talks to again waste time on minor questions, and that efforts should first be devoted to settling the fundamental issues between China and the United States, namely, the consent of the U.S. Government to settle disputes between China and the United States by peaceful negotiation without resorting to the use or threat of force and its consent to withdraw all its armed forces from China's territory Taiwan and the Taiwan Straits area. Although the U.S. side has up to now failed to display the least sincere desire, the Chinese side will continue to exert its utmost efforts in the talks as it has done in the past five years.

[PRC Foreign Ministry Statement, September 13, 1960, in *Peking Review*, No. 37, September 14, 1960, pp. 30–31.]

Why the US Rejected the PRC Draft Proposal, September 6, 1960

In rejecting the United States draft, the Chinese Communists put forward a proposal of their own. This draft was rejected by Ambassador Beam because it (1) maintained the Communists' insistence that the United States set aside its laws and regulations if these would bar a newsman selected by the Chinese Communists; (2) required the United States to guarantee the professional conduct of American correspondents; (3) tied in the admission of American correspondents with political conditions; and (4) contained provisions restrictive of legitimate press freedom. For example, it would require the United States to "guarantee" that American newsmen would not write reports contrary to Chinese Communist objectives, including the "withdrawal of all US armed forces from China's territory of Taiwan and the Taiwan Strait area."

The rejection of Ambassador Beam's proposal follows the similar rejection by the Chinese Communists of every other initiative of the United States Government designed to make possible an exchange of newsmen. As a consequence the Department of State is reluctantly compelled to conclude that Communist China, whatever its reasons may be, has no serious interest either in reporting by its own newsmen from the United States or reporting by American newsmen from the China mainland. By refusing to issue a statement that the United States newsmen will be admitted to mainland China in accordance with the principles of equality and reciprocity along the lines of the statement proposed by Ambassador Beam, and by putting forward their totally unacceptable counterproposal, the Chinese Communist regime has again demonstrated that it is opposed to a reciprocal exchange of newsmen.

Despite Chinese Communist obstruction, the representatives of the United States will continue to press for a satisfactory solution to this problem.

[State Department Press Release, September 8, 1960, in Department of State, *Bulletin,* XLIII, No. 1109, September 26, 1960, p. 498.]

V. Talking at Cross-Purposes

PRESIDENT KENNEDY, according to his most trusted adviser, "felt dissatisfied with his administration's failure to break new ground" in China policy.[1] He "began and remained throughout his presidency disturbed and baffled by Peking's instant and constant antagonism,"[2] appalled apparently that the Chinese had "spewed unremitting vituperation upon him" since his inauguration.[3] The unkindest cut of all seems to have been that Mao said he was worse than Eisenhower."[4] Kennedy concluded that any American initiative toward negotiations, diplomatic recognition, or UN admission would be regarded by the Chinese as rewarding their aggressiveness. He was also concerned about how such moves would go down in Congress and in the country as a whole. Kennedy decided to postpone reconsidering policy toward China until his second term.[5]

The bewilderment of the Kennedy administration is understandable. The New Frontiersmen were willing to re-examine pragmatically the foreign policy of the Dulles era toward every area of the world. They wished to discard the rigidities of the cold war and, with the Communist countries, "explore what problems unite us instead of belaboring those problems which divide us."[6] But

[1] Theodore C. Sorensen, *Kennedy* (London: Hodder & Stoughton, 1965), p. 665.
[2] Young, *op. cit.*, p. 239.
[3] Sorensen, *loc. cit.*
[4] Roger Hilsman, *To Move a Nation* (New York: Delta, 1968), p. 304.
[5] Sorensen, *op. cit.*, pp. 665–66.
[6] See Kennedy's Inaugural Address in President John F. Kennedy, *To Turn the Tide* (London: Hamish Hamilton, 1962), p. 9.

though his mind was wide-ranging and flexible, Kennedy, too, had been shaped by the cold war, "disciplined by a hard and bitter peace," as he put it in his inaugural address.[7] The attitudes toward China that he brought to the presidency did not differ markedly from those of his campaign opponent, Eisenhower's Vice-President, Nixon (**46**).

There was, however, one significant policy difference between Kennedy and his predecessor. As a Senator, Kennedy had expressed from his sickbed his strong opposition to the "Formosa resolution" of January, 1955 (**19**), because he felt the offshore islands should be abandoned.[8] During the 1960 presidential campaign he reaffirmed this position, clashing with Nixon on the issue when they debated on television. Kennedy's stand placed him among liberals who wanted to remove possible threats to peace in the Far East. It also signified his disbelief in Dulles's concept of the evanescence of the Communist regime (**32**).[9] Ironically, it was precisely this "liberal" stand on the offshore islands question that must have made him seem more dangerous than Eisenhower to Mao.

As we have seen, the Chinese Communists had indicated their concern about the effect of a Nationalist withdrawal from the offshore islands as early as the Taiwan Strait crisis of 1958.[10] But at least Dulles seemed committed to the idea of a single China embracing Taiwan, although he would have preferred it ruled by Chiang Kai-shek—indeed, Dulles's general position worried the Chinese more when he began to show what in Western eyes was greater realism and acknowledged that there were two Chinese regimes in existence.[11] Kennedy, on the other hand, had indicated even before his election that he was prepared to think in terms of some form of two-Chinas solution; and, as the Chinese noted, some of his top foreign policy advisers were also on record as favoring such a policy (**47**). By July, 1961, the Chinese decided

[7] *Ibid.*, p. 7.
[8] Eisenhower, *op. cit.*, I, p. 468.
[9] Hilsman, *op. cit.*, pp. 302–3.
[10] See introduction to Chapter Four.
[11] *Peking Review*, No. 34, August 25, 1961, p. 11.

that the two-successor-states formula was the option favored by Kennedy and strongly condemned it (48).

One area of China policy in which the Kennedy administration was forced to make a change was with respect to the UN seat. Since 1951, the Americans had secured a majority in the General Assembly to postpone discussion of a Soviet resolution to seat the PRC. But the US majority on this vote had been declining over the years and could have disappeared in 1961. The Kennedy administration therefore changed America's tactics in the 1961 General Assembly, abstained on the resolution to postpone discussion (which did not pass), and instead secured a favorable vote on a proposal to make Chinese representation an "important question" that required a two-thirds majority to be passed.[12] The "important-question" device was to be successful in excluding the PRC from the UN for another ten years.

Contacts between the American and Chinese governments now occurred far less often than in the Dulles era. Foreign Minister Ch'en Yi hinted in October, 1961, that China was still interested in ministerial-level discussions with the United States, something the Chinese had been very keen on in the mid-1950s. But Kennedy and Secretary of State Dean Rusk "somewhat lamely" deflected the suggestion by pointing out that the two countries were already engaged in negotiations at the Geneva conference on Laos and in the ambassadorial meetings in Warsaw.[13] In fact, bilateral US-PRC discussions did not take place in Geneva,[14] and from 1961 on the frequency of the Warsaw meetings declined noticeably.[15]

However, the Warsaw link proved useful in defusing a potential offshore islands crisis in mid-1962. Earlier that year, refugees from the economic setbacks of China's "three bitter years" (1959–61) had begun pouring into Hong Kong. Kennedy hinted that the

12 Hilsman, *op. cit.*, pp. 307–10.
13 *Ibid.*, p. 309.
14 Young, *op. cit.*, p. 249.
15 *Ibid.*, p. 247.

United States would consider lifting the trade embargo in order to ship food to China, but Ch'en Yi replied curtly that the Chinese did not need to beg.[16]

The domestic problems that the refugee exodus pointed up encouraged the Nationalists. Their propaganda directed toward the mainland became increasingly threatening. The Chinese, presumably fearing that Chiang was finally going to try to reverse the verdict of 1949, brought in considerable reinforcements to the coastal provinces opposite Taiwan. Anxious that Peking should not misjudge the situation, Kennedy had the Chinese representative at the Warsaw talks informed on June 26 that the United States would not support any Nationalist attack; but he also issued a public warning that US policy on the offshore islands remained what it had been since 1955. The Seventh Fleet was reinforced to drive the message home.[17] Tension gradually diminished.

Chinese suspicion of Kennedy persisted. Peking was particularly aroused by his grand strategy of the flexible response, outlined in an interview with Stewart Alsop early in 1962 (**49**). Ch'en Yi immediately condemned the new doctrine that the United States might in some circumstances strike first with nuclear weapons (**50**), and Chinese writers attacked Kennedy's emphasis on training American and allied troops in counterinsurgency techniques to fight guerrillas, a doctrine particularly relevant to the struggle in Vietnam where the United States was becoming increasingly involved (**51**).

For his part, Kennedy continued to deplore Chinese aggressiveness. He sent Averell Harriman, the Assistant Secretary of State for Far Eastern Affairs, with a top-level mission to New Delhi on the outbreak of the Sino-Indian border war in November, 1962, to arrange military assistance for India.[18] Mao Tse-tung's decision to issue a personal denunciation of the Kennedy administration's handling of the racial issue in the United States could

16 Hilsman, *op. cit.,* pp. 315–17.
17 *Ibid.,* pp. 317–20.
18 *Ibid.,* 327–31.

only have irritated him (52).[19] But Kennedy's severest comment on the Peking government came after the Chinese had denounced the partial test-ban treaty as an attempt to bind their hands (53 & 54).

Nevertheless, the Kennedy administration did start to rethink its China policy in preparation for his second term. The Sino-Soviet dispute forced American policy-makers finally to discard the old hypothesis of one united enemy called "Communism."[20] The way in which the Peking government had surmounted the internal difficulties of the "three bitter years" had exposed the wishful thinking in Dulles's theory of an evanescent Communist regime; the theory had to be abandoned. Some official analysts hopefully suggested that the next generation of Chinese leaders might be easier to deal with. All these ideas went into a major speech on China policy prepared before Kennedy's assassination but delivered three weeks after it by Roger Hilsman, who had replaced Harriman as Assistant Secretary for Far Eastern Affairs (55).[21] Hilsman's rewriting of Dulles was noticed in Peking, but his speech and those of other American policy-makers were denounced by the Chinese in February, 1964, as an attempt to pursue old policies in a new way (56).

Eight months later, on October 16, 1964, the long-awaited first Chinese nuclear test took place. Premier Chou En-lai used the occasion to repeat the call for a world-wide summit conference made by the Chinese at the time of the partial test-ban treaty. He also stated that China would never be the first to use nuclear weapons (57). President Lyndon Johnson condemned the defiance of the partial test-ban treaty and ridiculed China's "nuclear pretensions" (58). At the next ambassadorial meeting on November 25, the Chinese proposed a "no-first-use" agreement between

[19] This was the first of a series of personal statements made by Mao over the course of two years condemning U S. policy in, for instance, the Congo, Vietnam, Panama, and the Dominican Republic.

[20] Hilsman, *op. cit.*, p. 344.

[21] *Ibid.*, pp. 350–57.

the two sides. This was the first time since 1960 that the Chinese had offered to conclude any agreement prior to an agreement on Taiwan.[22] It was an indication of the degree to which they had been alarmed by Kennedy's grand strategy of flexible response. The Americans did not abandon that strategy on this occasion.

[22] Young, *op. cit.*, pp. 261–68.

46. UPI Report on Campaign Statements on China Policy, September 22, 1960

Washington, Sept. 22.—Democratic Presidential candidate John F. Kennedy said today that the United States' China policy should concentrate on building a strong and successful Japan and India and promoting a broad Southeast Asia alliance against Communist aggression.

Sen. Kennedy and Republican Presidential candidate Richard M. Nixon stated their China-policy views in written answers to a question submitted by the Scripps-Howard newspapers.

They were asked: "In what circumstances would you recognize Red China?" Both opposed recognition as long as Communist China pursues its present policies.

Mr. Nixon said recognition of the Peking Government or American support for its admission to the United Nations "must wait for a basic change in her foreign policy."

"As long as the Chinese Communists continue their present hostile and aggressive policies toward the free world and refuse to live in peace with the family of nations, there can be no question of our recognizing them," Mr. Nixon said.

'Opposite Direction'

Sen. Kennedy said: "I don't see any evidence that Red China desires to live in comity with us. In fact, she is moving in the opposite direction. Therefore, I do not advocate recognition of Red China."

However, Sen. Kennedy said: "Recognition is not really the crux of our foreign policy. The real question is what should be done about the harsh fact that China is a powerful and aggressive nation.

"The dangerous situation now existing can be remedied only by a strong and successful India, a strong and successful Japan, and some kind of regional group over Southeast Asia which gives these smaller countries the feeling that, in spite of their distaste for a military alliance, they will not be left to be picked off one by one at the whim of the Peking regime."

[UPI report in *New York Herald Tribune* (European Edition), September 23, 1960.]

47. *Peking Review.* "A Brief Account of the US 'Two-Chinas' Plot," August 25, 1961 (Extract)

Before he was elected president, Kennedy himself and other Democratic politicians who are now high-ranking officials in the present Democratic administration, actively advocated the creation of "two Chinas." In an interview with a correspondent of the British *Sunday Times* on July 3, 1960, Kennedy said that "it might be possible that Formosa would be recognized as an independent country."

Since the Kennedy Administration was inaugurated last January, there has been a stepping up of U.S. plots designed to create "two Chinas." This was because, as the U.S. press pointed out, the question of his China policy is "one of Mr. Kennedy's toughest" (Washington *Evening Star*). The Kennedy Administration is attempting by the creation of "two Chinas" to find new tactics for its China policy "to take some of the heat off Washington," but it "contemplates no change in basic policy" (UPI).

Various Formulas for "Two Chinas"

U.S. ruling circles and their idea men, both before and after the inauguration of the Kennedy Administration, have been cooking up various formulas for the creation of "two Chinas." This includes old stuff inherited from the Republican administration and new tricks devised by the Democratic administration. These "formulas" can be summarized in general as follows:

No. 1. "An independent state of Taiwan." According to this formula, the United States will make the Chiang Kai-shek clique withdraw its troops from Quemoy and Matsu Islands, and then Taiwan will be declared "independent" and made a new member of the United Nations, while China will be "admitted" into the United Nations and the Security Council on condition of undertaking "not to liberate Taiwan by force."

In an article in the April 1960 issue of the American quarterly *Foreign Affairs*, the present U.S. Under Secretary of State

Bowles urged the formation of "an independent Sino-Formosan nation" predominantly Chinese by culture but Formosan in outlook. He stressed that only by beginning with imaginative policies based on "two Chinas" could the United States start to "exert a constructive influence" on Asia.

No. 2. Placing Taiwan under U.N. "trusteeship" or "protection." According to this formula, the United States will leave the Kuomintang clique in the lurch. The status of Taiwan will remain "unsettled for the time being" and it will be placed under U.N. "trusteeship" or "protection" for a number of years, at the expiration of which time a "plebiscite" will be held to decide its future.

In last year's January issue of *Foreign Affairs*, Adlai Stevenson, now permanent representative of the Kennedy administration to the United Nations, advocated "acceptance of the right of the inhabitants of Formosa to determine their own destiny by plebiscite supervised by the United Nations."

In collusion with the reactionary circles in Japan which have been attempting to lay their fingers once again on Taiwan, the United States has for years been fostering the Chinese traitor Liao Wen-yi as a ready tool for pushing ahead this plan. The *Taiwan Kung Ping Pao,* published in Japan, said that there already existed openly in Japan a so-called "Provisional Government of the Taiwan Republic" and a "Taiwan Independence and Freedom Party." According to reports circulated in the United States recently, Liao Wen-yi is planning to visit the United States. This throws fresh light on the U.S. plot.

No. 3. "One and a half Chinas." The main idea of this formula is, in the name of recognizing so-called Chinese "suzerainty" over Taiwan, to turn Taiwan into an "autonomous" area which would retain the right of handling its foreign affairs independently; and to restore to China its seat in the United Nations while giving Taiwan a separate seat in the U.N. General Assembly.

This formula was proposed by John Fairbank, former Director of the U.S.I.S. office in China, on January 20, this year. Fairbank admitted that the "two Chinas" concept was unpopular, so he proposed that "instead of imposing the obnoxious term 'two Chinas' from the outside, we might better describe the situation realistically in Chinese terms as one of Peking's 'suzerainty' and Taipei's 'autonomy.'"

No. 4. The "two successor states" formula. This is the latest

U.S. formula for creating "two Chinas." In the latter part of
June this year, just around the time when Japanese Prime Minister Hayato Ikeda was visiting the United States, the new, so-
called "successor states" formula was reported in the U.S. press.
As the American journal *Newsweek* (July 10) disclosed, the
author of this formula is Chester Bowles, U.S. Under-Secretary
of State. This scheme envisages that both the People's Republic
of China and the Kuomintang clique in Taiwan, which has been
repudiated by the Chinese people, will be regarded "as 'successors' to the China that entered the United Nations at its founding"; the Kuomintang clique will be allowed to continue to usurp
the position of permanent member of the U.N. Security Council
and the seat in the U.N. General Assembly, while the People's
Republic of China will "apply to the Credentials Committee of
the General Assembly for approval to occupy an assembly
seat."

[*Peking Review,* No. 34, August 25, 1961, pp. 11–12.]

48. *People's Daily* Editorial, "There Is Only One China, Not Two," July 14, 1961 (Extracts)

The Kennedy Administration of the United States, in pursuance
of its "two Chinas" policy, is now playing a new trick—the so-
called "successor state" formula . . .

Still fresh in everybody's memory is the fact that Eisenhower
and Dulles, in the earlier days of their power, utterly refused to
recognize the existence of the People's Republic of China. In
the later days of their rule, they regarded the Kuomintang clique
in Taiwan as an "independent political entity"; in other words,
they wanted to name it a small China so as to create a situation of
a big China and a small China existing side by side. Kennedy is
now attempting to name the Kuomintang clique a "successor
state" to China in the United Nations so as to create a situation
of two Chinas existing side by side and on a par with each
other. Like its predecessor, the Kennedy Administration, while
continuing to "recognize" on the one hand the Kuomintang
clique discarded by the Chinese people, tries on the other to
create "two Chinas." The only difference is that Kennedy's
predecessor used the "half-and-half" division method to break
China up into two, while Kennedy is using the "two-times-one-

is-two" multiplication method to transform one China into two Chinas. Kennedy may think he is smarter than his predecessor, but his proposition, in fact, is more absurd. After all when was this other China suddenly dropped from the heavens, adding 9.6 million square kilometres of land and 650 million people to the earth? What else can this be if not day-dreaming? . . .

The "two Chinas" policy of the United States is a continuation of the U.S. policy of aggression and hostility towards China. It is essentially an attempt to occupy China's territory of Taiwan permanently and a threat to the security of China and the peace in Asia. Therefore, anyone who has national self-respect and cares for peace in Asia will firmly oppose, as the Chinese people do, this criminal policy of the United States. There is only one China. Taiwan is China's territory. The Chinese people are determined to liberate Taiwan. They will never tolerate any interference in China's internal affairs, any encroachment on China's sovereignty or the splitting of China's territory. The attempt of any state or person to create "two Chinas" in whatever way and under whatever circumstances will only be an illusion that can never be realized.

[*Peking Review,* No. 29, July 21, 1961, pp. 5–6.]

KENNEDY'S GRAND STRATEGY IS CONDEMNED BY THE CHINESE

49. Stewart Alsop on Kennedy's Grand Strategy, March 31, 1962 (Extract)

The essential purpose of the Kennedy grand strategy is that *we* should choose how to respond to Khrushchev's challenges, rather than have the choice forced upon us. The underlying principles of the strategy are all designed to this end.

Kennedy inherited two basic doctrines on nuclear warfare. One, as we have seen, was that any war bigger than a brush-fire war would be a nuclear war from the outset. The other was that the United States would never strike first with the nuclear weapon. Under the Kennedy grand strategy, both doctrines have been quietly discarded.

The aim now is to convince Khrushchev on one point, and

leave him uncertain on another. This country must maintain a sufficient margin of superiority in nuclear striking power so that Khrushchev will be certain that, if he strikes first, he will receive a devastating counterblow. But Khrushchev must *not* be certain that, where its vital interests are threatened, the United States will never strike first. As Kennedy says, "in some circumstances we might have to take the initiative." In these way Khrushchev is to continue to be convinced that "global thermonuclear war" is something to avoid.

It was for this reason that Kennedy decided that he had no alternative to resuming nuclear tests in the atmosphere. It was for the same reason that more than a third of the Kennedy Administration's $9,000,000,000 increase in defense spending has been allocated to nuclear striking power. The rest of the money has been used to give the President that "choice" upon which he insists—the choice *not* to initiate a nuclear holocaust, if he so wills. The Army, for example, has been increased from eleven combat-ready divisions to sixteen, and nonnuclear fighting power has been beefed up all along the line.

One purpose is to convince Khrushchev that he cannot extend his empire by proxy, by the oblique thrust, as Stalin tried to do in Korea. Khrushchev must be convinced that any military thrust, in Europe or elsewhere, will mean the direct confrontation of Soviet and American troops, and will thus involve the risk of "global thermonuclear war."

A further purpose is to give the United States the means of dealing directly, if essential in the national interest, with those Communist-supported guerrilla wars which are the main military means of Communist expansion under the Khrushchev grand strategy. The United States must have sufficient forces to prevent a Communist take-over in a country like Laos or Vietnam. And if such intervention is decided upon, the Presdent must have left enough nonnuclear chips—enough conventional power—to continue to play the global poker game.

But direct intervention is a sanction to be applied only when there is no other way of dealing with the Communist-guerrilla threat. In Vienna Khrushchev complacently told Kennedy that outside intervention to deal with internal uprisings is always ineffective. Kennedy was too tactful to mention Hungary, but he is quite aware that the use of foreign troops against an internal resistance movement is by no means the ideal way of dealing with such a movement.

If a Communist-supported guerrilla movement is to be re-sisted effectively, there must be a solid base of resistance *within* the threatened country. But the weapons and the military ex-pertise can be provided from outside. This is the chief reason why Kennedy has insisted on a greatly expanded guerrilla and antiguerrilla training program. . . .

[*Saturday Evening Post*, March 31, 1962. Reprinted by permission.]

50. Foreign Minister Ch'en Yi Comments on Kennedy's Grand Strategy, April 4, 1962

U.S. President Kennedy's threat about the United States not scrupling to take the initiative in using nuclear weapons has been sharply condemned by Vice-Premier Chen Yi.

At the reception to celebrate the 17th anniversary of Hungary's liberation given by the Hungarian Ambassador Martin Ferenc on April 4 in Peking, Vice-Premier Chen Yi said: "At a time when the people of the world are fervently hoping for positive results at the Geneva disarmament conference, the United States is threatening to resume nuclear tests in the atmosphere. President Kennedy's statement that the United States will not scruple to take the initiative in using nuclear weapons and thus launching a 'preventive' nuclear war is particularly outrageous. It thoroughly exposes Kennedy for what he really is."

"With the daily increasing strength of the socialist camp and the vigorous growth of the national-liberation movement, U.S. imperialism has become more cunning and more adventurist than ever. It persists in its military occupation of West Berlin, and continually commits military provocations and creates tension. In Asia, it has already gone into an undeclared war in south Viet Nam," the Vice-Premier added.

"The socialist camp is powerful and will never be cowed," the Vice-Premier stressed. "The world's people all oppose nuclear war. We socialist countries will make every possible effort to safeguard world peace. We believe that world war can be averted."

In conclusion, Vice-Premier Chen Yi pointed out: "If U.S. imperialism should first use nuclear weapons and impose a nu-clear war on the people of the world, it can be said with certainty that it is U.S. imperialism, as the first to use nuclear weapons, that will be destroyed."

[*Peking Review*, No. 15, April 13, 1962, p. 6.]

51. *Peking Review* Comments on Kennedy's Grand Strategy, August 10, 1962 (Extracts)

Kennedy has summed up his experience in suppressing the national and democratic revolutionary movements during the period since his inauguration. He has paid special attention to the lesson of Cuba. Writing about this, Stewart Alsop, a spokesman for U.S. monopoly capital, said: "One thought was obvious. This country's great stock of nuclear weapons had no direct bearing on the Cuban situation at all." He added: "As in the case of Cuba, not one of Kennedy's advisers has ever suggested that the way to deal with the Pathet Lao or the Viet Cong is to begin dropping nuclear weapons in the jungle." He also declared that Kennedy had time and again discovered that "all these experiences pointed inexorably to the same conclusions. The West's near-total reliance on the nuclear weapon could be fatal in the end. The West must have other means of exerting its power with limited means for limited ends." This explains the emphasis in the U.S. "grand strategy" on the capability to make a "choice" short of an all-out nuclear war; this also explains the demand for the effective use of "limited war" and "special war" to defend the so-called "frontiers of freedom."

The Kennedy Administration is turning south Viet Nam and Southeast Asia into testing grounds for its "special warfare." It intends to apply its "experiences" of buccaneering in this region to other parts of Asia and to Africa and Latin America. In order to extend the application of this "strategy" to various parts of the world, Kennedy openly called upon U.S. military men to learn how to fight guerrilla war. In his address to the West Point Military Academy graduates on June 6, he declared that the way to deal with guerrilla war is a "challenge" that will face the United States "in the next decade," that the graduates of the U.S. military academies must be capable of conducting "special warfare" and that the special forces under the command of the U.S. military officers in the next decade will be "growing in number and importance and significance." . . .

The Kennedy Administration is stepping up its preparations for three kinds of war—all-out nuclear war, "limited war," and "special warfare." It is playing the role of a world gendarme, attempting to defend the "frontiers of freedom," achieve "a closing off of areas of vulnerability" and suppress revolutionary struggles in all parts of the world. It will inevitably find itself falling into a position of increasing isolation as Enemy No. 1 of the people of the world. Militarily, this "strategy" can only result in such weaknesses as a long frontline, a distant rear, scattered strength and extreme passivity. Economically, since it requires both a speedy development of nuclear weapons and the expansion of conventional armaments, it will inevitably add to the burdens of military expenditure and aggravate the deepening financial crisis of the United States.

Although Kennedy's "grand strategy" sums up the lessons of defeat suffered so far during his term of office and lays down a series of still more cunning, sinister and adventurist principles for its policies of aggression and war, it is beyond doubt that U.S. imperialism can never overcome its weaknesses nor solve its inherent contradictions. It will never be able to resist the trend of historical development.

In face of this counter-revolutionary "grand strategy" of the Kennedy Administration, all the peace-loving people of the world must heighten their vigilance and wage a blow-for-blow struggle against it. They must remain on guard and not make light of it. So long as the people of the whole world strengthen their unity and fight resolutely, they will surely defeat this counter-revolutionary "grand strategy" of U.S. imperialism, safeguard the independence and freedom of the peoples and secure lasting world peace and social progress for mankind.

[Jen Ko-ping, "US Imperialists' 'Grand Strategy,' " *Peking Review,* No. 32, August 10, 1962, pp. 13, 15.]

MAO TSE-TUNG SUPPORTS THE AMERICAN NEGROES

52. Mao's Statement on the Racial Situation in the United States, August 8, 1963 (Extracts)

An American Negro leader now taking refuge in Cuba, Mr. Robert Williams, the former President of the Monroe, North

Carolina Chapter of the National Association for the Advancement of Coloured People, has twice this year asked me for a statement in support of the American Negroes' struggle against racial discrimination. I wish to take this opportunity, on behalf of the Chinese people, to express our resolute support for the American Negroes in their struggle against racial discrimination and for freedom and equal rights. . . .

The speedy development of the struggle of the American Negroes is a manifestation of the sharpening of class struggle and national struggle within the United States; it has been causing increasing anxiety to the U.S. ruling circles. The Kennedy Administration has resorted to cunning two-faced tactics. On the one hand, it continues to connive at and take part in the discrimination against and persecution of Negroes; it even sends troops to suppress them. On the other hand, it is parading as an advocate of the "defence of human rights" and "the protection of the civil rights of Negroes," is calling upon the Negro people to exercise "restraint," is proposing to Congress the so-called "civil rights legislation," in an attempt to lull the fighting will of the Negro people and deceive the masses throughout the country. However, these tactics of the Kennedy Administration are being seen through by more and more of the Negroes. The fascist atrocities committed by the U.S. imperialists against the Negro people have laid bare the true nature of the so-called democracy and freedom in the United States and revealed the inner link between the reactionary policies pursued by the U.S. Government at home and its policies of aggression abroad.

I call upon the workers, peasants, revolutionary intellectuals, enlightened elements of the bourgeoisie and other enlightened personages of all colours in the world, white, black, yellow, brown, etc., to unite to oppose the racial discrimination practised by U.S. imperialism and to support the American Negroes in their struggle against racial discrimination. In the final analysis, a national struggle is a question of class struggle. In the United States, it is only the reactionary ruling circles among the whites who are oppressing the Negro people. They can in no way represent the workers, farmers, revolutionary intellectuals and other enlightened persons who comprise the overwhelming majority of the white people. At present, it is the handful of imperialists, headed by the United States, and their supporters, the reactionaries in different countries, who are carrying out oppression, aggression and intimidation against the overwhelming majority of the nations and peoples of the world. We are in the majority and they are in the minority. At most, they make up less than 10 per cent of the 3,000 million population of the world. I am firmly convinced that, with the support of more than 90 per cent of the people of the world, the American Negroes will be victorious in their just struggle. The evil system of colonialism and imperialism grew up along with the enslavement of Negroes and the trade in Negroes, it will surely come to its end with the thorough emancipation of the black people.

[*Peking Review,* No. 33, August 16, 1963, pp. 6–7.]

CHINA CONDEMNS THE PARTIAL TEST-BAN TREATY

53. Chinese Government Statement on the Partial Test-Ban Treaty, July 31, 1963 (Extracts)

This is a treaty signed by three nuclear powers. By this treaty they attempt to consolidate their nuclear monopoly and bind the hands of all the peace-loving countries subjected to the nuclear threat.

This treaty signed in Moscow is a big fraud to fool the people of the world. It runs diametrically counter to the wishes of the peace-loving people of the world.

The people of the world demand general disarmament and a complete ban on nuclear weapons; this treaty completely divorces the cessation of nuclear tests from the total prohibition of nuclear weapons, legalizes the continued manufacture, stock-piling and use of nuclear weapons by the three nuclear powers, and runs counter to disarmament.

The people of the world demand the complete cessation of nuclear tests; this treaty leaves out the prohibition of underground nuclear tests, an omission which is particularly advantageous for the further development of nuclear weapons by U.S. imperialism.

The people of the world demand the defence of world peace and the elimination of the threat of nuclear war; this treaty actually strengthens the position of nuclear powers for nuclear blackmail and increases the danger of imperialism launching a nuclear war and a world war.

If this big fraud is not exposed, it can do even greater harm.

It is unthinkable for the Chinese Government to be a party to this dirty fraud. The Chinese Government regards it as its unshirkable and sacred duty to thoroughly expose this fraud.

The Chinese Government is firmly opposed to this treaty which harms the interests of the people of the whole world and the cause of world peace.

Clearly, this treaty has no restraining effect on the U.S. policies of nuclear war preparation and nuclear blackmail. It in no way hinders the United States from proliferating nuclear weapons, expanding armament or making nuclear threats. The central purpose of this treaty is, through a partial ban on nuclear tests, to prevent all the threatened peace-loving countries, including China, from increasing their defence capability, so that the United States may be more unbridled in threatening and blackmailing these countries. . . .

For these reasons, the Government of the People's Republic of China hereby proposes the following:

(1) All countries in the world, both nuclear and nonnuclear, solemnly declare that they will prohibit and destroy nuclear weapons completely, thoroughly, totally and resolutely. Concretely speaking, they will not use nuclear weapons, nor export, nor import, nor manufacture, nor test, nor stockpile them; and they will destroy all the existing nuclear weapons and their means of delivery in the world, and disband all the existing establishments for the research, testing and manufacture of nuclear weapons in the world.

(2) In order to fulfill the above undertakings step by step, the following measures shall be adopted first:

a. Dismantle all military bases, including nuclear bases, on foreign soil, and withdraw from abroad all nuclear weapons and their means of delivery.

b. Establish a nuclear weapon–free zone of the Asian and Pacific region, including the United States, the Soviet Union, China and Japan; a nuclear weapon–free zone of Central Europe; a nuclear weapon–free zone of Africa; and a nuclear weapon–free zone of Latin America. The countries possessing nuclear weapons shall undertake due obligations with regard to each of the nuclear-free zones.

c. Refrain from exporting and importing in any form nuclear weapons and technical data for their manufacture.

d. Cease all nuclear tests, including underground nuclear tests.

(3) A conference of the government heads of all the countries

of the world shall be convened to discuss the question of complete prohibition and thorough destruction of nuclear weapons and the question of taking the above-mentioned four measures in order to realize step by step the complete prohibition and thorough destruction of nuclear weapons. . . .

[*Peking Review,* No. 31, August 2, 1963, pp. 7–8.]

54. Kennedy's Assessment of the Chinese Threat at His Press Conference, August 1, 1963

Q. Some reputable experts estimate that it will be at least 10 years before Communist China could become a full-fledged nuclear power. Against that background, could you expand a little bit your answer to a previous question on just how we assess the power and the threat of Communist China today.

THE PRESIDENT. Well, we assess its power at 700 million people, increasing at 14 million or 15 million a year, surrounded by countries which are, in every case but one, much smaller, which are faced with very difficult geographic and social problems, which do not have a strong national history. So that we find a great, powerful force in China, organized and directed by the government along Stalinist lines, surrounded by weaker countries. So this we regard as a menacing situation.

In addition, as I said, that government is not only Stalinist in its internal actions, but also has called for war, international war, in order to advance the final success of the Communist cause. We regard that as a menacing factor. And then you introduce into that mix, nuclear weapons. As you say, it may take some years, maybe a decade, before they become a full-fledged nuclear power, but we are going to be around in the 1970's, and we would like to take some steps now which would lessen that prospect that a future President might have to deal with.

I would regard that combination, if it is still in existence in the 1970's, of weak countries around it, 700 million people, a Stalinist internal regime, and nuclear powers, and a government determined on war as a means of bringing about its ultimate success, as potentially a more dangerous situation than any we faced since the end of the Second War, because the Russians pursued in most cases their ambitions with some caution. Even in the case of the most overt aggression, which was the North

Korean invasion of South Korea, other forces were used and not the Russians.

So what we are anxious to do, and one of the reasons why we have moved into the limited test ban, even though we recognize its limitations, is because we don't want to find the world in as great a danger as it could be in the 1970's, for the reasons that I have described.

[*Public Papers of the Presidents of the United States: John F. Kennedy, 1963* (Washington D.C.: U.S. Government Printing Office, 1964), p. 320.]

THE UNITED STATES ACCEPTS THAT THE CHINESE COMMUNIST REGIME IS HERE TO STAY

55. Assistant Secretary of State for Far Eastern Affairs Roger Hilsman's Speech on China Policy to the Commonwealth Club, San Francisco, December 13, 1963 (Extracts)

Let me begin by disposing of a myth: it is frequently charged that the United States Government is "ignoring" China and its 700 million people.

This is simply untrue. We do not ignore our ally, the Government of the Republic of China. We do not ignore the 12 million people in Taiwan. Nor, in fact, do we ignore the people on the mainland. We are very much aware of them, and we have a deep friendship for them. Nor, finally, do we ignore the Communist leadership which has established itself on the mainland. We meet with them from time to time, as at the periodic talks between our Ambassadors in Warsaw. We should like to be less ignorant of them and for them to be less ignorant of us. To this end, we have been striving for years to arrange an exchange of correspondents; but we have been put off with the assertion that, so long as the "principal issue"—which they define in terms of their absurd charge that we are "occupying" Taiwan—is unresolved, there can be no progress on "secondary issues."

If we have not persuaded the Chinese Communists to allow an exchange of correspondents and to lower the wall of secrecy with which they surround themselves, we have nevertheless spent considerable effort in trying to understand what manner of men the Chinese Communists are, what are their ambitions, and what are the problems which stand in their way. We have tried to be objective, and to see to it that dislike of Communism does not becloud our ability to see the facts.

What is the essence of our analysis? What sort of people are the Chinese Communists? What kind of power is at their disposal?

These are important questions. We shall be in danger if we let our policies be guided by emotionalism, our own thought processes by clichés. Our policies flow from the answers to these questions, and it is not enough that we prove ourselves properly anti-Communist by repeating anti-Communist phrases.

First and foremost, the Chinese Communist leaders have shown themselves to be dangerously overconfident and wedded to outdated theories, but pragmatic when their existence is threatened.

Take the example of the so-called "great leap forward" of 1958–1960. You have undoubtedly heard that it was a catastrophe, and so it was. . . .

Nevertheless, the Communists did correct the most dangerous mistakes of the "great leap forward." When their survival depended upon it, they showed flexibility in meeting the threat, and we have no reason to believe that there is a present likelihood that the Communist regime will be overthrown. . . .

A second major fact about Communist China's leaders is their parochialism: they have seen extraordinarily little of the outside world, and their world view is further constricted by their ideology. . . . Mao and his colleagues are simply unaware of some of the vital ideas which have moved civilisation. For them, there is no problem of the relationship between man and society: the individual must yield. These men know nothing of the genuine purposes of democracy, or of constitutional government. These are men who say that "all progressive wars are just, and all wars that impede progress are unjust," and who then reserve the right to decide what is "progress." These are men who comfortably clothe their own dictatorship in a cloak of doctrinal righteousness. Where such men triumph, some of civilisation's most precious values are eclipsed. And they have proclaimed their determination to spread their system everywhere.

Is this permanent? Must we live indefinitely with such men?

Perhaps I am too optimistic; but there is some evidence of evolutionary forces at work in mainland China. As I have said, the present leaders have seen remarkably little of the outside world. They have conquered mainland China. They may believe that, with concepts unchanged, they can go on to conquer the world. These leaders, however, were deep in rural China when the rest of the world was debating Keynes and sharpening the tools of economic analysis. They may not yet have absorbed all the lessons of the "great leap forward": but the more sophisticated second echelon of leadership undoubtedly knows that it was simple ignorance of the techniques of administering a complex economy which led to many of the mistakes of 1958. This economic example is particularly striking; it could be repeated throughout the sciences and humanities. The leaders may not know it, but the intellectuals know that the official explanation is not adequate as a description of reality. As these ideas seep upward or as the present leaders retire, this awareness may eventually profoundly erode the present simple view with which the leadership regards the world. . . .

What about the appeal of the Chinese Communists to the new nations of the world? They have scored some successes with extremists everywhere in identifying themselves as the radical end of the Communist movement. Peking has been alert to the world-wide opportunities for playing on nationalistic differences and prejudices and gaining toeholds within the so-called National Liberation Movements or among the dissatisfied and disgruntled. We may expect this process to continue. These successes, however, may be more apparent than real. As extremists approach power, they may become less radical and may weigh more heavily the questions as to who can offer them more support and more protection. . . .

You have expected me to talk about American policy, and I have talked mostly about Communist China's prospects. I have had a reason for doing this. Policies based upon a misapprehension of reality may lead us far from the goals we seek. There has perhaps been more emotion about our China policy than about our policy toward any single country since World War II. Yet our nation must look squarely at China, pursuing policies which will protect the interests of our country, of the free world, and of men of good will everywhere.

Our prime objective concerning Communist China is that it should not subvert or commit aggression against its free world neighbours. It must not be allowed to accomplish for Communism through force of arms that success which it has rarely achieved at the ballot box.

President Kennedy called our purposes in the Far East "peaceful and defensive." And so they remain. . . .

Our military assistance in the Far East has been given with the objective of permitting Asian nations to develop the forces to defend their own borders and to protect themselves against probing attacks and paramilitary challenges. This is a necessary and grave responsibility. . . .

We believe that the policies which have proved their worth with Moscow are equally valid for our long-term relations with Peking. But we also believe that our approach should be adapted to the differences in behaviour between the two, as they relate to our own national objectives.

First and foremost, we fully honour our close and friendly ties with the people of the Republic of China on Taiwan, and with their Government. We conceive of this relationship not as an historical accident but as a matter of basic principle. So long as Peking insists on the destruction of this relationship as the sine qua non for any basic improvement in relations between ourselves and Communist China, there can be no prospect for such an improvement.

Our differing policies toward the Soviet Union and Communist China derive, secondly, from their differing attitudes towards negotiations, as such, even in limited areas. Faced with the realities of the nuclear age, the Soviet Union appears to recognise that certain interests—notably survival—are shared by all mankind. Peking, however, remains wedded to a fundamentalist form of Communism which emphasises violent revolution, even if it threatens the physical ruin of the civilised world. It refuses to admit that there are common interests which cross ideological lines.

Third, United States policy is influenced by Chinese Communism's obsessive suspicion of the outside world, far exceeding even that of the Soviet Union. Whereas Moscow appears to have learned that free world readiness to negotiate limited common interests is not a sign of weakness, Peking regards any conciliatory gesture as evidence of weakness and an opportunity for exploitation.

Perhaps the best evidence of this paranoid view of the world came from Peking's Foreign Minister Chen Yi, who declared, at the height of China's food crisis in 1962, that his Government would never accept any aid from America because this would mean "handing our vast market over to America." Given the near-subsistence level of the society and the limited purchasing power of the government, this view of American intentions could only be conjured up by men possessed of an unremitting distrust of all external peoples and a naive sense of their own economic prospects.

Fourth are the differing circumstances and opportunities on the peripheries of the Soviet Union and 'Communist China. The Soviet Union and European members of its bloc border on long-established, relatively stable states defended by powerful, locally based—as well as more distant—deterrent and defensive forces. Communist China's neighbours, on the other hand, include newly established states struggling to maintain their independence, with very limited defence forces. There is a wider range of opportunities for aggression and subversion available to Peking, which renders it even more important that in dealing with Peking we do not permit that regime to underestimate free world firmness and determination. . . .

We are confronted in Communist China with a regime which finds no ground of common interest with those whose ideals it does not share, which has used hatred as an engine of national policy. The United States is the central figure in their demonology, and the target of a sustained fury of invective. After President Kennedy's assassination, while other nations—Communist and free—shared our grief, the Chinese Communist "Daily Worker" published a cartoon of a man sprawled on the ground, with the caption "Kennedy bites the dust." If this speaks for the Chinese Communist leadership, I am confident that it does not speak for most Chinese. . . .

We do not know what changes may occur in the attitudes of future Chinese leaders. But if I may paraphrase a classic canon of our past, we pursue today towards Communist China a policy of the open door; we are determined to keep the door open to the possibility of change, and not to slam it shut against any developments which might advance our national good, serve the free world, and benefit the people of China. Patience is not unique to the Chinese. We, too, can maintain our positions without being provoked to unseemly action or despairing of what the future may hold. We will not sow the dragon's seed of hate which may bear bitter fruit in future generations of China's millions. But neither will we betray our interests and those of our Allies to appease the ambitions of Communist China's leaders. . . .

[U.S. Information Service, London, Press Release, January 7, 1964.]

56. *People's Daily* Article by "Observer," "US Policy Towards China Is in a Blind Alley," February 19, 1964 (Extracts)

Close upon each other's heels in the past three months, Dean Rusk, Averell Harriman, Roger Hilsman, Adlai Stevenson, and other responsible officials of the U.S. Administration have made speeches or statements on U.S. policy towards China and towards Asia in general. U.S. press reports disclose that the keynote of these speeches and statements was set by the Kennedy-Johnson Administration after three years of study. It can be summed up as follows:

1. China pursues "aggressive and lone-wolf policies" and is "an increasing threat to the rest of the world";

2. The "prime objective" of U.S. China policy is to prevent China from "subverting or committing aggression against its free world neighbours";

3. The United States will examine its China policy "dispassionately, objectively, and coolly," attaching importance to "flexibility" and "keeping the door open to the possibility of change";

4. China would have to make "very fundamental and very far-reaching" changes before the United States could consider "the possibility of a break" in its relations with her;

5. The United States has seen "no modification of their [China's] attitude or policy," so "there is no present prospect for any significant change" in U.S. China policy.

It is almost 15 years since the founding of the People's Republic of China. During this period, the United States has consistently followed a policy of hostility towards China. What, then, is the aim of the U.S. ruling group in suddenly unburdening themselves of this spate of empty words about their policy towards China?

The matter is crystal clear. With U.S. China policy on its last legs and U.S. aggressive policy towards Asia running up against a stone wall, the policy-makers in Washington want to extricate themselves from a position of isolation and passivity by means of a new anti-China propaganda campaign. . . .

Much as it desires to do so, U.S. imperialism cannot overthrow, "contain" or isolate China, nor deny its existence. Suffice it to point out that while Dulles, a fierce anti-China warrior who bore an inveterate hatred for the Chinese people, arrogantly declared seven years ago that communist rule in China was "a passing and not a perpetual phase," his disciple Hilsman had to admit reluctantly that "we have no reason to believe that there is a present likelihood that the communist regime will be overthrown." Meanwhile, the U.S. imperialist policy of hostility towards China has become more and more an object of derision and opposition in all parts of the world. U.S. policy towards China has been universally condemned as stupid. So it is not difficult to imagine the agony of mind and anxiety of the U.S. ruling group as they dither in their anti-China blind alley.

U.S. China policy is only part of the U.S. policy of aggression in Asia. In its bid to rule the roost in Asia since the end of World War II, U.S. imperialism has been following a policy of aggression and expansion in a most truculent form. Its tactics are varied but they may be boiled down to:

1. Buying over and fostering the most reactionary forces, putting its puppets in power, enslaving the people of the countries and territories concerned and reducing them to the status of U.S. colonies;

2. By means of military alliances and blocs, binding a number of countries to its war chariot, building military bases and posting aggressor troops to intimidate these countries and keep them under its control;

3. Political, military and economic infiltration and control over the lifelines of other countries through "aid";

4. Interfering in the internal affairs of other countries by political subversion, military threats and even direct armed aggression;

5. Intriguing to make "Asians fight Asians." . . .

U.S. imperialism is running into a package of troubles in south Viet Nam, Laos, Japan, Cambodia, Indonesia and Pakistan. It is, in short, surrounded by its enemies, forsaken by its friends and deserted by its followers in Asia.

The present situation in Asia is characterized by the irresistible momentum of the struggle of the people to win and uphold national independence and the outbreak of anti-U.S. imperialist storms everywhere. "U.S. imperialism, get out of Asia!" has become a catch-word of the Asian peoples. No wonder responsible officials in Washington cry out in alarm that in the Asian countries "the passions of nationalism . . . are at flood tide."

Precisely because the U.S. ruling circles are confronted with the irreversible situation in China and Asia described above, they are compelled to defend the U.S. policy of aggression against China and Asia and to make excuses for its defeat. They attempt to shift on to China the responsibility for strained Sino-U.S. relations and for the threat to peace in Asia.

The Chinese and Asian peoples are only too familiar with such U.S. imperialist tricks. . . .

The U.S. imperialists have tried to force others to believe that their policy towards China is not stiff. They have lately made a special effort to appear "flexible," pretending that they have adopted a "policy of the open door" towards China. From "burying its head in the sand" to "keeping the door open to the possibility of change," the United States seems to have taken a step forward. But, just a minute. Let's see what kind of stuff is this "policy of the open door" advocated by the U.S. ruling group. . . .

One is told that this time it is not China that is asked to "open its door," but that the United States itself will "open its door." What strange talk is this! It turns out that though the door seems to open in a different direction, there is, in essence, no change whatsoever in the nature of U.S. aggression against China. It is not a door of friendship such as is desired by the Chinese and American peoples that the United States has opened. That door has long been shut tight by the U.S. Government. What it has opened is a door for accepting surrender—a demand that China should completely change its policy towards the United States. First of all, it demands that China should accept a situation of "two Chinas" in which the United States will be permitted to occupy China's territory of Taiwan permanently; and secondly, China should drop its support for the national-liberation movements in the other Asian countries. In short, the U.S. policy of hostility to China and aggression against Asia will remain unchanged while China must capitulate to the United States.

These conditions have on one occasion been explained fairly clearly by Adlai Stevenson. He said: "Our position is very clear. The Chinese Communists still claim Taiwan. They still are bombarding the islands. They are still encouraging the Viet Cong. They are still at war in Korea. They are still stirring up the Pathet Lao. These are all policies that originate in Peking. Until this attitude changes, until the present aggressive position of the Chinese People's Republic is altered, there can be no change in our policy toward them."

The preconditions advanced by U.S. imperialism for improving Sino-U.S. relations are utterly preposterous. Everybody knows that the tension in Sino-U.S. relations stems from the forcible occupation by U.S. imperialism of China's territory of Taiwan and its threats against China. Therefore, to improve Sino-U.S. relations, it is necessary for U.S. imperialism to get out of Taiwan and the Taiwan Straits, and not for China to relinquish its sovereign rights and territory. Likewise, tension in Asia derives from the U.S. imperialist policies of aggression and war there. Therefore, to relax tension in Asia, it is necessary for U.S. imperialism to get out of Asia and not for China to refrain from supporting the peoples in their struggles to win and uphold national independence. . . .

[*Peking Review,* No. 9, February 28, 1964, pp. 9–12.]

CHINA BECOMES A NUCLEAR POWER

57. Chou En-lai's Cable to All Heads of Government Proposing a World Summit Conference on the Prohibition and Destruction of All Nuclear Weapons, October 17, 1964

On October 16, 1964, China exploded an atom bomb, thus successfully making its first nuclear test. On the same day, the Chinese Government issued a statement on this event, setting forth in detail China's position on the question of nuclear weapons.

The Chinese Government consistently stands for the complete prohibition and thorough destruction of nuclear weapons. China has been compelled to conduct nuclear testing and develop nuclear weapons. China's mastering of nuclear weapons is entirely for defence and for protecting the Chinese people from the U.S. nuclear threat.

The Chinese Government solemnly declares that at no time and in no circumstances will China be the first to use nuclear weapons.

The Chinese Government will continue to work for the complete prohibition and thorough destruction of nuclear weapons through international consultations and, for this purpose, has put forward in its statement the following proposal:

That a summit conference of all the countries of the world be convened to discuss the question of the complete prohibition and thorough destruction of nuclear weapons, and that as the first step, the summit conference should reach an agreement to the effect that the nuclear powers and those countries which may soon become nuclear powers undertake not to use nuclear weapons, neither to use them against non-nuclear countries and nuclear-free zones, nor against each other.

It is the common aspiration of all peace-loving countries and people of the world to prevent a nuclear war and eliminate nuclear weapons. The Chinese Government sincerely hopes that its proposal will be given favourable consideration and positive response by your Government.

Please accept the assurances of my highest consideration.

[*Peking Review,* No. 43, October 23, 1964, p. 6.]

58. President Lyndon Johnson's Comments on China's First Nuclear Test in a Television Broadcast, October 18, 1964 (Extract)

No American should treat this matter lightly. Until this week, only four powers had entered the dangerous world of nuclear explosions. Whatever their differences, all four are sober and serious states, with long experience as major powers in the modern world. Communist China has no such experience. Its nuclear pretensions are both expensive and cruel to its people. It fools no one when it offers to trade away its first small accumulation of nuclear power against the mighty arsenals of those who limit Communist Chinese ambitions. It shocks us by its readiness to pollute the atmosphere with fallout. But this explosion remains a fact, sad and serious. We must not, we have not, and we will not ignore it.

I discussed the limited meaning of this event in a statement on last Friday. The world already knows that we were not surprised; that our defense plans take full account of this development; that we reaffirm our defense commitments in Asia; that it is a long, hard road from a first nuclear device to an effective weapons system; and that our strength is overwhelming now and will be kept that way.

But what I have in my mind tonight is a different part of the meaning of this explosion at Lop Nor. Communist China's expensive and demanding effort tempts other states to equal folly. Nuclear spread is dangerous to all mankind. What if there should come to be 10 nuclear powers, or maybe 20 nuclear powers? What if we must learn to look everywhere for the restraint which our own example now sets for a few? Will the human race be safe in such a day?

The lesson of Lop Nor is that we are right to recognize the danger of nuclear spread, that we must continue to work against it—and we will.

First: We will continue to support the limited test ban treaty, which has made the air cleaner. We call on the world—especially Red China—to join the nations which have signed that treaty.

Second: We will continue to work for an ending of all nuclear tests of every kind, by solid and verified agreement.

Third: We continue to believe that the struggle against nuclear spread is as much in the Soviet interest as in our own. We will be ready to join with them and all the world in working to avoid it.

Fourth: The nations that do not seek national nuclear weapons can be sure that, if they need our strong support against some threat of nuclear blackmail, then they will have it. . . .

[*AFP,* 1964, p. 885.]

VI. The Impact of the War in Vietnam

THE GROWING American involvement in Vietnam after the 1964 presidential election caused considerable concern in Peking. The regular bombing of North Vietnam from March, 1965, and the dispatch of increasing numbers of US troops to South Vietnam threatened to pose for the Chinese a problem similar to the one they had had to face during the Korean War. The dangers of the situation sparked a major debate in Peking during 1965 over the strategy China should adopt. There was disagreement over the precise nature of the American threat to China: Was it really going to be Korea all over again with the Americans sending ground troops across the north-south frontiers toward the Chinese border? Was there a possibility of an American attack on China? What was the best form of defense in the event of such an attack?

The debate was intense; it helped lose the Chinese chief-of-staff his job.[1] The view that prevailed was Mao's. It was explained by Defense Minister Lin Piao in a major article commemorating the twentieth annniversary of the defeat of Japan. Entitled "Long Live the Victory of People's War!" the article prescribed guerrilla

---

[1] See Harry Harding and Melvin Gurtov, *The Purge of Lo Jui-ch'ing: The Politics of Chinese Strategic Planning* (Santa Monica: RAND, R-548-PR, February, 1971). Some analysts have suggested that there were further disagreements over whether China should patch up its quarrel with the Soviet Union and send troops to Vietnam; see Uri Ra'anan, "Peking's Foreign Policy 'Debate,' 1965–1966," and Donald Zagoria, "The Strategic Debate in Peking," in Tang Tsou (ed.), *China in Crisis: II. China's Policy in Asia and America's Alternatives* (Chicago: Unversity of Chicago Press, 1968).

warfare as the main form of struggle against a formidable foe, asserted that this kind of "people's war" must be conducted primarily by the inhabitants of the country in question, and warned that if America attacked China then Peking would be free to decide how and where the war should be fought (59). The implications of the article were that the National Liberation Front (NLF) could win in South Vietnam by themselves if they used the correct (i.e., Maoist) strategy and tactics, and that the NLF would have to win by themselves even though they would get Chinese assistance. The Chinese would only fight if attacked, or, probably, if North Vietnam were invaded, but then might expand the war through Southeast Asia. In fact, Lin did not seem to rate the direct threat to China very high.[2] Another top Chinese leader, Foreign Minister Ch'en Yi, taunted the Americans, daring them to attack China, but warning again that if they did the war would have no boundaries (60).

Those Chinese leaders who did not think a direct American attack likely were presumably encouraged by the hearings held by the Senate Foreign Relations Committee during March, 1966. The testimony of a galaxy of China scholars showed that there had developed over the years among those particularly concerned a strong desire for changes in US China policy—not radical changes perhaps, but changes nevertheless. Columbia University Professor A. Doak Barnett characterized US China policy over the previous seventeen years as "containment and isolation." He called for "containment but not isolation." [3]

It was perhaps in response to this mood that the American Government announced in April that it would now permit Chinese scholars and scientists to visit the United States, a goodwill gesture that was promptly rejected.[4] A more important sign that America did not intend to attack China was the long statement by Secre-

---

[2] See Harding and Gurtov, *op. cit.*, pp. 41–42.

[3] *U.S. Policy with Respect to Mainland China: Hearings before the Committee on Foreign Relations, U.S. Senate, 89th Congress, 2nd Session* (Washington, D.C.: U.S. Government Printing Office, 1966), p. 4.

[4] *China and U.S. Far East Policy, 1945–1966* (Washington, D.C.: Congressional Quarterly Service, 1967), p. 184.

tary of State Dean Rusk on China policy released on April 17 (**61**). Though there was much in the statement that the Chinese disliked, it did indicate a desire for better relations and did not contain threats of attack.

However, wars are often difficult to contain. On April 23, American fighters shot down two North Vietnamese MIG-17s 70 miles north of Hanoi in the first major air battle of the war in Vietnam. A 1965 statement by Rusk that there would be no sanctuary in this war was reiterated for the benefit of China. On April 28, after Senator Robert Kennedy had warned about the dangers of expanding the war in this way, it was announced that the decision to send American aircraft in pursuit of Chinese planes over China would be taken by the President himself.[5]

On May 9, China conducted its third nuclear test, its first involving thermonuclear material, a step toward an H-bomb.[6] In the light of the new dangers of Sino-American aerial warfare— the first clash took place on May 12, according to Peking—the Chinese may have felt there was some possibility of an American pre-emptive strike against their nuclear installations. This could account for the publication on May 10 of a four-point statement by Chou En-lai of China's policy toward the United States (**62**). The first sentences of the four points added up to the message and the warning Chou was trying to get across: "China will not take the initiative to provoke a war with the United States. . . . The Chinese mean what they say. . . . China is prepared. . . . Once the war breaks out, it will have no boundaries." [8]

Concern over a pre-emptive strike may also have accounted for Chou En-lai's revelation on May 10 of China's eighteen-month-old proposal for a Sino-American agreement on no-first-use of

[5] *Ibid.,* pp. 185–86.
[6] *Peking Review,* No. 20, May 13, 1966, p. 4.
[7] *Ibid.,* p. 5.
[8] According to an editorial note, *ibid.,* Chou's statement had been made on April 10 in an interview given to Mr. Ejaz Husain of the Pakistani paper *Dawn.* However, the four-point statement does not appear in what is described as the full text of the interview in *Dawn,* April 27, 1966.

nuclear weapons.[9] Questioned at his press conference, Dean Rusk stated that "mere declarations on such matters would not be adequate" (63). But it was apparently felt necessary to make a more positive response. At the ambassadorial meeting on May 25, the American side inquired whether the Chinese would be prepared to sign the partial test-ban treaty in return for an American signature on a no-first-use pledge.[10] China's response was an indignant negative (64).

The Americans continued to evidence a desire for better relations. In a speech on July 12, President Johnson called for reconciliation and cooperation with China (65). However, the deepening American involvement in the Vietnam war effectively prevented the Chinese from making any response at this time, especially in view of Soviet insinuations that Peking talked belligerently about Vietnam but was in reality quite happy to continue negotiating with Washington. Such Soviet taunts led the Chinese Government to authorize their delegate to the Sino-American ambassadorial talks to break the agreement on confidentiality and release his statement at the meeting on September 7, 1966 (66). The statement rejected all recent American friendly overtures and strongly condemned US actions in Vietnam.

By this time, China was already involved in the convulsion of the Cultural Revolution. For the next year and more, Peking's leaders had little time to spare for foreign relations. All China's ambassadors abroad—except for Huang Hua in Cairo—were recalled for re-education. Foreign Minister Ch'en Yi came under strong criticism from the Red Guards and eventually ceased to exercise his office. The most prominent aspect of Chinese foreign relations of the time was a succession of clashes, of varying degrees of severity, between the Red Guards and foreign diplomats in Peking. The worst incident was the sack of the British mission and the beating up of its personnel in the summer of 1967.

[9] In a speech at a banquet for the visiting Albanian Premier on May 10; see *Peking Review,* No. 21, May 20, 1966, p. 17.
[10] Young, *op. cit.,* pp. 266–67.

There was, of course, no American mission in Peking to suffer. The United States and China were therefore able to continue to keep their careful distance in Vietnam without the complications of diplomatic incidents. In mid-1968, as the turmoil of the Cultural Revolution was dying down, the Johnson administration made a final gesture toward Peking by inviting Chinese correspondents to cover the forthcoming presidential campaign (**67**). Under Secretary of State Nicholas Katzenbach made a major speech on China policy on May 21, 1968, but although he reiterated American interest in contracts and stressed strongly that there was no need for China to fear an American threat to China's security, he did not break any new ground (**68**). Nor could any major initiative have been expected in the last months of an unhappy administration.

59. Lin Piao, "Long Live the Victory of People's War!" September 2, 1965 (Extracts)

During the War of Resistance Against Japan, on the basis of his comprehensive analysis of the enemy and ourselves, Comrade Mao Tse-tung laid down the following strategic principle for the Communist-led Eighth Route and New Fourth Armies: "Guerrilla warfare is basic, but lose no chance for mobile warfare under favourable conditions." He raised guerrilla warfare to the level of strategy, because, if they are to defeat a formidable enemy, revolutionary armed forces should not fight with a reckless disregard for the consequences when there is a great disparity between their own strength and the enemy's. If they do, they will suffer serious losses and bring heavy setbacks to the revolution. Guerrilla warfare is the only way to mobilize and apply the whole strength of the people against the enemy, the only way to expand our forces in the course of the war, deplete and weaken the enemy, gradually change the balance of forces between the enemy and ourselves, switch from guerrilla to mobile warfare, and finally defeat the enemy. . . .

War of annihilation is the fundamental guiding principle of our military operations. This guiding principle should be put into effect regardless of whether mobile or guerrilla warfare is the primary form of fighting. It is true that in guerrilla warfare much should be done to disrupt and harass the enemy, but it is still necessary activity to advocate and fight battles of annihilation whenever conditions are favourable. In mobile warfare superior forces must be concentrated in every battle so that the enemy forces can be wiped out one by one. Comrade Mao Tse-tung has pointed out:

> A battle in which the enemy is routed is not basically decisive in a contest with a foe of great strength. A battle of annihilation, on the other hand, produces a great and immediate impact on any enemy. Injuring all of a man's ten fingers is not as effective as chopping off one, and routing ten enemy divisions is not as effective as annihilating one of them.

Battles of annihilation are the most effective way of hitting the enemy; each time one of his brigades or regiments is wiped out, he will have one brigade or regiment less, and the enemy forces will be demoralized and will disintegrate. By fighting battles of annihilation, our army is able to take prisoners of war or capture weapons from the enemy in every battle, and the morale of our army rises, our army units get bigger, our weapons become better, and our combat effectiveness continually increases. . . .

Comrade Mao Tse-tung has provided a masterly summary of the strategy and tactics of people's war: You fight in your way and we fight in ours; we fight when we can win and move away when we can't.

In other words, you rely on modern weapons and we rely on highly conscious revolutionary people; you give full play to your superiority and we give full play to ours; you have your way of fighting and we have ours. When you want to fight us, we don't let you and you can't even find us. But when we want to fight you, we make sure that you can't get away and we hit you squarely on the chin and wipe you out. When we are able to wipe you out, we do so with a vengeance; when we can't, we see to it that you don't wipe us out. It is opportunism if one won't fight when one can win. It is adventurism if one insists on fighting when one can't win. Fighting is the pivot of all our strategy and tactics. It is because of the necessity of fighting that we admit the necessity of moving away. The sole purpose of moving away is to fight and bring about the final and complete destruction of the enemy. This strategy and these tactics can be applied only when one relies on the broad masses of the people, and such application brings the superiority of people's war into full play. However superior he may be in technical equipment and whatever tricks he may resort to, the enemy will find himself in the passive position of having to receive blows, and the initiative will always be in our hands. . . .

The Chinese people enjoyed the support of other peoples in winning both the War of Resistance Against Japan and the People's Liberation War, and yet victory was mainly the result of the Chinese people's own efforts. Certain people assert that China's victory in the War of Resistance was due entirely to foreign assistance. This absurd assertion is in tune with that of the Japanese militarists.

The liberation of the masses is accomplished by the masses themselves—this is a basic principle of Marxism-Leninism. Revolution or people's war in any country is the business of the masses in that country and should be carried out primarily by their own efforts; there is no other way. . . .

It must be emphasized that Comrade Mao Tse-tung's theory of the establishment of rural revolutionary base areas and the encirclement of the cities from the countryside is of outstanding and universal practical importance for the present revolutionary struggles of all the oppressed nations and peoples in Asia, Africa, and Latin America against imperialism and its lackeys. . . .

Taking the entire globe, if North America and Western Europe can be called "the cities of the world," then Asia, Africa and Latin America constitute "the rural areas of the world." Since World War II, the proletarian revolutionary movement has for various reasons been temporarily held back in the North American and West European capitalist countries, while the people's revolutionary movement in Asia, Africa and Latin America has been growing vigorously. In a sense, the contemporary world revolution also presents a picture of the encirclement of cities by the rural areas. In the final analysis, the whole cause of world revolution hinges on the revolutionary struggles of the Asian, African and Latin American peoples who make up the overwhelming majority of the world's population. The socialist countries should regard it as their internationalist duty to support the people's revolutionary struggles in Asia, Africa and Latin America. . . .

Today, the conditions are more favourable than ever before for the waging of people's wars by the revolutionary peoples of Asia, Africa and Latin America against U.S. imperialism and its lackeys. . . .

Everything is divisible. And so is this colossus of U.S. imperialism. It can be split up and defeated. The peoples of Asia, Africa and Latin America and other regions can destroy it piece by piece, some striking at its head and others at its feet. That is why the greatest fear of U.S. imperialism is that people's wars will be launched in different parts of the world, and particularly in Asia, Africa and Latin America, and why it regards people's war as a mortal danger.

U.S. imperialism relies solely on its nuclear weapons to intimidate people. But these weapons cannot save U.S. imperialism from its doom. Nuclear weapons cannot be used lightly. U.S. imperialism has been condemned by the people of the whole world for its towering crime of dropping two atom bombs on Japan. If it uses nuclear weapons again, it will become isolated in the extreme. Moreover, the U.S. monopoly of nuclear weapons has long been broken; U.S. imperialism has these weapons, but others have them too. If it threatens other countries with nuclear weapons, U.S. imperialism will expose its own country to the same threat. For this reason, it will meet with strong opposition not only from the people elsewhere but also inevitably from the people in its own country. Even if U.S. imperialism brazenly uses nuclear weapons, it cannot conquer the people, who are indomitable. . . .

The spiritual atom bomb which the revolutionary people possess is a far more powerful and useful weapon than the physical atom bomb.

Viet Nam is the most convincing current example of a victim of aggression defeating U.S. imperialism by a people's war. The United States has made south Viet Nam a testing ground for the suppression of people's war. It has carried on this experiment for many years, and everybody can now see that the U.S. aggressors are unable to find a way of coping with people's war. On the other hand, the Vietnamese people have brought the power of people's war into full play in their struggle against the U.S. aggressors. The U.S. aggressors are in danger of being swamped in the people's war in Viet Nam. They are deeply worried that their defeat in Viet Nam will lead to a chain reaction. They are expanding the war in an attempt to save themselves from defeat. But the more they expand the war, the greater will be the chain reaction. The more they escalate the war, the heavier will be their fall and the more disastrous their defeat. The people in other parts of the world will see still more clearly that U.S. imperialism can be defeated, and that what the Vietnamese people can do, they can do too. . . .

The Khrushchov revisionists maintain that a single spark in any part of the globe may touch off a world nuclear conflagration and bring destruction to mankind. If this were true, our planet would have been destroyed time and time again. There have been wars of national liberation throughout the twenty years since World War II. But has any single one of them developed into a world war? Isn't it true that the U.S. imperialists' plans for a world war have been upset precisely thanks to the wars of national liberation in Asia, Africa and Latin America? By contrast, those who have done their utmost to stamp out the "sparks" of people's war have in fact encouraged U.S. imperialism in its aggressions and wars. . . .

The U.S. imperialists are now clamouring for another trial of strength with the Chinese people, for another large-scale ground war on the Asian mainland. If they insist on following in the footsteps of the Japanese fascists, well then, they may do so, if they please. The Chinese people definitely have ways of their own for coping with a U.S. imperialist war of aggression. Our methods are no secret. The most important one is still mobilization of the people, reliance on the people, making everyone a soldier and waging a people's war.

We want to tell the U.S. imperialists once again that the vast ocean of several hundred million Chinese people in arms will be more than enough to submerge your few million aggressor troops. If you dare to impose war on us, we shall gain freedom of action. It will then not be up to you to decide how the war will be fought. We shall fight in the ways most advantageous to us to destroy the enemy and wherever the enemy can be most easily destroyed. Since the Chinese people were able to destroy the Japanese aggressors twenty years ago, they are certainly still more capable of finishing off the U.S. aggressors today. The naval and air superiority you boast about cannot intimidate the Chinese people, and neither can the atom bomb you brandish at us. If you want to send troops, go ahead, the more the better. We will annihilate as many as you can send, and can even give you receipts. The Chinese people are a great, valiant people. We have the courage to shoulder the heavy burden of combating U.S. imperialism and to contribute our share in the struggle for final victory over this most ferocious enemy of the people of the world. . . .

If the U.S. imperialists should insist on launching a third world war, it can be stated categorically that many more hundreds of millions of people will turn to socialism; the imperialists will then have little room left on the globe; and it is possible that the whole structure of imperialism will collapse. . . .

[*Peking Review,* No. 36, September 3, 1965, pp. 18–19, 24, 26–27, 29.]

60. Ch'en Yi Tells His Press Conference That China Will Be Prepared If an Attack Comes, September 29, 1965 (Extracts)

The Chinese people are ready to make all necessary sacrifices in the fight against imperialism. It is up to the U.S. President and the Pentagon to decide whether the United States wants a big war with China today. We cherish no illusions about U.S. imperialism. We are fully prepared against U.S. aggression. If the U.S. imperialists are determined to launch a war of aggression against us, they are welcome to come sooner, to come as early as tomorrow. Let the Indian reactionaries, the British imperialists and the Japanese militarists come along with them! Let the modern revisionists act in co-ordination with them from the north! We will still win in the end. . . .

For sixteen years we have been waiting for the U.S. imperialists to come in and attack us. My hair has turned grey in waiting. Perhaps I will not have the luck to see the U.S. imperialist invasion of China, but my children may see it, and they will resolutely carry on the fight. Let no correspondent think that I am bellicose. It is the U.S. imperialists who are brutal and vicious and who bully others too much. They are bullying the Chinese, the Koreans, the Vietnamese, the Khmers, the Laotians, the Indonesians, the Congolese and the Dominicans. Even their ally France is being bullied by them. Those who are bullied by them have risen against them and become friends of China. This is of the United States' own making.

Should the U.S. imperialists invade China's mainland, we will take all necessary measures to defeat them. By then, war will have no boundaries. It is the United States, and not China, that will have broken down the boundaries. We are willing to respect boundaries, but the United States willfully violates boundaries and drives in wherever it likes. With the defeat of U.S. imperialism, the time will come when imperialism and colonialism will be really liquidated throughout the world.

[*Peking Review,* No. 41, October 8, 1965, p. 14.]

RUSK'S CHINA POLICY; CHOU EN-LAI'S AMERICA POLICY

61. Rusk's Statement Before the Subcommittee on the Far East and the Pacific of the House Committee on Foreign Affairs, March 16, 1966 (Extracts)

We expect China to become some day a great world power. Communist China is a major Asian power today. In the ordinary course of events, a peaceful China would be expected to have close relations—political, cultural, and economic—with the countries around its borders and with the United States.

It is no part of the policy of the United States to block the peaceful attainment of these objectives. . . .

We look forward hopefully—and confidently—to a time in the future when the government of mainland China will permit the restoration of the historic ties of friendship between the people of mainland China and ourselves.

What should be the main elements in our policy toward Communist China?

We must take care to do nothing which encourages Peiping —or anyone else—to believe that it can reap gains from its aggressive actions and designs. It is just as essential to "contain" Communist aggression in Asia as it was, and is, to "contain" Communist aggression in Europe.

At the same time, we must continue to make it plain that, if Peiping abandons its belief that force is the best way to resolve disputes and gives up its violent strategy of world revolution, we would welcome an era of good relations.

More specifically, I believe, there should be 10 elements in our policy.

First, we must remain firm in our determination to help those Allied nations which seek our help to resist the direct or indirect use or threat of force against their territory by Peiping.

Second, we must continue to assist the countries of Asia in building broadly based effective governments, devoted to progressive economic and social policies, which can better withstand Asian Communist pressures and maintain the security of their people.

Third, we must honor our commitments to the Republic of China and to the people on Taiwan, who do not want to live under communism. We will continue to assist in their defense and to try to persuade the Chinese Communists to join with us in renouncing the use of force in the area of Taiwan.

Fourth, we will continue our efforts to prevent the expulsion of the Republic of China from the United Nations or its agencies. So long as Peiping follows its present course it is extremely difficult for us to see how it can be held to fulfill the requirements set forth in the charter for membership, and the United States opposes its membership. It is worth recalling that the Chinese Communists have set forth some interesting conditions which must be fulfilled before they are even willing to consider membership:

The United Nations resolution of 1950 condemning Chinese Communist aggression in Korea must be rescinded;

There must be a new United Nations resolution condemning U.S. "aggression";

The United Nations must be reorganized;

The Republic of China must be expelled;

All other "imperialist puppets" must be expelled. One can only ask whether the Chinese Communists seriously want membership, or whether they mean to destroy the United Nations. We believe the United Nations must approach this issue with the utmost caution and deliberation.

Fifth, we should continue our efforts to reassure Peiping that the United States does not intend to attack mainland China. There are, of course, risks of war with China. This was true in 1950. It was true in the Taiwan Straits crises of 1955 and 1958. It was true in the Chinese Communist drive into Indian territory in 1962. It is true today in Vietnam. But we do not want war. We do not intend to provoke war. There is no fatal inevitability of war with Communist China. The Chinese Communists have, as I have already said, acted with caution when they foresaw a collision with the United States. We have acted with restraint and care in the past and we are doing so today. I hope they will realize this and guide their actions accordingly.

Sixth, we must keep firmly in our minds that there is nothing eternal about the policies and attitudes of Communist China. We must avoid assuming the existence of an unending and inevitable state of hostility between ourselves and the rulers of mainland China.

Seventh, when it can be done without jeopardizing other U.S. interests, we should continue to enlarge the possibilities for unofficial contacts between Communist China and ourselves—contacts which may gradually assist in altering Peiping's picture of the United States.

In this connection, we have gradually expanded the categories of American citizens who may travel to Communist China. American libraries may freely purchase Chinese Communist publications. American citizens may send and receive mail from the mainland. We have in the past indicated that if the Chinese themselves were interested in purchasing grain we would consider such sales. We have indicated our willingness to allow Chinese Communist newspapermen to come to the United States. We are prepared to permit American universities to invite Chinese Communist scientists to visit their institutions.

We do not expect that for the time being the Chinese Communists will seize upon these avenues of contact or exchange. All the evidence suggests Peiping wishes to remain isolated from the United States. But we believe it is in our interests that such channels be opened and kept open. We believe contact and communication are not incompatible with a firm policy of containment.

Eighth, we should keep open our direct diplomatic contacts with Peiping in Warsaw. While these meetings frequently provide merely an opportunity for a reiteration of known positions, they play a role in enabling each side to communicate information and attitudes in times of crisis. It is our hope that they might at some time become the channel for a more fruitful dialogue.

Ninth, we are prepared to sit down with Peiping and other countries to discuss the critical problems of disarmament and non-proliferation of nuclear weapons. Peiping has rejected all suggestions and invitations to join in such talks. It has attacked the test ban treaty. It has advocated the further spread of nuclear weapons to non-nuclear countries. It is an urgent task of all countries to persuade Peiping to change its stand.

Tenth, we must continue to explore and analyze all available information on Communist China and keep our own policies up to date. We hope that Peiping's policies may one day take account of the desire of the people of Asia and her own people for peace and security. We have said, in successive administrations, that when Peiping abandons the aggressive use of force and shows that it is not irrevocably hostile to the United States, then expanded contacts and improved relations may become possible. This continues to be our position.

These, I believe, are the essential ingredients of a sound policy in regard to Communist China.

I believe that they serve the interests not only of the United States and of the free world as a whole—but of the Chinese people. We have always known of the pragmatic genius of the Chinese people, and we can see evidence of it even today. The practices and doctrines of the present Peiping regime are yielding poor returns to the Chinese people. I believe that the Chinese people, no less their neighbors and the American people, crave the opportunity to move toward the enduring goals of mankind: a better life, safety, freedom, human dignity, and peace.

[Department of State, *Bulletin,* LIV, No. 1401, May 2, 1966, pp. 693–95.]

62. Chou En-lai's Four-Point Statement on China's Policy Toward the United States, April 10, 1966

(1) China will not take the initiative to provoke a war with the United States. China has not sent any troops to Hawaii; it is the United States that has occupied China's territory of Taiwan Province. Nevertheless, China has been making efforts in demanding, through negotiations, that the United States withdraw all its armed forces from Taiwan Province and the Taiwan Straits, and she has held talks with the United States for more than ten years, first in Geneva and then in Warsaw, on this question of principle, which admits of no concession whatsoever. All this serves as a very good proof.

(2) The Chinese mean what they say. In other words, if any country in Asia, Africa or elsewhere meets with aggression by the imperialists headed by the United States, the Chinese Government and people definitely will give it support and help. Should such just action bring on U.S. aggression against China, we will unhesitatingly rise in resistance and fight to the end.

(3) China is prepared. Should the United States impose a war on China, it can be said with certainty that once in China, the United States will not be able to pull out, however many men it may send over and whatever weapons it may use, nuclear weapons included. Since the 14 million people of southern Vietnam can cope with over 200,000 U.S. troops, the 650 million people of China can undoubtedly cope with 10 million of them. No matter how many U.S. aggressor troops may come, they will certainly be annihilated in China.

(4) Once the war breaks out, it will have no boundaries. Some U.S. strategists want to bombard China by relying on their air and naval superiority and avoid a ground war. This is wishful thinking. Once the war gets started with air and sea action, it will not be for the United States alone to decide how the war will continue. If you can come from the sky, why can't we fight back on the ground? This is why we say the war will have no boundaries once it breaks out.

[*Peking Review,* No. 20, May 13, 1966, p. 5.]

THE QUESTION OF A NO-FIRST-USE AGREEMENT ON NUCLEAR WEAPONS

63. Rusk Tells His Press Conference Why the United States Rejects a No-First-Use Agreement, May 17, 1966 (Extract)

Q. Mr. Secretary, in that same connection, Chou En-lai claimed that the United States has turned down or rejected an offer by him or by China to agree not to strike each other first in a nuclear attack. Would you have any comment on that?

A. Well, we are aware of their proposal on that. But we did not—and that proposal has been made by others and it has been made publicly from time to time. But we did not accept the Chinese Communist proposal because we believe that these disarmament measures should be carried out under strict and effective international control so that all parties can be assured of honoring their obligations. Mere declarations on such matters would not be adequate.

And so we are very much concerned about that, that any measures that involve the prohibition or the control of nuclear weapons should deal with the question of verification and inspection. We have ourselves put forward some very far-reaching proposals about limiting nuclear weapons and freezing and possibly reducing nuclear weapons delivery vehicles. You recall that the first Chinese proposal was made in connection with their own nuclear tests. They had refused to sign the nuclear test ban treaty, and they have made certain suggestions which seem to be an attempt to soften the impact upon world opinion of their gross failure to cooperate in a worldwide effort to limit the further spread of these weapons.

Now, we have suggested that they ought to be associated with a preparatory committee, the so-called exploratory group, which might try to work out arrangements for a world disarmament conference. But we have had no indication from the Chinese that they are willing to do that. . . .

[Department of State, *Bulletin,* LIV, No. 1406, June 6, 1966, pp. 884–85.]

64. *People's Daily* Article by "Observer," "Exposing New US Fraud over Nuclear Weapons," June 20, 1966 (Extracts)

China successfully conducted its third nuclear test on May 9. The next day, at Comrade Mehmet Shehu's farewell banquet, Premier Chou En-lai in his speech again expounded China's consistent stand on the question of nuclear weapons. He pointed out that China had already proposed to the United States that the two countries undertake the obligation of not being the first to use nuclear weapons against each other. But U.S. imperialism had rejected China's proposal. China's third successful nuclear test and Premier Chou En-lai's speech dealt another heavy blow at U.S. imperialism, caused a turmoil in the United States, and threw the U.S. Government into a very awkward position.

In these circumstances, at the Sino-American ambassadorial talks on May 25 the U.S. Government proposed that the Chinese Government consider linking its non-first use of nuclear weapons draft agreement to the U.S.-British-Soviet treaty on partial cessation of nuclear testing. Then on June 3, the U.S. Government disclosed the content of this proposal through the *New York Times* to the effect that "neither would be the first to use nuclear weapons, providing the Chinese would agree to stop their atomic testing."

This card played by the U.S. Government was just another of its big frauds on the question of nuclear weapons. . . .

The U.S. promise that it will consider the question of not using nuclear weapons first is false; its real intention is to fasten China to the tripartite partial nuclear test ban treaty.

Just what is the tripartite treaty? It is a criminal concoction by the two nuclear overlords—the United States and the Soviet Union—to consolidate their nuclear monopoly, to bind all the peace-loving countries hand and foot and to hoodwink the people of the world. It is a gross betrayal of the interests of the people of the Soviet Union and other peoples of the world by the leaders of the Communist Party of the Soviet Union. The Chinese Government was the first to oppose the treaty and oppose it most firmly. At no time and in no circumstances shall we subscribe to it. This solemn position taken by China is known to the whole world and the U.S. Government, too, is well aware of it.

Why then should the U.S. Government bring this preposterous proposal forward now and publicize it widely round the world? The reason is quite simple. The rapidity of China's progress in developing nuclear weapons has gone far beyond U.S. expectations, and has accelerated the bankruptcy of its nuclear monopoly and nuclear blackmail policy. Thus, Washington thought up this scheme to snare China into accepting the tripartite treaty with the bait that it may "consider" the non-first use question. By this it hopes to restrict China's development of nuclear weapons while it continues to develop them in a big way. This is a scheme to save its nuclear monopoly. If China refuses to be taken in, the United States would have a plausible excuse to refuse to undertake the obligation that it will not be the first to use nuclear weapons, and put all blame on China. . . .

[*Peking Review,* No. 26, June 24, 1966, pp. 27–28.]

JOHNSON'S CALL FOR RECONCILIATION WITH CHINA REJECTED AS A FRAUD

65. Johnson's Speech to the American Alumni Council, July 12, 1966 (Extract)

There is a fourth essential for peace in Asia which may seem the most difficult of all: reconciliation between nations that now call themselves enemies.

A peaceful mainland China is central to a peaceful Asia.

A misguided China must be encouraged toward understanding of the outside world and toward policies of peaceful cooperation.

A hostile China must be discouraged from aggression.

For lasting peace can never come to Asia as long as the 700 million people of mainland China are isolated by their rulers from the outside world.

We have learned in our relations with other such states that the weakness of neighbors is a temptation, and only firmness, backed by power, can really deter power that is backed by ambition. But we have also learned that the greatest force for opening closed minds and closed societies is the free flow of ideas and people and goods.

For many years now, the United States has attempted in vain to persuade the Chinese Communists to agree to an exchange of newsmen as one of the first steps to increased understanding between our people.

More recently, we have taken steps to permit American scholars, experts in medicine and public health, and other specialists to travel to Communist China. And only today we, here in the Government, cleared a passport for a leading American businessman to exchange knowledge with Chinese mainland leaders in Red China.

All of these initiatives, except the action today, have been rejected by Communist China.

We persist because we know that hunger and disease, ignorance and poverty, recognize no boundaries of either creed or class or country.

We persist because we believe that even the most rigid societies will one day awaken to the rich possibilities of a diverse world.

And we continue because we believe that cooperation, not hostility, is really the way of the future in the 20th century. . . .

[*Documents on American Foreign Relations* (New York: Council on Foreign Relations and Harper & Row, 1967), pp. 281–82.]

66. PRC Ambassador's Press Statement on the Sino-American Talks and the Text of His Main Statement at the 131st Meeting of the Talks, September 7, 1966 (Extracts)

Press Statement

Recently, the U.S. Government has time and again violated the agreement between China and the United States by unilaterally revealing the contents of the Sino-U.S. Ambassadorial Talks. The Soviet revisionist leading clique has followed up by conducting a great deal of propaganda about a "Sino-U.S. dialogue." Singing a duet, they have spread deceptive propaganda in a vain attempt to create an impression of Sino-U.S. reconciliation, cover up the U.S. imperialist policies of aggression and war and obscure the banner of opposition to U.S. imperialism held aloft by the Chinese people. I am now instructed to make public my main statement at the 131st meeting of the Sino-U.S. Talks held today. From this statement all the just-minded people of the world will surely be able to see clearly the solemn and just stand taken by the Chinese Government in the Sino-U.S. Talks. The U.S. Government's deceptive propaganda and the Soviet revisionist leading clique's profuse nonsense will only serve further to expose their sinister features.

Main Statement at 131st Meeting

Mr. Ambassador, today I would like first of all to speak on the question of Sino-U.S. relations.

(1) Throughout the past 17 years the U.S. Government has all along pursued a policy of hostility and aggression with respect to China. This policy has met with the strongest condemnation by the Chinese people and the people of the world and has gone completely bankrupt. However, unreconciled to its failure, the U.S. Government is employing its counter-revolutionary dual tactics in every possible way in order to cover up its criminal acts of hostility against the Chinese people.

Of late, one U.S. official after another has indicated a wish for "reconciliation," "building a bridge" and entering into "peaceful cooperation" with China. The U.S. Government thinks that the Chinese people and the people of the world will be hoodwinked by these high-sounding words it has uttered. This is sheer wishful thinking. Armed with Mao Tse-tung's thought, the 700 million Chinese people neither fear intimidation by the United States nor believe in its lies. The iron-clad facts in the past 17 years, and particularly in the recent period, prove that the U.S. Government's talk about "easing" Sino-U.S. relations is not worth a penny.

(2) The U.S. Government's military provocation and war threats against China have not only never stopped, they have become more and more unbridled. Since the last meeting, U.S. military aircraft and warships have again intruded into China's airspace and territorial waters on many occasions. Against this, the Chinese Ministry of Foreign Affairs has served the 403rd-411th serious warnings on the U.S. Government. In the meantime, U.S. military aircraft have repeatedly harassed and attacked Chinese merchant ships and fishing boats on the high seas. On May 23, U.S. military aircraft wildly attacked Chinese fishing boats engaged in fishing in the high seas area of the Bac Bo Gulf, killing and wounding as many as 21 Chinese fishermen. . . . The great Chinese people are not to be trifled with. The debts of blood incurred by the U.S. Government must be cleared and repaid. I am now instructed once again to address the most serious warning and the strongest protest to you and through

you to the U.S. Government against its above-mentioned military provocations against China.

The U.S. Government is still occupying Chinese territory, the province of Taiwan, by armed force and has increasingly turned it into a colony and military base. Not long ago, U.S. Secretary of State Dean Rusk personally went to Taiwan for secret talks with the Chiang Kai-shek gang to hatch criminal plots against the Chinese people. It was at this juncture that the Chiang Kai-shek gang clamoured for "counter-attack on the mainland." The forcible occupation of the Chinese province of Taiwan by the U.S. Government absolutely cannot be tolerated by the Chinese people. The recent scheming activities of U.S. Secretary of State Dean Rusk in Taiwan have further aroused the boundless indignation of the Chinese people. I am now instructed to reaffirm that the Chinese people are determined to liberate Taiwan and that the U.S. Government must withdraw all its armed forces from Taiwan and the Taiwan Straits. . . .

For a long time, the U.S. Government has set up military bases around China and rigged up military blocs. Furthermore, it is now energetically tightening its military encirclement of China. Recently, it summoned some of its vassals in Asia and the Pacific region, including the Chiang Kai-shek gang, for a meeting in Seoul, in an attempt to organize a new military alliance directed against China. Immediately afterwards, it collaborated with the Soviet revisionist leading clique and Japanese militarism in plotting a new "Holy Alliance" against communism, against the people, against revolution and against China. The U.S. Government's attempt to encircle China is futile. The Chinese people who hold high the banner of opposition to U.S. imperialism will never be encircled. It is definitely not China, but the United States, which has been besieged ring upon ring by the people of the whole world. The Chinese people are confident that together with the oppressed peoples and nations of Asia, Africa, Latin America and the rest of the world, they can thoroughly smash any scheme of the U.S. Government for aggression, and are determined to do so. . . .

(3) What the U.S. Government has done to China irrefutably proves that the U.S. Government does not have the slightest sincerity about easing Sino-U.S. relations. On the contrary, it is carrying out its policies of hostility and aggression against China with redoubled efforts, shifting the centre of gravity of its global

strategy eastward and regarding the Chinese people as its main enemy.

Twenty years ago, Chairman Mao Tse-tung, the great leader of the Chinese people, put forward his brilliant thesis that imperialism and all reactionaries are paper tigers. We would like to take this opportunity to warn the U.S. Government: The Chinese people have already had trials of strength with you and we know full well what you are capable of. We have made preparations. Should you dare to impose a war on the Chinese people, we will surely take you on and keep you company to the end.

Mr. Ambassador, the affairs of any country in the world should be managed by its people themselves. Asian affairs should be managed by the Asian people themselves and definitely not by the United States. U.S. aggression against Asia can only arouse the broad and resolute resistance of the Asian people. In coming to Asia to perform its so-called duty, the United States will only run against a brick wall and have itself badly battered. It is now high time that the U.S. Government should realize this point. The U.S. aggressors must get out of Taiwan and the Taiwan Straits. They must get out of Asia.

Mr. Ambassador, I would now like to make some comments on the U.S. Government's expansion of its war of aggression against Vietnam.

(1) Make trouble, fail, make trouble again, fail again . . . till their doom; that is the logic of the imperialists and all reactionaries the world over in dealing with the people's cause. The U.S. Government will never go against this logic in its actions in Vietnam.

Since the last meeting, the U.S. Government has flagrantly extended its bombing of the Democratic Republic of Vietnam to Hanoi, the capital of Vietnam, and Haiphong, its important harbour, carrying out the most despicable and most shameless war blackmail against the Democratic Republic of Vietnam and pushing its war of aggression against Vietnam to a new and still graver stage. At the same time, the U.S. Government has increased the number of its aggressor troops in Vietnam to over 300,000 and with increasing vigour pursued its scorched earth policy of "burn all, kill all, destroy all"* against the south Vietnamese

* A reference to Japan's highly destructive "Three-All" campaign in China in 1941–42—Ed.

people. Furthermore, the U.S. Government has instigated its south Vietnamese puppets, the Thai reactionaries and the Laotian Rightists to make military provocations against Cambodia and launch frantic attacks on the liberated areas of Laos in its attempt to spread the flames of war to the whole of Indo-China.

The U.S. Government has done its utmost to make trouble in Vietnam, but all it gains or can gain is the most disgraceful failure. . . .

(2) In order to maintain their rule and carry out expansion abroad, reactionary ruling classes have always resorted to the dual tactics of butcher-like suppression and priest-like deception. This is exactly what the U.S. Government has been doing in Vietnam.

Each time the U.S. Government throws a faggot into the flames of war in Vietnam, it always follows this up with a prayer for peace. Recently, while widening the war, the U.S. Government has spread another smokescreen of "peace talks" with the collaboration of the Soviet revisionist leading clique and reactionaries in various countries. They plead energetically for "de-escalation" of the Vietnam war. They loudly advocate a settlement of the Vietnam question on the basis of the Geneva agreements. . . .

As everyone knows, escalation, or de-escalation, the U.S. war against Vietnam is a war of aggression. The crux of the Vietnam question at present is absolutely not the gradual de-escalation of the war, but the immediate and complete withdrawal of the U.S. aggressors from southern Vietnam. The U.S. Government can never succeed in its scheme of "forcing peace talks through bombing." As everyone knows, the Geneva agreements were torn to shreds by the U.S. Government long ago. The attempt to use the Geneva agreements to tie the hands of the people of Vietnam, China and the whole world will never succeed.

The U.S. Government's peace talks swindle has already been discredited, and is bound to be thoroughly discredited. The U.S. Government will never be able to obtain at the conference table what it has failed to obtain on the battlefield. By playing its counter-revolutionary dual tactics, the U.S. Government absolutely cannot deceive the Vietnamese people and the people of the world; on the contrary, it will only further reveal its sinister features before the whole world.

(3) The Vietnamese people's struggle against U.S. aggression and for national salvation is a just one; it has won the firm support of the people throughout the world and is sure to be victorious.

The Vietnamese people's war is an iron bastion which it is impossible, and absolutely impossible, for any force on earth to smash. . . .

The Chinese people most warmly and most resolutely support the Appeal of President Ho Chi Minh of the Democratic Republic of Vietnam and firmly support the Vietnamese people in carrying the fight through to the end until not a single American soldier remains on the sacred soil of Vietnam and final victory is won in the war of resistance against U.S. aggression and for national salvation. The Chinese Government has time and again solemnly stated that U.S. imperialist aggression against Vietnam is aggression against China. The 700 million Chinese people provide powerful backing for the Vietnamese people. The vast expanse of China's territory is the reliable rear area of the Vietnamese people. In order to support the Vietnamese people in winning thorough victory in the war of resistance against U.S. aggression, the Chinese people are ready to undertake maximum national sacrifices.

The Chinese people mean what they say. If you underestimate the strong determination of the Chinese people to support the Vietnamese people in carrying the fight through to the end and if you underestimate the actions which the Chinese people will take to this end, then you will be committing a grave historical blunder and will find it too late to repent.

[*Peking Review,* No. 38, September 16, 1966, pp. 7–10.]

JOHNSON'S LAST OVERTURES

67. The Director of the US Information Agency Invites Chinese Correspondents to Cover the 1968 Presidential Campaign, May 2, 1968

Los Angeles, California, May 3rd—The United States has invited correspondents from Communist China to cover the 1968 Presidential election campaign.

In a speech yesterday (Thursday, May 2nd) to the 17th annual convention of American Women in Radio and Television, Mr. Leonard H. Marks, Director of the United States Information Agency offered Chinese Communist journalists "prime time" on Voice of America to send their reports home uncensored.

Mr. Marks made the invitation in discussing the challenge facing America and the world—"the challenge of communication with our foreign neighbours."

Technical achievements in communications had made the earth a tiny planet, he said, and there was little happening anywhere that was not the common concern of all people.

Yet, said Mr. Marks, the challenge of global communication was complicated by closed societies such as Communist China.

"We can only talk to the Chinese people by shortwave radio," said Mr. Marks, "and this is jammed." "However," said Mr. Marks, "no jamming has ever been 100 per cent successful. There are people in China today who listen to our programs; we know this."

Making his offer of uncensored election coverage, Mr. Marks stated:

"I say to the leaders in Peking: Let your journalists come to this country to see how Americans choose their President. We guarantee them full freedom to observe and report the campaign.

"The Voice of America will make prime listening time available daily to these Chinese journalists for broadcast to their homeland.

"In our tradition of free speech, we in the United States will not attempt in any manner to censor these broadcasts. The Chinese can express themselves as they wish in any language.

"Hopefully this initial effort will lead to further exchange between our respective countries. We stand ready to discuss such exchanges on a broad general basis or on specific points."

Mr. Marks said he hoped the offer would be considered seriously by Peking and that it would be accepted.

"We would expect Chinese observers to be critical and to look for the worst; but I am confident that any observer will find in our election processes the true flavour of a free society."

Mr. Marks asked the women's group to act as hostesses for the Chinese if Peking accepted the offer. . . .

[US Information Service, London, Press Release, May 2, 1968.]

68. Under Secretary of State Nicholas Katzenbach's Speech on Relations with China to the National Press Club, Washington, D.C., May 21, 1968 (Extract)

Chinese Communist Security Interests in Asia

Does the United States, through its bilateral and multilateral security arrangements with Asian countries, and by the existence of U.S. bases in Asia, threaten Peking? Do we fail to recognize that Peking has legitimate security interests of its own in Asia? Concern about an American threat to their security is undoubtedly felt by some leaders in Peking. I cannot stress too strongly, however, for their information, or for that of anyone else who may be interested, that no basis for such a fear exists.

We have made this clear over and over again. As President Johnson said in his State of the Union address last year: "We have no intention of trying to deny [Communist China's] legitimate needs for security and friendly relations with her neighbouring countries."

If we actually wanted to threaten Communist China, would not repeated opportunities have presented themselves? Could we not have attacked it on the many occasions when the mainland was weak or racked by internal problems?

Legitimate historical reasons for the Chinese people to be fearful of outside threats do exist, as I earlier indicated. We recognize these and understand them.

Fears and threats can work in both directions, however. The countries around China's borders have the same right to feel secure and free from external threat as the People's Republic of China. But these countries do, in fact, feel threatened—not by the United States, but by Peking.* The most reasonable avenue to security for mainland China in Asia is not through threats or bluster but through acts of goodwill which will reassure its neighbours.

The Military Threat From Communist China

The military threat posed by Peking can be, and perhaps at times has been, exaggerated. But there is no question that on

* An illustration of the gradual US shift from Nationalist nomenclature (Peiping) to Communist usage (Peking). In Chinese, Peiping means "northern peace," while Peking stands for "northern capital." The Nationalists, of course, do not recognize Peking as China's capital—Ed.

occasion Peking has been prepared to use armed force across its frontiers. Certainly there is no doubt of this fact in the minds of the people of India or Korea.

Although Peking has reached agreements with India, Burma, and Indonesia disavowing interference in each other's internal affairs, this has not prevented the Chinese from openly urging the overthrow of their governments by armed insurrection. Nor has it prevented Peking from translating words into actions by assisting insurrectionary groups in those countries.

A whole series of other Asian, as well as African and Latin American, nations have become aware of the financial assistance and training in guerrilla tactics offered by Peking to revolutionaries in their own countries. A number of them have severed diplomatic relations with Peking in protest.

Please do not take what I am saying to mean that I believe Peking is preparing to pour troops across its borders in great waves to occupy all the rimland of Asia. While Peking's large army and modern weapons make this a potential danger, we doubt anything like this is imminent. The fact remains, however, that most Asians—from the Himalayas to Japan—see Communist China today as a potential danger to their security.

Peking's Isolation in the International Community

It is often argued that we are isolating Peking from the international community by opposing its participation in the United Nations and other international groups, and by discouraging other states from establishing diplomatic relations or conducting trade with it.

But, once again, it is not the attitude of the United States but that of the People's Republic of China which isolates it. The United States, influential though it may be, does not control and govern the organs of the United Nations or of other international bodies.

The Government of the United States cannot accept Peking's demand for participation in international organisations to the exclusion of the Republic of China. This view is shared by a majority of the members of the United Nations.

Under present circumstances, Communist China's participation in the Security Council particularly would weaken that body's ability to deal constructively with international problems.

The Chinese mistreatment of diplomats and diplomatic missions in Peking since 1967, including the entry or sacking of several embassies, and the highly undiplomatic activities of many of Peking's own officials abroad have hardly helped its cause in the international community.

Peking has declined to participate even in totally non-political international activities, such as the International Geophysical Year. It rarely permits its scientists to attend even those international scientific meetings in which national membership is not a factor.

The Chinese have quarrelled even with fellow Communist nations with consequences for international Communist unity that are familiar to you. They have withdrawn from most of the organisations which formerly were known under the general label of the "World Peace Movement" and attempted either to set up rival organisations or disrupt already existing ones.

The United States would welcome a change in Peking's position which might indicate a shift in its attitude on the general conduct of international affairs. Few signs of any shift are discernible. Under these circumstances any isolation which Peking senses is of its own choosing.

Embargo on Trade with Communist China

But what about the embargo on U.S. trade with Peking? Are not the Chinese able to obtain virtually whatever they need from other countries anyway?

Since our present restrictions on trade were established China has grown increasingly able to produce many industrial materials which it needs. And gradually more and more states, including many such as Japan, Australia, and West Germany which do not recognize the Peking regime, have steadily increased their trade with mainland China in non-strategic goods and commodities.

At the same time, Peking has shown little interest in trading with the United States. In 1961 it turned a cold shoulder on President Kennedy when he indicated that the United States would consider Chinese interest in the purchase of food grains. Last year it rejected out of hand this administration's indication of willingness to permit the export of drugs and medical supplies for the treatment of certain epidemic diseases.

We have from time to time reviewed our trade policy to see if it would be feasible and in our interest to reduce the barriers on our side to mutually beneficial trade in non-strategic goods with the mainland. We have undertaken this review to determine whether such peaceful trade might be possible without harming our interests in the area. In view of Peking's attitudes, however, I cannot be optimistic about any early or significant practical result in terms of trade.

We have said many times in recent years that we are willing to move toward reciprocal (or even unilateral) person-to-person contacts and exchanges with mainland China. Just last week Leonard Marks invited Communist Chinese journalists here to observe and report on this year's election campaign.

We have informed numerous non-governmental organisations which wish to invite representatives from mainland China to meetings in this country, that we have no objection. We would also be happy to see exchanges of cultural exhibits and articles.

We are prepared to issue visas to Chinese visitors from the mainland who may wish to come to the United States, subject only to legislation applying to all visitors.

The Danger of U.S.-Chinese Communist Confrontation

Is it true that the degree of antagonism between the United States and Communist China is so great and so irreconcilable that there must inevitably take place a major military confrontation between our two countries?

Our entire policy and philosophy aims to avoid such a calamity. War is never inevitable. Given normal and sensible restraint on both sides, there is absolutely no reason why the United States and Communist China should come into conflict. . . .

[US Information Service, London, Press Release, May 22, 1968.]

VII. Light at the End of the Tunnel

POLITICS is the art of the impossible; the possible can be left to the bureaucrats. That surely is the lesson of the Nixon visit to China. No one imagined President Nixon would go to China. He had been a hard-liner toward Communism at home and abroad and especially toward China (**46**). The 1968 Democratic presidential candidate, Vice-President Hubert Humphrey, attempted to dissociate himself from President Johnson's foreign policy; but no one remembered Nixon dissociating himself from Dulles-style policies when he had last run for President in 1960. The success of his second campaign for the presidency therefore inspired great gloom among American liberals, who did not believe that the old "tricky Dick" was now the "new Nixon."

In his inaugural address, Nixon indicated some of the rethinking he had done on his many foreign trips during his eight years in the wilderness (**69**). He believed that an era of negotiation was now succeeding the period of confrontation. However, his remarks on China policy at his first press conference on January 27, 1969, held out no prospects of change; China had to change first (**70**).

The first contact between the new administration and the Chinese Government was scheduled to take place at the Warsaw ambassadorial talks on February 20. There had been no talks for a year,[1] but the Chinese had proposed a resumption after

---

[1] The Chinese had responded to the goodwill gestures made in the last year of the Johnson administration (see introduction to previous chapter) by stating in late May, 1968, that they would hold no more talks at Warsaw until after the election and would ignore all overtures; see Harold Hinton, *China's Turbulent Quest* (New York: Macmillan, 1970), p. 269.

Nixon's victory. At the last moment, they cancelled the meeting on the grounds that a Chinese defector had been given asylum in the United States. From about the time of Nixon's first press conference, Chinese comment on his administration became increasingly critical.[2] Mao issued another critical statement on the US racial situation on the occasion of the murder of Martin Luther King.[3]

At the same time, developments were taking place in China that probably encouraged its leaders to think again about relations with America. In April, 1969, the Ninth Congress of the CCP formally brought the Cultural Revolution to an end. China's interest in foreign relations resumed; ambassadors returned to their posts. In the major address to the Congress, Lin Piao—who was named Mao's successor in the new Party constitution—spent far more time denouncing the Soviet Union than the United States, though he did have harsh things to say about Nixon (71). This concentration on the Soviet Union was not surprising since the previous month there had been a grave clash on the Sino-Soviet border, along the Ussuri River. There was a subsequent clash on the Sinkiang border in August, and rumors emanating from East European sources suggested that the Russians had been sounding out their allies as to their views on a Soviet pre-emptive strike against China. In the light of the invasion of Czechoslovakia in 1968 and its justification by the "Brezhnev Doctrine"—which seemed designed to provide a sanction for the Soviet Union to overthrow governments in other Communist states—the Chinese may well have felt it advisable to reopen negotiations with the Americans.

Another factor would surely have been Nixon's evolving Asian policy. At Guam in July, 1969, the President had enunciated what became known as the "Nixon Doctrine," which seemed to foreshadow a lessening American commitment to Asia.[4] Certainly,

---

[2] *Ibid.*, p. 270.

[3] *Peking Review*, No. 16 (April 19, 1968).

[4] *See Public Papers of the Presidents of the United States: Richard Nixon, 1969* (Washington, D.C.: U.S. Government Printing Office, 1971), pp. 544–56.

it meant that in future Vietnam-type situations, America would "look to the nation directly threatened to assume the primary responsibility of providing the manpower for its defense." [5] This must have seemed a hopeful development in Peking, but China's satisfaction would have been diminished by a hint that Nixon might be expecting Japan to fill gaps left by America. Certainly, Chinese policymakers would have been aroused by the way Taiwan was mentioned in the communiqué issued by President Nixon and Japan's Premier Sato on November 21, 1969. The crucial passage read: "The Prime Minister said that the maintenance of peace and security in the Taiwan area was also a most important factor for the security of Japan." [6] Two months later, the first Warsaw meeting of the Nixon administration was held and it was quickly followed by a second in February, 1970. Then developments in Indochina intervened, and the third meeting scheduled for May 20 was cancelled.[7]

The coup in Cambodia on March 18, 1970, resulted in the overthrow of China's closest friend among non-Communist statesmen, Prince Sihanouk. The Prince took up residence in Peking, and American support for his successors effectively prevented the Chinese from continuing their dialogue with Washington. On May 20, the day the American and Chinese ambassadors should have met in Warsaw, Mao personally denounced the actions of the United States (72). A year later, the intervention of South Vietnamese troops, supported by the Americans, in Laos caused even more concern in Peking than the Cambodian coup, presumably because Laos bordered on China. Chou En-lai flew to Hanoi and issued a warning that recalled his statement on the eve of Chinese intervention in Korea (73). But it soon became clear, when the South Vietnamese troops had to execute a hasty withdrawal, that Nixon had no intention of putting US troops into Laos and so escalating the war. In fact, by May, 1971, the Nixon administration had almost halved the number of troops in

[5] See Secretary of State, *United States Foreign Policy, 1969–1970* (Washington, D.C.: U.S. Government Printing Office, March, 1971), p. 36.

[6] *Ibid.*, p. 503.

[7] *Ibid.*, p. 43.

Vietnam compared with the number there when it assumed office two years earlier.

The gradual reduction of American military strength in Vietnam must have been encouraging to Chinese leaders.[8] Nixon had also been taking a series of small steps to relax travel and trade restrictions with China since July, 1969, clearly signalling to Peking his hopes of a genuine dialogue (74). In his foreign-policy message to the Congress on February 25, 1971, Nixon had underlined the need to draw China into a "constructive relationship with the world community" (75). Suddenly, when the Laotian situation was clearly no longer critical, the Chinese responded with a major gesture of "people's diplomacy," inviting the American table-tennis team, along with others that had been competing in a world tournament in Japan, to come and play in China. The American players were received, like the other teams, by Premier Chou En-lai (76). American correspondents went in at the same time. Nixon immediately responded with new trade and travel relaxations (77). A few days later, he hinted that he would like to go to China one day, though he was not sure it would be while he was still in office.[9] Then, on April 30, *Life* magazine published a report by the American journalist Edgar Snow of a conversation he had had with Mao Tse-tung late in 1970 (78).[10] It contained Mao's imprimatur on a Nixon visit to China. Six weeks later, Nixon went on television to reveal that his Assistant for National Security Affairs, Henry Kissinger, had just returned from a secret visit to Peking during which a journey to China by the President had been agreed (79).

The news staggered the world. An era of unrelenting Sino-

[8] For a brief account of the reduction, see *ibid.*, p. 49.

[9] *Sunday Telegraph* (London), April 18, 1971.

[10] An earlier hint of Mao's attitude toward a *détente* with the Americans had been provided by the publication, on the front page of the *People's Daily* on Christmas Day, 1970—a date chosen presumably to signal goodwill to Americans—of a picture of Mao and Snow taken three months earlier. (Snow had a special relationship with Mao. His classic work, *Red Star over China,* a report of his visit to the Communist-held areas in 1936, contained Mao's autobiography as told to Snow. He had revisited China in 1960 and 1964.)

American hostility had ended. Even though many concrete problems remained—and some would certainly persist after the Nixon visit—the leaders of China and America had agreed to meet to talk about them. At the least, and at last, it was the beginning of a beginning.

69. President Nixon's Inaugural Address, January 20, 1969 (Extract)

Let us take as our goal: where peace is unknown, make it welcome; where peace is fragile, make it strong; where peace is temporary, make it permanent.

After a period of confrontation, we are entering an era of negotiation.

Let all nations know that during this administration our lines of communication will be open.

We seek an open world—open to ideas, open to the exchange of goods and people, a world in which no people, great or small, will live in angry isolation.

We cannot expect to make everyone our friend, but we can try to make no one our enemy.

Those who would be our adversaries, let us invite to a peaceful competition—not in conquering territory or extending dominion, but in enriching the life of man. . . .

[US Information Service, London, Press Release, January 21, 1969.]

70. Nixon's Answer on Improving Relations with China at His First Press Conference, January 27, 1969

Q. Mr. President, now that you are President, could you be specific with us about what your plans are for improving relations with Communist China and whether you think they will be successful or not?

The President: Well, I have noted, of course, some expressions of interest on the part of various Senators and others in this country with regard to the possibility of admitting Communist China to the United Nations.

I also have taken note of the fact that several countries—including primarily Italy among the major countries—have indicated an interest in changing their policy and possibly voting to admit Communist China to the United Nations.

The policy of this country and this administration at this time will be to continue to oppose Communist China's admission to the United Nations.

There are several reasons for that:

First, Communist China has not indicated any interest in becoming a member of the United Nations.

Second, it has not indicated any intent to abide by the principles of the U.N. Charter and to meet the principles that new members admitted to the United Nations are supposed to meet.

Finally, Communist China continues to call for expelling the Republic of China from the United Nations, and the Republic of China has, as I think most know, been a member of the international community and has met its responsibilities without any question over these past few years.

Under these circumstances, I believe it would be a mistake for the United States to change its policy with regard to Communist China in admitting it to the United Nations.

Now, there is a second immediate point that I have noted: That is the fact that there will be another meeting in Warsaw. We look forward to that meeting. We will be interested to see what the Chinese Communist representatives may have to say at that meeting, whether any changes of attitude on their part on major substantive issues may have occurred.

Until some changes occur on their side, however, I see no immediate prospect of any change in our policy.

[Department of State, *Bulletin,* LX, No. 1547, February 17, 1969, p. 141.]

CHINA'S ATTITUDE TOWARD THE UNITED STATES AFTER THE CULTURAL REVOLUTION

71. Lin Piao's Report to the CCP's Ninth Congress, April 1, 1969 (Extract)

The nature of U.S. imperialism as a paper tiger has long since been laid bare by the people throughout the world. U.S.

imperialism, the most ferocious enemy of the people of the whole world, is going downhill more and more. Since he took office, Nixon has been confronted with a hopeless mess and an insoluble economic crisis, with the strong resistance of the masses of the people at home and throughout the world and with the predicament in which the imperialist countries are disintegrating and the baton of U.S. imperialism is getting less and less effective. Unable to produce any solution to these problems, Nixon, like his predecessors, cannot but continue to play the counter-revolutionary dual tactics, ostensibly assuming a "peace-loving" appearance while in fact engaging in arms expansion and war preparations on a still larger scale. The military expenditures of the United States have been increasing year by year. To date the U.S. imperialists still occupy our territory Taiwan. They have dispatched aggressor troops to many countries and have also set up hundreds upon hundreds of military bases and military installations in different parts of the world. They have made so many airplanes and guns, so many nuclear bombs and guided missiles. What is all this for? To frighten, suppress and slaughter the people and dominate the world. By doing so they make themselves the enemy of the people everywhere and find themselves besieged and battered by the broad masses of the proletariat and the people all over the world, and this will definitely lead to revolutions throughout the world on a still larger scale . . .

[*Peking Review,* Special Issue, April 28, 1969, pp. 26–27.]

US ACTION IN INDOCHINA COMPLICATES SINO-AMERICAN RELATIONS

72. Mao's Statement on Cambodia, May 20, 1970 (Extracts)

Unable to win in Viet Nam and Laos, the U.S. aggressors treacherously engineered the reactionary coup d'état by the Lon Nol–Sirik Matak clique, brazenly dispatched their troops to invade Cambodia and resumed the bombing of North Vietnam, and this has aroused the furious resistance of the three Indo-

Chinese peoples. I warmly support the fighting spirit of Samdech Norodom Sihanouk, head of state of Cambodia, in opposing U.S. imperialism and its lackeys. I warmly support the joint declaration of the summit conference of the Indo-Chinese peoples. I warmly support the establishment of the Royal Government of National Union under the leadership of the National United Front of Kampuchea. Strengthening their unity, supporting each other and persevering in a protracted people's war, the three Indo-Chinese peoples will certainly overcome all difficulties and win complete victory. . . .

The Nixon government is beset with troubles internally and externally, with utter chaos at home and extreme isolation abroad. The mass movement of protest against U.S. aggression in Cambodia has swept the globe. . . .

U.S. imperialism, which looks like a huge monster, is in essence a paper tiger, now in the throes of its death-bed struggle. In the world of today, who actually fears whom? It is not the Vietnamese people, the Laotian people, the Cambodian people, the Palestinian people, the Arab people or the people of other countries who fear U.S. imperialism; it is U.S. imperialism which fears the people of the world. It becomes panic-stricken at the mere rustle of leaves in the wind. Innumerable facts prove that a just cause enjoys abundant support while an unjust cause finds little support. A weak nation can defeat a strong, a small nation can defeat a big. The people of a small country can certainly defeat aggression by a big country, if only they dare to rise in struggle, take up arms and grasp in their own hands the destiny of their country. This is a law of history.

People of the world, unite and defeat the U.S. aggressors and all their running dogs!

[New China News Agency, May 20, 1970.]

73. Chou En-lai's Speech at a Hanoi Rally, March 6, 1971 (Extract)

Chairman Mao has pointed out: "The 700 million Chinese people provide a powerful backing for the Vietnamese people; the vast expanse of China's territory is their reliable rear area." This is the firm and unshakable principle of the Chinese Party and Government as well as a guide to action of the entire Chinese people.

Your struggle is our struggle, your difficulty is our difficulty and your victory is our victory. Viet Nam, Laos and Cambodia are close neighbours of China and we will never allow U.S. imperialism to do whatever it pleases there. If U.S. imperialism should obdurately go down the road of expanding its war of aggression in Indochina, the Chinese people will take all necessary measures, not flinching even from the greatest national sacrifices, to give all-out support and assistance to the Vietnamese people's war against U.S. aggression and for national salvation and give all-out support and assistance to the three peoples of Indochina in their war against U.S. aggression and for national salvation until the thorough defeat of the U.S. aggressors. The Chinese people and the peoples of Viet Nam, Laos and Cambodia are brothers and comrades-in-arms sharing weal and woe and going through thick and thin together. We will always unite together, fight together and win victory together! . . .

[*Peking Review*, No. 11, March 12, 1971, p. 17.]

PING-PONG DIPLOMACY

74. Last US Restrictions on Travel to China Lifted, March 15, 1971

Washington—The United States has lifted the last remaining passport restriction on travel by Americans to the People's Republic of China.

In announcing yesterday that U.S. citizens will no longer need special passport stamps to visit mainland China, State Department spokesman Charles Bray noted that this action was consistent with President Nixon's "publicly stated desire to improve communications with the mainland."

Mr. Bray announced that the State Department ban on travel by Americans to Cuba, North Vietnam and North Korea remains in effect. . . .

Washington restricted travel of U.S. citizens to mainland China in 1952, to North Korea and North Vietnam in 1955 and to Cuba in 1961.

Reviewing unilateral steps taken by the United States in attempts to ease tensions between Washington and Peking, Mr. Bray listed the following:

July, 1969—Washington relaxed restrictions related to travel to allow almost anyone with a legitimate purpose to travel to mainland China on an American passport.

December, 1969—Permission was granted to U.S. tourists to make unlimited purchases of Chinese goods and to enable collectors, museums and universities to import Chinese products.

December, 1969—The U.S. Government allowed American-controlled subsidiaries abroad to conduct trade in non-strategic goods with mainland China.

April, 1970—The United States announced selective licensing of American-made components and related spare parts for non-strategic foreign goods exported to mainland China.

August, 1970—Restrictions were lifted on American oil companies abroad fuelling free world ships bearing non-strategic cargoes to Chinese mainland ports.

Asked by correspondents if Peking had ever responded to the U.S. initiatives, Mr. Bray said there had been no visible response, but "we would hope that lifting these restrictions on travel would result in greater travel to the mainland."

The spokesman also reaffirmed that Washington had "made it perfectly clear, publicly and privately, that we are prepared to resume the Warsaw talks at any time."

The last time U.S. and Chinese diplomats conferred in Warsaw was February 20th, 1970. The talks were suspended by Peking.

[US Information Service, London, Press Release, March 16, 1971.]

75. Nixon's Foreign Policy Message to Congress, February 25, 1971 (Extracts)

The twenty-two-year-old hostility between ourselves and the People's Republic of China is another unresolved problem, serious indeed in view of the fact that it determines our relationship with 750 million talented and energetic people.

It is a truism that an international order cannot be secure if one of the major powers remains largely outside it and hostile toward it. In this decade, therefore, there will be no more important challenge than that of drawing the People's Republic of China into a constructive relationship with the world community, and particularly with the rest of Asia. . . .

We are prepared to establish a dialogue with Peking. We cannot accept its ideological precepts, or the notion that Communist China must exercise hegemony over Asia. But neither do we wish to impose on China an international position that denies its legitimate national interests.

The evolution of our dialogue with Peking cannot be at the expense of international order or our own commitments. Our attitude is public and clear. We will continue to honor our treaty commitments to the security of our Asian allies. An honorable relationship with Peking cannot be constructed at their expense.

Among these allies is the Republic of China. . . . I do not believe that this honorable and peaceful association need constitute an obstacle to the movement toward normal relations between the United States and the People's Republic of China. As I have tried to make clear since the beginning of my Administration, while I cannot foretell the ultimate resolution of the differences between Taipei and Peking, we believe these differences must be resolved by peaceful means.

In that connection, I wish to make it clear that the United States is prepared to see the People's Republic of China play a constructive role in the family of nations. The question of its place in the United Nations is not, however, merely a question of whether it should participate. It is also a question of whether Peking should be permitted to dictate to the world the terms of its participation. For a number of years attempts have been made to deprive the Republic of China of its place as a member of the United Nations and its Specialized Agencies. We have opposed these attempts. We will continue to oppose them. . . .

In the coming year, I will carefully examine what further steps we might take to create broader opportunities for contacts between the Chinese and American peoples, and how we might remove needless obstacles to the realization of these opportunities. We hope for, but will not be deterred by a lack of reciprocity.

We should, however, be totally realistic about the prospects. The People's Republic of China continues to convey to its own people and to the world its determination to cast us in the devil's role. Our modest efforts to prove otherwise have not reduced Peking's doctrinaire enmity toward us. So long as this is true, so long as Peking continues to be adamant for hostility, there is little we can do by ourselves to improve the relationship. What we can do, we will. . . .

[Richard M. Nixon, *U.S. Foreign Policy for the 1970's: Building for Peace*. A Report to the Congress, February 25, 1971, pp. 105–9.]

76. "Premier Chou Meets Table Tennis Delegations of Canada, Colombia, England, Nigeria, and United States," April 14, 1971 (Extracts from Report)

Premier Chou En-lai met all the members of the table tennis delegations of Canada, Colombia, England, Nigeria and the United States on the afternoon of April 14 and had a friendly conversation with them. These delegations were invited to visit China after taking part in the 31st World Table Tennis Championship. . . .

When the guests of the various countries entered the meeting hall, Premier Chou and leading members of the Chinese People's Association for Friendship with Foreign Countries and the All-China Sports Federation shook hands with them in welcome, and had photographs taken with each of the delegations.

At the meeting, Premier Chou first of all welcomed the delegations' visit to China on behalf of the Chinese people and Government. . . .

In his conversation with the U.S. Table Tennis Delegation, Premier Chou said: Contacts between the people of China and the United States had been very frequent in the past but later they were broken off for a long time. Your visit to China on invitation has opened the door to friendly contacts between the people of the two countries. We believe that such friendly contacts will be favoured and supported by the majority of the two peoples. Delegation leader Graham Steenhoven and members of the delegation spoke highly of the hospitality of the Chinese people and said they were glad that their delegation was able to visit China. . . .

[*Peking Review*, No. 17, April 23, 1971, pp. 4–5.]

77. Nixon Announces Further Relaxation of Trade and Travel Restrictions, April 14, 1971

In my second annual foreign policy report to the Congress on February 25, 1971, I wrote, "in the coming year, I will carefully examine what further steps we might take to create broader opportunities for contacts between the Chinese and American peoples, and how we might remove needless obstacles to the realization of these opportunities."

I asked the Under Secretaries Committee of the National Security Council to make appropriate recommendations to bring this about.

After reviewing the resulting study and recommendations, I decided on the following actions, none of which requires new legislation or negotiation with the People's Republic of China:

—The United States is prepared to expedite visas for visitors or groups of visitors from the People's Republic of China to the United States.

—U.S. currency controls are to be relaxed to permit the use of dollars by the People's Republic of China.

—Restrictions are to be ended on American oil companies providing fuel to ships or aircraft proceeding to and from China except on Chinese-owned or Chinese-chartered carriers bound to or from North Vietnam, North Korea, or Cuba.

—U.S. vessels or aircraft may now carry Chinese cargoes between non-Chinese ports and U.S.-owned foreign flag carriers may call at Chinese ports.

—I have asked for a list of items of a non-strategic nature which can be placed under general licence for direct export to the People's Republic of China. Following my review and approval of specific items on this list, direct imports of designated items from China will then also be authorized.

After due consideration of the results of these changes in our trade and travel restrictions, I will consider what additional steps might be taken.

Implementing regulations will be announced by the Department of State and other interested agencies.

[US Information Service, London, Press Release, April 15, 1971.]

A JOURNEY IS ARRANGED

78. Edgar Snow's Report of His Conversation with Mao Tse-tung on December 18, 1970, in *Life*, April 30, 1971 (Extract)

At this point we were interrupted by the arrival of some glasses of *mao t'ai*, a fiery rice liquor made in Kweichow Province. We drank a toast. To my mortification the chairman noticed that I had omitted to toast the ladies present. How could I have done so? I had not yet accepted women as equals.

It was not possible, said the chairman, to achieve complete equality between men and women at present. But between Chinese and Americans there need be no prejudices. There could be mutual respect and equality. He said he placed high hopes on the peoples of the two countries.

If the Soviet Union wouldn't do [point the way], then he would place his hopes on the American people. The United States alone had a population of more than 200 million. Industrial production was already higher than in any other country and education was universal. He would be happy to see a party emerge there to lead a revolution, although he was not expecting that in the near future.

In the meantime, he said, the foreign ministry was studying the matter of admitting Americans from the left, middle and right to visit China. Should rightists like Nixon, who represented the monopoly capitalists, be permitted to come? He should be welcomed because, Mao explained, at present the problems between China and the U.S.A. would have to be solved with Nixon. Mao would be happy to talk with him, either as a tourist or as President.

I, unfortunately, could not represent the United States, he said: I was not a monopoly capitalist. Could *I* settle the Taiwan question? Why such a stalemate? Chiang Kai-shek had not died yet. But what had Taiwan to do with Nixon? That question was created by Truman and Acheson.

It may be relevant to mention—and this is not a part of my talk with Chairman Mao—that foreign diplomats in Peking were aware last year that messages were being delivered from Washington to the Chinese government by certain go-betweens. The purport of such communications was to assure Chinese leaders of Mr. Nixon's "new outlook" on Asia. Nixon was firmly determined, it was said, to withdraw from Vietnam as speedily as possible, to seek a negotiated international guarantee of the independence of Southeast Asia, to end the impasse in Sino-American relations by clearing up the Taiwan question and to bring the People's Republic into the United Nations and into diplomatic relations with the United States. . . .

[Edgar Snow, "A Conversation with Mao Tse-tung," *Life*, April 30, 1971, p. 47. © Copyrighted by Edgar Snow, 1971, and reprinted by his permission.]

79. Nixon's Announcement on Television of His Planned Visit to Peking, July 15, 1971

Good evening. I have requested this television time tonight to announce a major development in our efforts to build a lasting peace in the world.

As I have pointed out on a number of occasions over the past three years, there can be no stable and enduring peace without the participation of the People's Republic of China and its 750 million people. That is why I have undertaken initiatives in several areas to open the door for more normal relations between our two countries.

In pursuance of that goal, I sent Dr. Kissinger, my Assistant for National Security Affairs, to Peking during his recent world tour for the purpose of having talks with Premier Chou En-lai. The announcement I shall now read is being issued simultaneously in Peking and in the United States.

Premier Chou En-lai and Dr. Henry Kissinger, President Nixon's Assistant for National Security Affairs, held talks in Peking from July 9 to 11, 1971. Knowing of President Nixon's expressed desire to visit the People's Republic of China, Premier Chou En-lai, on behalf of the Government of the People's Republic of China, has extended an invitation to President Nixon to visit China at an appropriate date before May, 1972.

President Nixon has accepted the invitation with pleasure.

The meeting between the leaders of China and the United States is to seek the normalisation of relations between the two countries and also to exchange views on questions of concern to the two sides.

In anticipation of the inevitable speculation which will follow this announcement, I want to put our policy in the clearest possible context. Our action in seeking a new relationship with the People's Republic of China will not be at the expense of our old friends. It is not directed against any other nation. We seek friendly relations with all nations.

Any nation can be our friend without being any other nation's enemy. I have taken this action because of my profound conviction that all nations will gain from a reduction of tensions and a better relationship between the United States and the People's Republic of China.

It is in this spirit that I will undertake what I deeply hope will become a journey for peace—peace not just for our generation but for future generations on this earth we share together.

Thank you and good night.

[US Information Service, London, Press Release, July 16, 1971.]

Epilogue

THERE HAVE BEEN a number of important developments affecting Sino-American relations since President Nixon made his dramatic television announcement. The United States decided to change its policy on Chinese representation at the United Nations and backed Peking for the China seat on the Security Council. The American delegate to the United Nations made strenuous but unsuccessful efforts to retain UN membership for the Chinese Nationalist regime. In November, 1971, the PRC delegation arrived in New York and, in due course, its leader, Deputy Foreign Minister Ch'iao Kuan-hua, made a robust restatement of Chinese views on world problems. The People's Republic had finally joined the comity of nations. It represented a major victory for the new American policy of Mao and Chou En-lai.

There were signs, however, that this new policy was not acceptable to all their colleagues in Peking. Mao's heir apparent Lin Piao fell from grace sometime in the late summer or early autumn of 1971, and a number of other top political and military leaders disappeared at the same time. It seems unlikely that the major purge of the Chinese leadership, which quickly followed the radical change in relations with the United States, was coincidental. One possible explanation is that the disgraced men wanted to balance the opening to the Americans with an opening to the Soviet Union, which Mao might have opposed. Be that as it may, Chinese foreign policy continued on its new tack undisturbed. Kissinger revisited China in October to make final arrangements for the Nixon trip. At the end of November, the date for the start of the trip—February 21, 1972—was announced.

Nixon would be going with the UN representation issue resolved. There remained the overriding problem of Taiwan and, inevitably linked with it, mutual diplomatic recognition (quite apart from world problems on which the People's Republic and the United States held opposing positions). How could the two countries establish a permanent détente while the United States maintained its support of the Nationalist regime? [1] The answer to that question, and indeed documentation of all the developments since the announcement of the projected Nixon journey to China, belong in some future and, hopefully, less somber chronicle.

---

[1] One suggested answer is summed up in the phrase "one China but not now" and is outlined in Richard Moorsteen and Morton Abramowitz, *Remaking China Policy: U.S.–China Relations and Governmental Decision-Making* (Cambridge, Mass.: Harvard University Press, 1971). Abramowitz is a State Department China specialist and Moorsteen is with the semi-official Rand Corporation. Remarks made by Dr. Kissinger at his press conference on November 30, 1971, suggested that the Nixon administration might be thinking along similar lines. Dr. Kissinger stated: "The question which I was asked was: Will we settle the future of Taiwan in Peking? My answer to that was: It is our judgment that the future relationship between the People's Republic and Taiwan should be worked out between Taiwan and the People's Republic." (Official press release from the office of the White House Press Secretary, November 30, 1971, p. 7.) At a press conference only seven months earlier, President Nixon had described speculation about direct negotiation between Taiwan and China as "completely unrealistic" (*New York Times,* April 30, 1971.)

Bibliography

Background *

CLUBB, O. EDMUND. *Twentieth Century China*. New York: Columbia University Press, 1964.

FAIRBANK, JOHN KING. The United States and China. 3d ed. Cambridge, Mass.: Harvard University Press, 1971.

FITZGERALD, C. P. *The Chinese View of Their Place in the World*. New York: Oxford University Press, under the auspices of The Royal Institute of International Affairs, 1964.

FRANKE, WOLFGANG. *China and The West*. Columbia: University of South Carolina Press, 1967.

HSÜ, IMMANUEL C. Y. *The Rise of Modern China*. New York: Oxford University Press, 1970.

REISCHAUER, EDWIN O.; JOHN K. FAIRBANK; and ALBERT M. CRAIG. *East Asia: The Modern Transformation*. Cambridge, Mass.: Harvard University Press, 1964.

SCHRAM, STUART. *Mao Tse-tung*. New York: Simon & Schuster, 1967.

SCHURMANN, FRANZ, and ORVILLE SCHELL. *The China Reader: I. Imperial China; II. Republican China; III. Communist China*. New York: Random House, 1967.

SCHWARTZ, BENJAMIN. *In Search of Wealth and Power: Yen Fu and the West*. Cambridge, Mass.: Harvard University Press, 1964.

SNOW, EDGAR. *Red Star over China*. New York: Random House, 1938.

TENG, SSU-YÜ, and JOHN K. FAIRBANK. *China's Response to the West*. Cambridge, Mass.: Harvard University Press, 1954.

U.S.-China Relations, 1920–49

BARRETT, DAVID D. *Dixie Mission: The United States Army Observer Group in Yenan, 1944*. Berkeley, Calif.: Center for Chinese Studies, 1970.

BEAL, JOHN ROBINSON. *Marshall in China*. Garden City, N.Y.: Doubleday, 1970.

* The subdivisions of this bibliography are only intended as rough guides; many books could be classified under more than one heading.

Borg, Dorothy. *American Policy and the Chinese Revolution, 1925–1928.* New York: Institute of Pacific Relations, Macmillan, 1947.
———. *The United States and the Far Eastern Crisis of 1933–1938.* Cambridge, Mass.: Harvard University Press, 1954.

China and U.S. Far East Policy, 1945–1966. Washington, D.C.: Congressional Quarterly Service, 1967.

The China White Paper, August 1949. 2 vols. Stanford: Stanford University Press, 1967.

Feis, Herbert. *The China Tangle: The American Effort in China from Pearl Harbor to the Marshall Mission.* Princeton, N.J.: Princeton University Press, 1953.

Kerr, George H. *Formosa Betrayed.* Boston: Houghton Mifflin, 1966.

Liu, Kwang-ching. *Americans and Chinese: A Historical Essay and a Bibliography.* Cambridge, Mass.: Harvard University Press, 1963.

Mao Tse-tung. *Selected Works of Mao Tse-tung.* 4 vols. Peking: Foreign Languages Press, 1961, 1965.

Melby, John F. *The Mandate of Heaven.* Toronto: University of Toronto, 1968.

Peck, Graham. *Two Kinds of Time.* Boston: Houghton Mifflin, 1950.

Romanus, C. F., and R. Sunderland. *U.S. Army in World War II: The China-Burma-India Theater. I. Stilwell's Mission to China; II. Stilwell's Command Problems; III. Time Runs Out in CBI.* Washington, D.C.: Department of the Army, 1953, 1956, 1959.

Schram, Stuart. *The Political Thought of Mao Tse-tung.* Rev. ed. New York: Praeger Publishers, 1969.

Service, John S. *The Amerasia Papers: Some Problems in the History of U.S.–China Relations.* Berkeley, Calif.: Center for Chinese Studies, 1971.

Thomson, James C., Jr. *While China Faced West: American Reformers in Nationalist China, 1928–1937.* Cambridge, Mass.: Harvard University Press, 1969.

Tsou, Tang. *America's Failure in China, 1941–1950.* Chicago: University of Chicago Press, 1963.

Tuchman, Barbara. *Stilwell and the American Experience in China, 1911–45.* New York: Macmillan, 1971.

Vincent, John Carter. *The Extraterritorial System in China: The Final Phase.* Cambridge, Mass.: Harvard University Press, 1970.

White, Theodore H., and Annalee Jacoby. *Thunder out of China.* New York: Sloane, 1946.

Young, Arthur N. *China and the Helping Hand, 1937–1945.* Cambridge, Mass.: Harvard University Press, 1963.

US-PRC Relations

Acheson, Dean. *American Foreign Policy* (1950–1955, 1956, 1957 and subsequent annual volumes). Washington, D.C.: Department of State, 1957 and succeeding years.

ACHESON, DEAN. *Present at the Creation.* New York: Norton, 1969.

APPLETON, SHELDON. *The Eternal Triangle? Communist China, the United States and the United Nations.* East Lansing: Michigan State University Press, 1961.

BARNETT, A. DOAK. *A New U.S. Policy Towards China.* Washington, D.C.: Brookings Institution, 1971.

BARNETT, A. DOAK, and EDWIN O. REISCHAUER, eds. *The United States and China: The Next Decade.* New York: Praeger Publishers, for National Committee on U.S.-China Relations, 1970.

BLUM, ROBERT. *The United States and China in World Affairs.* Edited by A. DOAK BARNETT. New York: McGraw-Hill, for Council on Foreign Relations, 1966.

BOYD, R. G. *Communist China's Foreign Policy.* New York: Praeger Publishers, 1962.

CHEN, LUNG-CHU, and HAROLD D. LASSWELL. *Formosa, China, and the United Nations.* New York: St. Martin's, 1967.

CHINA INSTITUTE OF INTERNATIONAL AFFAIRS. *China and the United Nations.* New York: Manhattan for the Carnegie Endowment for International Peace, 1959.

CLARK, GREGORY. *In Fear of China.* New York: Humanities, 1966.

COHEN, JEROME ALAN, ed. *Dynamics of China's Foreign Relations.* Cambridge, Mass.: Harvard University Press, 1970.

COHEN, JEROME ALAN; EDWARD FRIEDMAN; HAROLD C. HINTON; and ALLEN S. WHITING. *Taiwan and American Policy: The Dilemma in U.S.–China Relations.* New York: Praeger Publishers, 1971.

COHEN, WARREN I. *America's Response to China: An Interpretative History of Sino-American Relations.* New York: Wiley, 1971.

DOUGLASS, BRUCE, and ROSS TERRILL, eds. *China and Ourselves: Explorations and Revisions by a New Generation.* Boston: Beacon, 1970.

DURDIN, TILLMAN; JAMES RESTON; and SEYMOUR TOPPING. *The New York Times Report from Red China.* New York: Quadrangle, 1971.

DUTT, VIDYA PRAKASH. *China's Foreign Policy.* New York: Praeger Publishers, 1966.

ECKSTEIN, ALEXANDER. *Communist China's Economic Growth and Foreign Trade: Implications for U.S. Policy.* New York: McGraw-Hill, for Council on Foreign Relations, 1966.

ECKSTEIN, ALEXANDER, ed. *China Trade Prospects and United States Policy.* New York: Praeger Publishers, for National Committee on U.S.–China Relations, 1971.

EISENHOWER, DWIGHT D. *The White House Years: I. Mandate for Change, 1953–1956; II. Waging Peace, 1956–1961.* Garden City, N.Y.: Doubleday, 1963, 1965.

FAIRBANK, JOHN K. *China: The People's Middle Kingdom and the U.S.A.* Cambridge, Mass.: Belknap, Harvard University Press, 1967.

FRIEDMAN, EDWARD, and MARK SELDEN, eds. *America's Asia: Dissenting Essays on Asian-American Relations.* New York: Vintage, 1971.

GEORGE, ALEXANDER L. *The Chinese Communist Army in Action: The Korean War and Its Aftermath.* New York: Columbia University Press, 1967.

GREENE, FELIX. *A Curtain of Ignorance—China: How America Is Deceived.* London: Cape, 1965.

GREENE, FRED. *U.S. Policy and the Security of Asia.* New York: McGraw-Hill, for Council on Foreign Relations, 1968.

HALPERIN, MORTON H. *China and the Bomb.* New York: Praeger Publishers, 1965.

HALPERIN, MORTON H., and DWIGHT H. PERKINS. *Communist China and Arms Control.* New York: Praeger Publishers, 1965.

HALPERN, A. M., ed. *Policies Towards China: Views from Six Continents.* New York: McGraw-Hill, for Council on Foreign Relations, 1965.

HARDING, HARRY, and MELVIN GURTOV. *The Purge of Lo Jui-ch'ing: The Politics of Chinese Strategic Planning.* Santa Monica, Calif.: Rand, R-548-PR, February, 1971.

HILSMAN, ROGER. *To Move a Nation.* New York: Delta, 1968.

HINTON, HAROLD C. *Communist China in World Politics.* Boston: Houghton Mifflin, 1966.

HSIEH, ALICE LANGLEY. *Communist China's Strategy in the Nuclear Era.* Englewood Cliffs, N.J.: Prentice-Hall, 1962.

HUCK, ARTHUR. *The Security of China.* New York: Columbia University Press, 1970.

KELLEY, JOSEPH. *The China Lobby Man: The Story of Alfred Kohlberg.* New Rochelle, N.Y.: Arlington House, 1969.

KOEN, ROSS Y. *The China Lobby in American Politics.* New York: Macmillan, 1960 (never officially published but copies are available in some American libraries).

LALL, ARTHUR. *How Communist China Negotiates.* New York: Columbia University Press, 1968.

LEE, LUKE T. *China and International Agreements: A Study of Compliance.* Durham, N.C.: Rule of Law Press, 1969.

LINDBECK, JOHN M. H. *Understanding China: An Assessment of American Scholarly Resources.* New York: Praeger Publishers for the Ford Foundation, 1971.

MEHNERT, KLAUS. *Peking and the New Left: At Home and Abroad.* Berkeley, Calif.: Center for Chinese Studies, 1969.

MENDEL, DOUGLAS. *The Politics of Formosan Nationalism.* Berkeley and Los Angeles: University of California Press, 1970.

MOORSTEEN, RICHARD, and MORTON ABRAMOWITZ. *Remaking China Policy: U.S.–China Relations and Governmental Decision-Making.* Cambridge, Mass.: Harvard University Press, 1971.

NORTH, ROBERT C. *The Foreign Relations of China.* Belmont, Calif.: Dickenson, 1969.

OJHA, ISHWER C. *Chinese Foreign Policy in an Age of Transition: The Diplomacy of Cultural Despair.* Boston: Beacon, 1969.

PANIKKAR, K. M. *In Two Chinas: Memoirs of a Diplomat.* London: Allen & Unwin, 1955.

RANKIN, KARL LOTT. *China Assignment.* Seattle: University of Washington Press, 1964.

RAVENAL, EARL C., ed. *Peace with China? U.S. Decisions for Asia.* New York: Liveright, 1971.

REES, DAVID. *Korea: The Limited War.* Baltimore: Penguin, 1970.

SIMMONDS, J. D. *China's World: The Foreign Policy of a Developing State.* New York: Columbia University Press, 1971.

SNOW, EDGAR. *The Other Side of the River: Red China Today.* New York: Random House, 1961.

SORENSEN, THEODORE C. *Kennedy.* New York: Harper and Row, 1965.

STEELE, A. T. *The American People and China.* New York: McGraw-Hill, for Council on Foreign Relations, 1966.

TSOU, TANG. *Embroilment over Quemoy: Mao, Chiang, and Dulles.* Salt Lake City: University of Utah Press, 1959.

TSOU, TANG, ed. *China in Crisis: II. China's Policies in Asia and America's Alternatives.* Chicago: University of Chicago Press, 1968.

U.S., Congress, House of Representatives, Subcommittee on Asian and Pacific Affairs of the Committee on Foreign Relations. *Hearings on United States-China Relations: A Strategy for the Future.* Washington, D.C.: U.S. Government Printing Office, 1970.

U.S., Congress, Senate, Committee on Foreign Relations. *Hearings on U.S. Policy with Respect to Mainland China.* Washington, D.C.: U.S. Government Printing Office, 1966.

VAN NESS, PETER. *Revolution and Chinese Foreign Policy.* Berkeley and Los Angeles: University of California Press, 1970.

WHITING, ALLEN S. *China Crosses the Yalu: The Decision to Enter the Korean War.* New York: Macmillan, 1960.

WU, YUAN-LI. *As Peking Sees Us.* Stanford, Calif.: Hoover Institution Press, 1969.

YOUNG, KENNETH T. *Negotiating with the Chinese Communists: The United States Experience, 1953–1967.* New York: McGraw-Hill, for Council on Foreign Relations, 1968.

ZAGORIA, DONALD S. *The Sino-Soviet Conflict, 1956–1961.* Princeton, N.J.: Princeton University Press, 1962.

Editor and Contributors

RODERICK MACFARQUHAR is a senior research fellow at the Royal Institute of International Affairs (Cratham House) where he is engaged in a study of the origins of the Chinese Cultural Revolution. Formerly editor of *The China Quarterly,* he is the author of *The Hundred Flowers Campaign and the Chinese Intellectuals* (1960), a joint author of *The Sino-Soviet Dispute* (1961), and editor of *China Under Mao* (1966).

MORTON H. HALPERIN became a senior fellow at the Brookings Institution in Washington, D.C., in 1969. Between 1967 and 1969, he served first as Deputy Assistant Secretary of Defense and then as a member of the senior staff of the National Security Council. A former Assistant Professor of Government at Harvard University and research associate at Harvard's Center for International Affairs, he is the author of *China and the Bomb* (1965), *Defense Strategies for the Seventies* (1971), and other books.

A. M. HALPERN is a senior professional staff member of the Center for Naval Analyses in Arlington, Virginia, specializing in Far Eastern international relations. He is the editor of *Policies Toward China* (1966) and the author of numerous articles in professional journals.

DONALD W. KLEIN, a research associate at the East Asian Institute of Columbia University, is the co-author, with Anne B. Clark, of *Biographic Dictionary of Chinese Communism, 1921–65* (1971). A frequent journal contributor of articles on Chinese politics, he is the general editor of the Praeger Library of Chinese Affairs. He is currently engaged in a study of the Chinese Foreign Ministry.